Innovation in East Asia

Business & Innovation

Vol. 37

The creation of new activities, of news production and consumption modes, of new goods and services, of new markets and new jobs (etc.) depends as much on the heroic action of entrepreneurs as on the strategies of big corporations which develop their activities at a global scale. Innovation and business are interlinked. The main themes of the books published in this series are: Entrepreneurship, enterprise and innovation; Innovation strategies in a global context; Innovation policies and business climate; Innovation, business dynamics and socio-economic change. The synergies between innovative entrepreneurship, firms' strategies and innovation policies is of major importance in the explanation of technological paradigms change and of the transformations in economic and social structures of wealthy and less wealthy countries. In this series are published books in English or in French specialized in economics, management and sociology of innovation and also dealing with change and entrepreneurship in a local, national or international perspective.

This series is supported by the Research Network on Innovation.

Series editors:

Dimitri UZUNIDIS, Blandine LAPERCHE, Sophie BOUTILLIER:
Université du Littoral (France), Seattle University (USA) et
Wesford Business School (Lyon, Genève, France, Switzerland),
Research Network on Innovation.
Viktor PROKOP: University of Pardubice, Czech Republic, Research
Network on Innovation.

Son Thi Kim LE (ed.)

Innovation in East Asia

Contexts and relevant cases

PETER LANG

Bruxelles - Berlin - Chennai - Lausanne - New York - Oxford

Library of Congress Cataloging-in-Publication Data
A CIP catalog record for this book has been applied for at the
Library of Congress.

**Bibliographic Information published by the
Deutsche Nationalbibliothek**
The Deutsche Nationalbibliothek lists this publication in the Deutsche
Nationalbibliografie; detailed bibliographic data is available online at
http://dnb.d-nb.de.

This book is funded by research funding of French Embassy in Vietnam
for the collaboration between University of Littoral Côte
d'Opale and Vietnam National University.

ISBN 978-2-87574-783-9 • ISSN 2034-5402
E-ISBN 978-2-87574-788-4 (ePDF) • E-ISBN 978-2-87574-789-1 (ePUB)
DOI 10.3726/b22190 D/2024/5678/41

2024 Peter Lang Group AG, Lausanne
Published by Peter Lang Éditions Scientifiques Internationales - P.I.E.,
Brussels, Belgium

info@peterlang.com - www.peterlang.com

This publication has been peer-reviewed.

Contents

General presentation. East Asian innovation performances: Antecedents and prospects

SON THI KIM LE

University of Littoral Côte d'Opale
Research Network on Innovation RNI

Historically, since the 1960s, East Asian countries have made great efforts to develop their industries, focusing on training a high-performance workforce, industrial investment and technological innovation. Today, to keep pace with the global economic model based on digital and green technologies, these countries are implementing policies of industrial, economic and social transformation. These reforms of East Asian countries resulted in "economic miracles", transforming East Asia region into home to some of the largest and most prosperous economies of the world, including Japan, South Korea, Mainland China, Hong Kong, Macau and Taiwan. East Asian countries are growing faster than the rest of the world with a regional GDP growth rate of 5.1 % by 2023 and are expected to experience a forecast growth rate of 4.5 % by 2024 (World Bank, 2024). The region's economic success has led the World Bank to call it the East Asian Renaissance. The debate over why they have grown so well has long been developed. Accordingly, the main growth factors highlighted include abundant natural resources and supplies of relatively low-cost and skilled labor, favorable political and legal environments to industry and trade, rapid productivity growth attributable to innovative technology, etc.

Among these factors, in the economic literature, innovation has indeed long been studied as a key driver for economic growth (Uzunidis, 2009). Beyond economic growth, the importance of innovation for long-term sustainable development has been receiving growing interest from academia, industry, and policy-makers (Laperche *et al.*, 2012). Precise, technological innovation can provide appropriate solutions to the challenges of sustainable development which has been defined as "*development that meets the needs of the present without compromising the ability of future generations to meet their own needs*" (Brundtland, 1987). With the desire to explore the importance of innovation for economic development in East Asian countries, this book focuses on discussing the antecedents and prospects of innovation in this region. Particular, this book provides an overview of the determining factors of innovation systems in East Asia, including the efforts from academia, industry to government (corresponding to the Trip helix model proposed by Etzkowitz, 2003). At the same time, this book also mentions the emergence of new innovation models and types towards sustainability in some East Asian countries.

East Asian region has been and is still being in the process of transforming from a manufacturing center of the global economy to a milieu of innovation for the knowledge economy (World Bank, 2021). The national or regional differences in terms of business environment, socio-economic environment (including institutions, markets, knowledge and innovation systems) and even culture condition leads to a variety of innovation approaches and perspectives (Boutillier *et al.*, 2021). This book provides valuable insights into the growing emergence of multi-level innovation systems in the East and South East Asia, and highlights research on: overview on regional and national innovation systems; the development of innovation ecosystems towards the creation, adoption and diffusion of innovation; the evolution of new innovation models due to the emergence of new societal challenges or opportunities.

Firstly, innovation capability of an enterprise heavily relies on regional and national systems of regulations, laws and policies, knowledge and physical infrastructure, and human capital development (Laperche & Uzunidis, 2023). Chapters 1 and 2 thus provide an overview about economic development strategies and the extent to which the role of innovation is emphasized. It then turns to the framework conditions for innovation, in particular on the regulatory frameworks supporting the development of technology. The importance of education investment in supporting for innovation activities has been explored in these chapters.

In particular, Chapter 1, written by Lebert and Anedda, examines the long-term evolution of innovation systems in ten East Asian developing countries: Burma (or Myanmar), Cambodia, China, Indonesia, Laos, Malaysia, Mongolia, the Philippines, Thailand, and Vietnam. To do that, the authors adopt a product space approach by considering the import and export flows linking these countries to their trading partners over the period from 1980 to 2018. As a result, the authors proposed indices of economic complexity to position countries in relation to each other, to identify significant developments, and to infer the capacity of a national innovation system. Doing so, the authors can classify these countries into three groups, including those with existing innovation systems that favor moving up the value chain, those caught in the middle-income trap and struggling to renew their innovation system, and those without a clearly structured innovation system.

Regarding the antecedents of developing innovation system in some specific countries in Asia, the Chapter 2 of Sun and his colleagues highlights the influencing factors of city innovative level and explore the effect of innovative city pilot policies on for building innovative cities of China from 2001 to 2021. This chapter mainly investigates and compares how R&D expenditure and education investment impact innovation system of 348 Chinese cities. Using the DID model, this chapter also shows that innovative cities pilot policy improved the innovation level across different regions of China. Their empirical analysis found that endogenous R&D emerged as a key driver to enhance the city's innovation whereas innovative cities pilot policy and education expenditure improved urban innovation. These results therefore suggest certain recommendations for policymakers to raise innovative level, including (1) increasing R&D expenditure for science and technology initiatives, (2) providing tax incentives for research and development, (3) expanding policies that support innovative city, and (4) prioritizing education as a critical component of urban innovation strategies. Further, policies aimed at enhancing innovation in cities need to be tailored to each city to stimulate the significance of policy interventions.

Given the importance of innovation for economic development, Chapter 3 of Chen and Yang proposed a national innovation performance evaluation index system that is synthesized from the dimensions of innovation input, innovation achievement and innovation benefit. Particular, innovation inputs include the innovative talents and R&D funding whereas innovation achievements are referred to the academic research results generated in innovation activities and the exclusive rights obtained from knowledge invention and creation, such as scientific and technological publications, top technology awards, and intellectual property rights achieved. Innovation benefit refers to the economic value generated by innovation activities, including intellectual property income, information and communication technology (ICT) service exports, creative products exports, and a proportion of these innovative outcomes in total trade. Analyzing innovation performance of China based on this index, the authors pointed out some weaknesses in Chinese innovation system, including low intensity of R&D investment, insufficient number of high-level innovative talents and lack of top science and technology awards. This chapter, then proposed directions for improving innovation performance in China, mainly through strengthening innovation resources and innovation entities, and optimize the innovation environment to enhance innovation momentum.

Secondly, the effectiveness of innovation system relies on the existence and evolution of innovation ecosystems (Lundvall, 1992; Grandstrand & Holgensson, 2020; Lundvall & Rikap, 2022). The following chapters thus explore the accumulation of knowledge capital in innovation ecosystems, paying particular attention to the diversity of Open innovation models among several stakeholders and the importance of protecting intellectual property rights in supporting multi-level innovation system. For instance, Chapter 4 of Vu and her colleagues analyzes the distinctive features of the Korean Innovation Model, unraveling the unique blend of government interventions, industry dynamics, and societal factors that have propelled South Korea into a global innovation powerhouse. By studying the evolution of innovation models through the improvement of policies over the historical timeline of Korea, the development of the innovation management system from the grassroots level to the national level, and some typical success case studies (including (1) Creative Economy programs are strategic initiatives designed to create vibrant and innovative communities, and (2) Free Semester Program and the SMART Initiative are the new programs of innovative and technology-driven education). This research sheds light on the adaptability and resilience associated with Korea's innovation model. Through a comparative analysis, this study aims to distill valuable lessons and principles that can inform innovation strategies and policy frameworks.

Regarding the importance of developing technology and intellectual property rights for innovation systems, a chapter written by Oh and Bai, analyzes the economic impact of innovation activities in the ICT industry of Korea. Particularly, this chapter analyzes the impact of patent applications by Korean manufacturing firms as a proxy for technological development on exports and sales over the period from 1999 to 2019. By classifying patent applications into overseas and domestic patents and comparing their effects on corporate performance, the authors realize that overseas patents include relatively higher technological capabilities compared to domestic patents. Further, by analyzing the flow and stock of patents, corporate performance can be affected not only by patents filed in the current year but also by those accumulated in the past.

Continuing to emphasize the role of multi-level innovation ecosystems for enhancing innovation level, a chapter of Nguyen and her colleagues analyzes the innovation system in a developed country of Asia – Japan. Japan possesses a flourishing startup ecosystem characterized by a progressively expanding community of entrepreneurs, investors, and support entities. This chapter presents the general innovative context in Japan and analyzes the innovation development management system at the national, local and enterprise level, with the emphasis on an ecosystem of startups. Particular, the authors focus on introducing local innovation system of certain big cities in Japan, such as Tokyo, Kansai, Osaka, Kyoto and Kobe. At the enterprise level, KEIDANREN (Japan Business Federation), a comprehensive economic organization whose members are companies and industry associations nationwide, is introduced as a typical example of innovation efforts. Japan Business Federation is considerably contributing on promoting sustainable growth of the Japanese economy. In addition, this chapter also presents a case study of PayPay – a Japanese company that develops innovative electronic payment services providing new technology solutions to change the payment habits of Japanese consumers.

Thirdly, innovation has been widely recognized in East and South East Asia as a key component of long-term sustainable growth. The global issues related to climate change and environmental pollution encourage the emergence of new innovation models towards the sustainable development, such as Durable innovation, Sustainable innovation (Oksanen & Hautamäki, 2015), Eco-innovation (Kemp & Pearson, 2007), etc. In another aspect, the emergence of unconventional innovation approaches recently in developing countries raises the question about the rationale, settings and conditions, and outputs of the innovation process in these countries. Resource-constrained innovation such as frugal innovation, bricolage, grassroot innovation, low-tech innovation, etc. are all evidence of local innovation approaches and outcomes.

For instance, to foster business innovations towards post Covid-19 economic recovery and sustainable development, Thai government emphasizes the importance of Bio-Circular-Green (BCG) economy by issuing a BCG action plan 2021–2027. A chapter written by Saelim

introduces Thailand's BCG action plan and policies as well as investment ecosystems supporting business innovations related to BCG. From
2021, Thai government has placed the BCG economy as the national
agenda and the core of Thailand's post Covid-19 economic recovery.
BCG is aimed at turning Thailand's comparative advantage in biological
and cultural diversity into new sustainable and inclusive growth engines
with technology and innovation. In addition, BCG is also in line with
Thailand's growth path towards achieving climate goals of carbon neutrality by 2050 and net-zero emissions by 2065. BCG focuses on four
strategic sectors, namely (1) agriculture and food; (2) wellness and medicine; (3) energy, materials and biochemicals; and (4) tourism and creative economy. Accordingly, the 2021–2027 BCG Action Plan consists
of several key strategies to promote sustainability of biological resources,
strengthen communities and grassroots, enhance the competitiveness of
Thai BCG industries and improve resilience to global changes by employing science, technology, and innovation. BCG policy measures include
supporting BCG startups, creating digital repositories and employing big
data analysis, creating demand for innovative goods and services through
the government procurement program, tax and investment incentives.
Finally, this chapter analyzes the lessons learned and proposes policy recommendations for fostering business innovations and sustainable development in Thailand.

Further, regarding the emergence of new innovation models towards
the sustainable development, a chapter written by Hoang and his colleagues analyzes the national innovation system of Vietnam with an
emphasis on startup innovation ecosystem and innovation strategy in the
agriculture sector as well as in rural areas. Several innovation programs
and projects at national and regional level have been highlighted in which
focus on Green Innovation, Circular Economy and Social Innovation.
Innovation activities emphasize sustainable development and focus
on: exploiting digital technology in production (Big Data, IoT, AI, new
generation biotechnology…); innovation in market access (e-commerce
platforms and online sales channels are widely deployed at the national
level); international cooperation in scientific research and technology
transfer (CGIAR, GIZ…). To clarify the effectiveness of these programs,
two case studies on Innovation in the agriculture sector and a startup
handicraft in rural areas have been explored.

The comprehensive coverage of different countries within East and
South East Asia regarding their innovation process will thus enrich the

existing literature about innovation at a changing global context. This book is expected to be a useful reference to scholars and students researching innovation, international business and entrepreneurship. This book will be of interest to innovation managers and public policy practitioners looking for a thorough guide on establishing a favorable regulatory environment conducive to innovation in East and South East Asia.

References

Boutillier, S., Casadella, V., & Laperche, B. (2021). Economy – Innovation economics and the dynamics of interactions. In *Innovation economics, engineering and management handbook 1: Main themes* (pp. 1–23). London: ISTE/Wiley.

Brundtland, G. (1987). *Report of the world commission on environment and development: Our common future.* United Nations General Assembly document A/42/427.

Etzkowitz, H. (2003). Innovation in innovation: The triple helix of university-industry-government relations. *Social science information, 42*(3), 293–337.

Granstrand, O., & Holgensson, M. (2020). Innovation ecosystems: A conceptual review and a new definition. *Technovation, 90,* 102098.

Kemp, R., & Pearson, P. (2007). Final report MEI project about measuring eco-innovation. *UM Merit, Maastricht, 10*(2), 1–120.

Laperche, B., & Uzunidis, D. (2023). Innovation ecosystems in core digital technologies. In Adatto, L., Aouinaït, C., Le, S. T. K, & Mongo, M. (Eds.), *Innovation ecosystems in the new economic era* (pp. 39–65). Peter Lang.

Laperche, B., Levratto, N., & Uzunidis, D. (Eds.). (2012). *Crisis, innovation and sustainable development: The ecological opportunity.* Edward Elgar Publishing.

Lundvall, B.- A. (Ed.). (1992). *National innovation systems: Towards a theory of innovation and interactive learning.* London: Pinter.

Lundvall, B.- A., & Rikap, C. (2022). China's catching-up in artificial intelligence seen as a co-evolution of corporate and national innovation systems. *Research Policy, 51,* 104395.

Oksanen, K., & Hautamäki, A. (2015). Sustainable innovation: A competitive advantage for innovation ecosystems. *Technology Innovation Management Review, 5*(10).

Uzunidis, D. (2009). Innovation, growth and sustainable development: General presentation. *Journal of Innovation Economics*, (1), 5–11.

World Bank. (2021). *The innovation imperative for developing East Asia.* Retrieved from: https://openknowledge.worldbank.org/server/api/core/bitstreams/439b29b8-0bb7-5ba2-9a7b-d826631aa71f/content

World Bank. (2024). *East Asia and Pacific to sustain growth amid global headwinds.* Retrieved from: https://www.worldbank.org/en/news/press-release/2024/03/31/east-asia-and-pacific-to-sustain-growth-amid-global-headwinds

Chapter 1

Long-term performance of innovation systems in East Asian developing countries: A structural analysis

RAFFAELE ANEDDA AND DIDIER LEBERT

Abstract: To measure the performance of East Asian developing countries' innovation systems, we adopt a product space approach by considering the import and export flows linking each country to its trading partners over the long term (1980–2018). We apply economic dominance theory to construct and analyze this space. Using an extension of Pavitt's (1984) taxonomy proposed by Castellacci (2008), we classify manufactured goods into categories distinguished by the technological intensity required for their development, production, and diffusion. We propose indices of economic complexity to position countries in relation to each other, to identify significant developments, and to infer the capacity of a national innovation system to deepen a country's insertion into the global value chain based on the mastery of complex technologies. In this way, we identify three groups of countries: those whose current innovation system favors moving up the value chain, those caught in the middle-income trap and struggling to renew their innovation system, and those without a clearly structured innovation system.

Keywords: National Innovation Systems, East Asian developing countries, Economic Complexity, Graph Theory

JEL Codes: C65, F14, O25

1. Introduction

This article examines the long-term evolution of innovation systems in ten East Asian developing countries: Burma (or Myanmar), Cambodia, China, Indonesia, Laos, Malaysia, Mongolia, the Philippines, Thailand, and Vietnam. According to a recent World Bank report (2021), these economies are now at a crossroads, facing new challenges. Two of these challenges seem important to us. First, total factor productivity in these countries remains low and has even tended to drift away from the best international standards since the 2008 financial crisis. Second, the advent of the Fourth Industrial Revolution (including embedded systems, cloud computing, artificial intelligence, and additive manufacturing) is challenging traditional global value chains and the position these countries once held in them, a key source of their past growth. These findings (and others) lead the institution to conclude that these countries *"need to move to a more innovation-led growth model"* (*idem*, p. 5).

The challenges faced by these countries are sometimes summarized by the term "middle-income trap". The World Bank (2012) notes that just over 10 % of middle-income economies in the 1960s managed to join the high-income club fifty years later. For Agénor (2016), these countries are currently "caught in the middle" between low-wage countries that dominate mature industries and innovative countries that dominate technology-intensive industries. In the case of Malaysia, for example, Hill *et al.* (2012) and Flaaen *et al.* (2013) note its inability to move up the value chain and generate strong growth focused on penetrating international markets for products derived from the intensive use of knowledge and innovation. Jimenez *et al.* (2012) make exactly the same observation for Thailand. Broader econometric studies (*e.g.*, Eichengreen *et al.*, 2012, 2014; Felipe *et al.*, 2017) also conclude that innovation is at the heart of the necessary transformation of these countries' production systems to break out of the middle-income trap.

Numerous factors have been identified as determining the difficulty of transformation through innovation. They relate to the factors of production and the physical, institutional and financial infrastructures of these countries. And public policy recommendations have been made to remove these obstacles: actions in favor of education, support for public and business research and development (R&D), strengthening of intellectual property legislation (Agénor, 2016).

Two main outcomes that reveal the capacity of these countries to generate innovation are regularly studied: the evolution of their international specialization, and their capacity to produce new technologies. With regard to the latter, Brahmbhatt and Hu (2007), for example, show China's tendency since the 2000s to register more patents, which, of course, absorb mainly Western scientific and technical knowledge, but also – and increasingly – knowledge produced locally and in the countries of the region. These countries are thus helping to lay the foundations of a "global innovation system" characterized by the formation of a dense network of international knowledge flows (Britto *et al.*, 2021). The first outcome is mainly understood in terms of the change in a country's position within a "product space", a space that synthesizes both the structure of international trade relations and the comparative advantages that the country possesses within it. According to this interpretation, escaping the middle-income trap depends on a country's ability to adapt its industrial and export structures to the demands of international product markets that emphasize innovation and differentiation.

It is the outcome "evolution of trade structure" over the long term (1980–2018) that we use in this article to assess the performance of a national innovation system, *i.e.,* its ability to generate new, sustainable sources of growth. To construct the international product space, we use a network representation of world trade. In addition, our analytical grid of product space dynamics is inspired by Pavitt's (1984) taxonomy of sectoral innovation trajectories and, more specifically, its development by Castellacci (2008). The idea is that the way in which manufacturing sectors generate their innovations by interacting with each other, and the way in which production is rethought following more or less radical technological, organizational and institutional evolutions, not only drive the reconfiguration of the social division of labor within these countries. They also affect the structuring of their international trade.

In adopting this approach, we differ from the literature presented above in one important respect. The network approach offers a different and complementary perspective on the characteristics of national innovation systems compared to monographic and econometric approaches. It focuses on one of the main outcomes of these systems, namely their capacity to transform production and exchange structures at the national level. In this sense, it is not sufficient on its own because it does not require an institutional description of each of these systems, while at the same time it must be complemented by quantitative studies to identify the factors at the source of the changes in trajectory that it observes. We therefore propose here an additional tool to enrich the study of national innovation systems. This tool provides a diagnosis, but not an explanation of its origin.

The paper is divided into two sections. The first section introduces and details the product space framework. The second section presents the methodology, data, and results.

2. Innovation trajectories and product space

We use economic dominance theory (EDT) to locate East Asian developing countries in the product space in the long run. This theory (Lantner, 1974; Lantner & Lebert, 2015) is a branch of network analysis (Freeman, 2004). It "draws" economic relationships between different entities in the form of mathematical objects – "graphs" – where the "nodes" represent these entities (here, countries) and the "links" between these nodes represent the relationships they have with each other (here, import and export flows). Applied to the analysis of international trade, this structural technique allows us to identify bifurcations within the product space (Hidalgo *et al.*, 2007).

The use of network analysis has become commonplace to study the structure and dynamics of international trade (see De Benedictis *et al.*, 2013, for a first overview). For Kim and Shin (2002), the most important evolution that has characterized world trade since the mid-1960s is the densification of intraregional linkages that has gone hand in hand with that of interregional linkages (the "globalization of trade"). The density of the world trade structure is measured by indicators of the "degree" of countries, *i.e.*, the number of links connecting nodes. For these authors, this intra- and interregional densification would run counter to the predictions of dependency theory (*e.g.*, Wallerstein, 1985), which emphasizes the difficulty of peripheral countries to reach central ones.

Mahutga (2006) revisits the study of Kim and Shin (2002). His own empirical investigation, conducted with tools that take into account the "strengths" (*i.e.*, intensities) of trade links between countries, shows that only a small fraction of the peripheral countries of the 1960s have been able to integrate into the center, while the situation of other peripheral countries has not changed fundamentally.

These first approaches in the form of graphs, however, do not specify the product content of trade relations. To integrate this content, we need to consider relations between countries as taking place in networks where the nodes are connected by multiple links (one link for each type of product). These are called "multigraphs" and are used to study international trade in two main ways.

Barigozzi *et al.* (2009) examine the degree of similarity between the trade structures of products, which requires the choice of a specific trade weighting scheme. Here, we use a different weighting scheme from these authors to allow us to analyze the same flow matrix from two different perspectives: from the perspective of "what enters" the nodes/countries (imports) and from the perspective of "what leaves" the nodes (exports). Comparisons of similarities from these two perspectives are often informative, especially for the study of the historical process of catching-up of core countries by emerging and developing countries. Lebert (2019), for example, has shown that the export structures of emerging economies now mimic those of developed countries quite well, while their import structures take longer to adjust.

However, the choice of weighting scheme is not the main criterion that distinguishes this article from Barigozzi *et al.* (2009). In studying the historical dynamics of similarities between products in international trade, these authors make a strong assumption by distinguishing between what they call an "intrinsic correlation" between products, reflecting the (dis)similarity of products at the level of their technical characteristics, which is assumed to be invariant over time (products with similar technical characteristics are assumed to have a similar international trade structure), and a "revealed correlation" through the empirical measurement of similarities in trade structures over time, which is a function of "institutional proximities" between countries. Any upward or downward movement in similarity between product layers (*i.e.*, within the product space) is thus interpreted in terms of a series of factors that involve transformations in the institutional organization of international trade: the entry of countries into free trade zones, changes in tariff and non-tariff barriers on some products, and so on. Over the period 1992–2003, the authors find that these factors have tended to slightly accentuate the international specialization of countries.

Our aim here is to reintroduce a logic of historical transformation of intrinsic correlations between product exchange structures. To do so, we mobilize a product taxonomy inspired by Keith Pavitt's (1984) article on sectoral trajectories of innovation. We structure a product space a priori (the categories of the taxonomy and the way they are articulated) and see how the components of this structure change over time for each country.

It is precisely the aim of the work of Hidalgo and his colleagues (Hidalgo *et al.*, 2007; Hidalgo, 2009; Hidalgo & Hausmann, 2009) to study the evolution of countries' historical positions within a product space that is itself evolving. This space is defined by these authors as the network that connects products according to the probability that countries export them simultaneously. The measurement of countries' positions in the product space is based on indicators of revealed comparative advantage by using a set of reticular information related to the "diversification of exports" of countries (by their "outdegree") and the "ubiquity of products" that these countries export (approximated by the number of countries exporting each product).

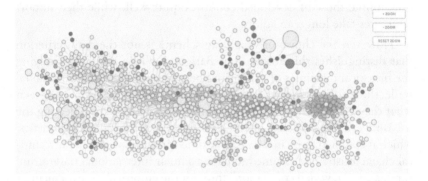

Figure 1.1: Indonesia's product space in 2021

Reading: The global map shows the proximity of products on a global scale, according to their export structure. In color are Indonesia's revealed comparative advantages (RCA) in 2021. The different colors represent metasectors (agriculture, textiles, minerals, etc.). The high density of Indonesia's RCAs in green, at the top right of the figure, concerns textile products.

Source: https://atlas.cid.harvard.edu/ (consulted in December 2023)

The product space has led to the development of an index of the economic complexity of countries (Hidalgo *et al.*, 2007). This index measures the knowledge intensity of country by taking into account the structure of its exports (Figure 1.1). The higher the index, the higher the knowledge/R&D intensity of its exports. The authors embed their measures in a theoretical argument based on the notion of "capability". Their argument is as follows: the complexity of a country's productive structure is revealed by its possession of specific, diversified tangible and intangible assets. This possession is captured by the richness of the country's export flows in products of diverse nature, *i.e.,* by the diversification index seen above, as well as by the ubiquity of the products it exports, on the assumption that a good produced by many countries requires less "internal capabilities" than a good produced by a small number of countries. According to the authors' empirical findings, this complexity in turn determines a country's development potential.

For emerging and developing countries, the realization of this potential is sometimes linked to the existence of considerable complexity in national production structures prior to the catching-up phase. This high level of complexity has been observed in China, South Korea and Singapore since the 1960s (the empirical study by Hidalgo and colleagues covers the period 1963–2005). In this case, public policies favoring decentralized adjustments that unleash existing potential would be more effective than those of the developmental state in the take-off phase. Sometimes, however, the level of complexity of production structures is low before the take-off phase. The authors observe this empirically in Brazil, Indonesia, and Turkey in the 1960s. In this case, the pendulum swings in favor of government intervention over private incentives. The goal is to create development potential ex nihilo. This second observation is very much in line with Rodrik's (2003) historiography of economic development over the last sixty years: very often, "unorthodox" institutional practices, in specific forms that are always difficult to replicate elsewhere, are associated with the take-off and sustainability phases of growth. These practices give a central role to proactive public policies and to a variety of institutions coordinating what Hall and Soskice (2001) call "producer groups" (public authorities, firms, social partners, the banking system, etc.). In other words, most of the successful development experiences since the 1960s have been based on the elaboration of national institutional arrangements characteristic of "coordinated economies".

Hidalgo and his colleagues have chosen to understand the dynamics of countries' trade structures solely through their export flows. In our view, the analysis of countries' import structures is also informative within the theoretical framework adopted by these authors. More specifically, it can be used to identify the source of a country's development potential. Indeed, the assets that foster development may have an external origin and be internally appropriated, "absorbed", according to specific modalities that reveal a particular nature of these national capabilities. For example, imports of capital goods often remain the dominant modality for modernizing industrial production capacities and transforming countries' export structures. Imports of intermediate goods, on the other hand, increase the variety of inputs, helping to diversify the production mix and promote local learning (Coe & Helpman, 1995; Keller, 2002). To paraphrase the title of the Hausmann *et al.* (2007) article, «what you import matters too».

We use Pavitt's (1984) taxonomy of sectoral innovation trajectories, as adapted by Castellacci (2008), to capture changes in countries' international production and consumption structures. The literature on sectoral innovation trajectories (see Archibugi, 2001; Carlsson *et al.*, 2002; Malerba, 2002, for summaries), following Pavitt's seminal article, initially set out to classify firms according to their technological capabilities. The underlying idea is that firms in the same category face similar dominant technological trajectories that affect their innovation strategies. Firms whose knowledge bases are closely linked to a set of emerging technological innovations are able to take advantage of market opportunities that are not available to firms less directly affected by these innovations.

Pavitt (1984) identifies four categories of firms in his taxonomy: supplier-dominated firms, active in traditional sectors, which innovate primarily by acquiring capital goods; specialized suppliers of capital goods and equipment, which supply firms in the previous category; science-based firms, whose innovation activity is driven by scientific discoveries explored and exploited most often within in-house R&D laboratories; finally, scale-intensive firms, active in mass production industries.

An important dimension of this taxonomy lies in the links that are established between the different categories. In Pavitt (1984), the vertical link between the first two categories is obvious, reflecting a traditional pattern of deepening of the social division of labor as already described by Adam Smith. Castellacci (2008) formalizes these links in a more complex way, integrating his thinking into a pattern of transformation of productive structures that has characterized Western economies since the 1960s: this transformation, often referred to as the «crisis of Fordism», affects the ways in which capital is valued and the forms of industrial and work organization. At the heart of this transformation is the growing role of knowledge and the intangible capital. The changes in forms of productive organization considered by Castellacci in his 2008 article concern, on the one hand, the rise of commercial service activities and their differentiated innovation trajectories, and, on the other hand, the role played by infrastructures (transport, telecommunications, energy) in supporting a growing number of economic activities. The relationships between these new categories and the old ones are summarized in a two-dimensional diagram. The first dimension is the intensity of technological content in the production processes of goods and services, and the second is the positioning of these production processes within the value chain.

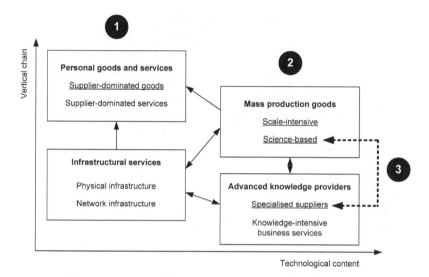

Figure 1.2: Castellacci's (2008) taxonomy

Figure 1.2 reproduces Castellacci's (2008) taxonomy. It identifies Pavitt's (1984) original categories (underlined) as well as the categories we rely on in the rest of the article, based on the data available to us for the empirical study (numbers circled in black). There are three categories of goods: (1) supplier-dominated goods, (2) scale-intensive goods, and (3) a fusion between specialized suppliers and science-based goods.

Castellacci (2008) uses a disaggregated level of the ISIC Rev. 2 nomenclature to isolate "office machines and computers" within electrical machinery, which he classifies as science-based, while other electrical machinery is classified as specialized suppliers. The CEPII data we use do not allow for this split. Rather than assigning the "electrical machinery" product layer to either Science-based or Specialized suppliers in order to maintain the original four categories, we prefer to merge these two categories for two reasons:

- Although these two categories operate at different points in the value chain, their technological content is comparable in intensity. The constraint imposed by this approximation will be to favor a technological reading of the dynamics of the product space rather than in terms of value chains.

 - In Castellacci's empirical attempt to qualify the technological regimes associated with each of these categories, based on a sample of European firms, we find a strong similarity between them for the categories of science-based and specialized suppliers (see Table 3, p. 988 of Castellacci, 2008). This applies to the general orientation of innovation – product rather than process innovation –, the frequency of product renewal, the organizational innovation index, the relatively low use of external knowledge sources, and all the other items that allow Castellacci to empirically qualify technological regimes.

The acronyms PGS for Personal Goods – Supplier-dominated goods, MPG for Mass Production goods/Scale-intensive manufacturing, and SSS for Science-based manufacturing and Specialized Suppliers manufacturing will hereafter designate these product categories.

As we trace the path from Pavitt's taxonomy to our article, several shifts have occurred. The original taxonomy is devoted to the classification of firms. Pavitt, in some respects, and many authors inspired by his taxonomy, classify industries. Castellacci and we classify products. This tendency to move away from the original project has been discussed in detail by Archibugi (2001). In particular, he describes the use of the grid at the product level as a "transfiguration", while noting the richness of the analyzes that can emerge. In doing so, we follow the approach of Guerrieri (1999), who applies Pavitt's taxonomy to the study of the dynamics of international specialization in some developed countries.

3. Data, method, and results

3.1. Data

To draw the product space, we use the TradeProd database published by CEPII. TradeProd covers 162 countries and 9 manufactured product categories (2-digit ISIC Rev. 3) over the period 1966–2018 (Mayer *et al.*, 2023). It provides information on import and export flows between countries in millions of current dollars, recorded at the point of exit from the exporting country and entry into the importing country. CEPII combines import and export declaration flows in the case of missing data to achieve a broader coverage.

We note the flow of information $X^C_{ij,t}$, the amount of exports from the country i to the country j for the product c in year t. For each product and each year, a flow matrix is constructed, X^c_t, an $N_t \times N_t$ matrix where N_t is the number of countries participating in world trade in t (from 124 countries in 1980 to 159 in 2018), with exporting countries in the rows and importing countries in the columns. These yearly flow matrices are aggregated in two different ways, by simple addition of product layers. At the general level:

$$X^G_t = \sum_{c=1}^{C} X^c_t,$$ (1)

where the superscript G indicates the aggregation of all product layers. At the level of the product categories defined below:

$$X^K_t = \sum_{c \in K} X^c_t,$$ (2)

where $K = \{PGS, MPG, SSS\}$.

In the literature using multigraphs to represent international trade, three weighting schemes are often used, depending on the topological indicators developed:

$$w^c_{ij,t} = x^c_{ij,t} / \sum_{h=1}^{N_t} \sum_{l=1}^{N_t} x^c_{hl,t}.$$ (a)

(a) is the weighting scheme used by Barigozzi *et al.* (2009).

$$w^{c,imp}_{ij,t} = x^c_{ij,t} . / M^{imp}_{j,t}.$$ (b)

$$w^{c,exp}_{ij,t} = x^c_{ij,t} . / M^{exp}_{i,t}.$$ (c)

$M^+_{i/j,t}$ (where $+ = \{exp, imp\}$) is the «margin» of the flow matrix, where "./" stands for "term-to-term division". The arguments of the vectors M correspond, in the rest of this article, to the maximum, for each country, of its import or export flows for a product, or a product category, or all product categories. This rule ensures "equal margins" in columns $\left(M_{j,t}^{imp}\right)$ or in rows $\left(M_{i,t}^{exp}\right)$ of the flow matrix by introducing two transfer vectors whose arguments correspond to the trade imbalances of the countries. Here, we use the weighting scheme (c).

The values of some indicators are presented in a normalized way. This normalization, for an indicator Q takes the form: $Q_i^{norm} \equiv \left(Q_i - min(Q)\right) / \left(max(Q) - min(Q)\right)$. The value of Q_i^{norm} is equal to 1 if it corresponds to the score of the leading country (which has the highest observed value), and to 0 if it corresponds to the minimum of the observed values. The main advantage of this normalization is that it puts the individual values into perspective with respect to the maximum value, and thus allows us to think in terms of "catching up" and "falling behind" over time.

We use classical network analysis indicators (especially degrees and strengths) as well as others derived from the economic dominance theory. The former are obtained from the matrix X_t^G and its associated Boolean matrix A_t^G where the non-zero cells of X_t^G take the value of 1. The latter are derived from (c) $W_t^{*,exp}$ with $* = \{G, k \in K\}$ through the determinant and cofactors of the matrix $E_t^{*,exp} \equiv I - W_t^{*,exp}$ where I is the identity matrix of the same size as W (see Lantner & Lebert, 2015, for an overview).

3.2. Lessons from classical network analysis

The degrees are determined by the products $A_t^G .1 \left(\equiv A_{out,t}^G\right)$ for outdegrees (number of outgoing connections of nodes, where 1 is a column vector $N_t \times 1$ whose cells take the value 1) and $^T A_t^G .1 \left(\equiv A_{in,t}^G\right)$, where the left exponent T denotes the transpose, for indegrees (number of incoming connection of nodes). Strengths are obtained by multiplying $X_t^G .1 \left(\equiv X_{out,t}^G\right)$ for outstrengths (intensity of outgoing node connections: total amount of exports) and $^T X_t^G .1 \left(\equiv X_{in,t}^G\right)$ for instrengths (intensity of incoming node connections: total amount of imports).

Opsahl *et al.* (2010) propose a measure of the relative importance of nodes in a weighted directed structure that combines information from matrices A_t^G and X_t^G. The idea is that traditional centrality indicators on these structures dilute information about either the number of node connections or the aggregate intensities of these connections. More precisely, very similar centrality scores can hide very different connection structures. To alleviate this problem, they present a composite indicator of the degrees and strengths. This indicator takes the form of a Cobb-Douglas function. For any node i :

$$ C_{in/out,i,t}^G = A_{in/out,i,t}^G \left(\frac{X_{in/out,i,t}^G}{A_{in/out,i,t}^G} \right)^{\alpha_t}. \tag{3} $$

The value of α is in the interval $[0;1]$. When α tends to 1, the value of C approaches that of X, while when it tends to 0, it approaches that of A. Opsahl *et al.* (2010) do not endogenize the value of α. We propose here a way to set α according to a characteristic of the network under study. Let's imagine that each country trades with all the others, in exports and imports. In this case, the information provided by A is zero, since it does not discriminate between countries. In this case, attention must be focused entirely on X. Conversely, when the trade structure is sparse, the country's ability to connect with more partners than others is very important information. Therefore, we propose to set α to the value of network density, which is the number of effective connections divided by the number of possible connections. We obtain:

$$ \alpha_t = \frac{\sum_i \sum_j A_{ij,t}^G}{N_t (N_t - 1)} \tag{4} $$

Figure 1.3 shows the graph of international trade in 2018, obtained from the matrix A_{2018}^G. This graph consists of 159 nodes/countries and 19,962 links, giving a density of 0.7946. The network is therefore very dense at this date, although at the periphery of the graph we can identify nodes connected to central countries and rarely connected to each other. This density has increased sharply since 1980, as shown in Figure 1.4. Kim and Shin's (2002) argument is valid at the beginning of the 21st century: the structure of international trade is constantly creating new

links, even if this does not automatically mean that the historical center/
periphery configuration is disappearing.

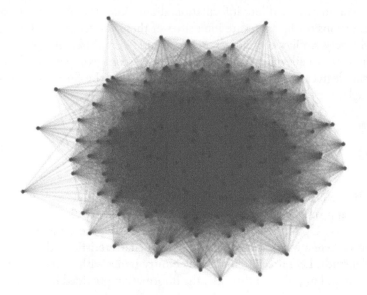

Figure 1.3: The international trade network in 2018

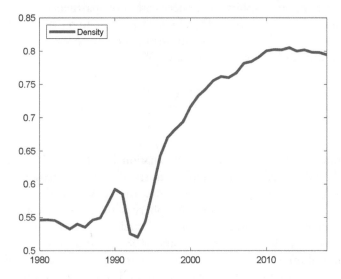

Figure 1.4: The density of the international trade network

This fact is important in itself and it also has a positive effect on the weight given to strengths in the Opsahl index. Table 1.1 shows the Top 10 countries according to the value of this index in terms of supply ($C^G_{out,i,2018}$, here Out_Opsahl) for 2018.

Table 1.1: Top 10 countries according to their importance in supply for their partners – 2018

	Country	Indegree	Outdegree	Instrength	Outstrength	In_Opsahl	Out_Opsahl
1	CHN	158	144	813649.9	1760104.9	140619.8	254707.7
2	DEU	158	144	806427.0	1102666.6	139627.0	175656.0
3	USA	157	144	1629225.9	987364.4	243830.2	160897.2
4	JPN	156	144	388436.8	580241.8	77938.1	105462.9
5	FRA	158	144	436069.0	421621.4	85664.9	81827.5
6	ITA	158	144	326366.0	405834.3	68045.9	79383.4
7	KOR	158	144	248930.5	339967.0	54870.1	68962.9
8	MEX	144	143	339720.5	335473.3	68923.1	68139.9
9	GBR	158	144	416598.8	282747.5	82611.4	59568.5
10	NLD	158	144	284988.4	270609.7	61096.7	57527.5

China is the most important country in terms of supply in world trade in 2018. Given the highly homogeneous link structures at the top of this ranking, this country occupies this position by the amount of its exports. China, on the other hand, is only second in terms of outlets. Three other East Asian developing countries appear in this ranking: Thailand (code: THA) in 15th place, Malaysia (MYS) in 18th place, and Vietnam (VNM) in 19th place. As for China, these two countries are less central in terms of outlets (in 22nd, 28th and 27th place, respectively). Some countries in this region are therefore well integrated into international trade in manufactured goods. Figure 1.5 shows the values of the Out_Opsahl index over the period 1980–2018 for nine developing countries in the region (IDN for Indonesia, KHM for Cambodia, LAO for Laos, MNG for Mongolia, MMR for Myanmar, PHL for Philippines). The observed increase in Out_Opsahl values is a function of the amount of trade. What counts here are the changes in the hierarchy. On the one hand, two groups of countries seem to stand out, one well integrated into world trade, the other lagging behind. Second, there is a scissor effect between two countries that change groups over the period, with Myanmar's relative place deteriorating and Vietnam's improving.

The economic dominance theory is useful to deepen these initial findings and to interpret them in terms of the ability of these countries to master an increasingly complex production system, exploiting more advanced technologies through innovation.

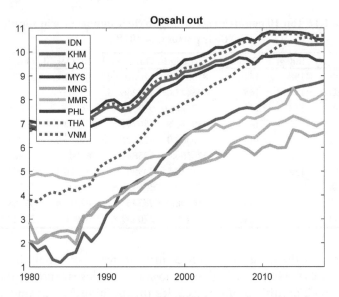

Figure 1.5: The evolution of Out_Opsahl values (in logarithm) for nine East Asian developing countries between 1980 and 2018

3.3. Lessons learned from EDT

Influence graphs are used to identify the contributions of manufactured products to the integration of East Asian developing countries into world trade, according to the technological intensity of their production processes, as in the product space approach of Hausmann *et al.* (2007). This intensity in turn reflects a country's ability to master complex knowledge, absorb it from other countries and disseminate it internationally. It is thus both an important input and output of an innovation system (Hartmann *et al.*, 2017; Laverde-Rojas & Correa, 2019). According to Qureshi *et al.* (2021), high-tech products account for a significant share of manufacturing exports in East Asian countries (close to 30 %), but have tended to stagnate since the turn of the century. The EDT approach integrates export flows with import flows to qualify a country's position in the global economy, including its ability to control and extract value from them.

Three product categories are considered here (Figure 1.1): PGS (low technology intensity), MPG (medium/high intensity) and SSS (high intensity). The TradeProd database distinguishes 9 kinds of manufactured products. Following Castellacci (2008), Table 1.2 associates these products to technology categories.

Table 1.2. Products and technology categories (ISIC Rev. 3)

Personal Goods – Supplier-dominated goods (PGS)
    Food (ISIC 15 to 16)
    Textiles (ISIC 17 to 19)
    Wood-Paper (ISIC 20 to 22)
Mass Production Goods – Scale-intensive manufacturing (MPG)
    Minerals (ISIC 26)
    Metals (ISIC 27 to 28)
    Vehicles (ISIC 34 to 35)
    Other (ISIC 36)
Science-based manufacturing – Specialized Suppliers manufacturing (SSS)
    Chemicals (ISIC 23 to 25)
    Machines (ISIC 29 to 33)

Note that only two specifications of the strength indicators make sense in the weighting schemes (b) and (c): $NS_{in,t}^{G,exp}$ (from $^{T}W_{t}^{G}.1$) and $NS_{out,t}^{G,imp}$ (from $W_{t}^{G}.1$, where NS stands for "node strength"). Indeed, the cells of $W_{t}^{G,exp}$ measure the shares of exports from i to j, and the sum in the columns of this matrix ultimately reflects the importance of any given country j for the total outlets of individual exporters i, and $NS_{in,t}^{G,exp}$ measures this importance. Symmetrically, the cells of $W_{t}^{G,imp}$ measure the share of imports of i from j, and the sum in the rows of $W_{t}^{G,imp}$ $\left(NS_{out,t}^{G,imp}\right)$ reflects the importance of any given country i in the total supply of the different importers j. To sum up, the degrees and strengths in a directed, weighted structure of international trade with weighting schemes (b) and (c) have two meanings:

    – In the case of *exp(/in)*, we use the term "outlet centrality" to indicate the importance of this country as an outlet for its partners.

– In the case of *imp(/out)*, we use the term "supply centrality" to indicate the importance of this country as a source of supply for its
partners.

To generate the subgraphs from the weighting scheme (c), we use the
same margin vector that applies to the aggregate structure X_t^G, so that:

$$w_{ij,t}^{G,exp} = \sum_{k \in K} w_{ij,t}^{k,exp} \tag{5}$$

The resulting graph can be divided into layers and parts. Here, a layer
corresponds to a product category, and a part corresponds to a country
or a group of countries. The goal of decomposing the graph is to measure
the "interdependencies" between its elements, *i.e.*, the intensity of the
synergies (circularities, or feedback effects) that their relationships inter-
nalize (Lantner & Lebert, 2015). To measure these synergies, we need
to know the determinants of $E_t^{*,exp}$. The determinant of $E_t^{G,exp}$ indicates
the weight of dependencies (asymmetric relationships between countries)
within the overall trade structure, while its difference from 1 measures
the weight of synergies. Figure 1.6 shows the value of this determinant.

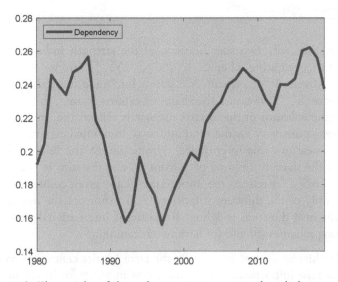

Figure 1.6: The weight of dependencies in international trade between 1980
and 2018

While the densification of international trade relations has remained almost constant over the period 1980–2018 (Figure 1.4), the forms of relations between countries have changed. As shown in Figure 1.3, interdependence dominates. However, the 1990s saw an accelerated homogenization of countries in international trade, while asymmetric relations have tended to increase since then. It's true that countries are becoming more interconnected, but trade imbalances are becoming more pronounced, returning to the levels of the 1980s, when the density of connections was much lower than today.

A country's place in international trade, in the EDT, depends on its ability to position itself at the center of trade circuits. To assess this ability, we measure the properties – always in terms of dependence and interdependence – of a subgraph that does not include the country under study. Removing the country's inflows and outflows will more or less redefine the paths and intensities between the remaining countries. The farther the properties of the subgraph are from those of the full graph, the more important the country under study is in international trade, as it internalizes flows that create binders/gateways within world trade. Conversely, if the elimination of flows originating or ending in the country under study has no impact on the main channels of this trade, we consider this country to be secondary.

Technically, this amounts to an analysis of the robustness of the graph to the deletion of one of its nodes. In network analysis, this corresponds to a "betweenness centrality" score, *i.e.,* a measure of flow control capacity in an exchange structure. Deletion of a node and detection of a gap between graphs in terms of the relationship between dependencies and synergies consists in reporting a diagonal cofactor of $E_t^{G,exp}$ (for the row and column corresponding to the evaluated node) to the determinant of this matrix. Since deleting a node reduces the number and intensity of circuits, the value of the cofactor-determinant ratio will necessarily be greater than or equal to 1. The greater the deviation from 1, the more synergy the node internalizes. If we call $d_t^{G,exp}$ the determinant of $E_t^{G,exp}$ and $d_{i,t}^{G,exp}$ the diagonal cofactor for node i, we obtain:

$$s_{i,t}^{G,exp} = \frac{d_{i,t}^{G,exp}}{d_t^{G,exp}} \geq 1 \qquad (6)$$

Figures 1.7 and 1.8 show the long-term normalized values of $s_{i,t}^{G,exp}$ for the Top 10 countries with regard to synergy internalization in

manufactured goods trade in 2018 (including China) and the nine other
East Asian developing countries, respectively.

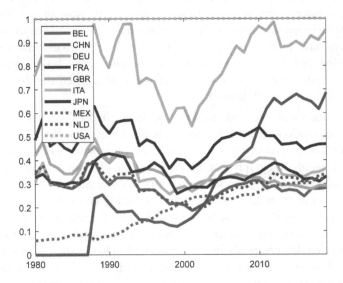

Figure 1.7: Major betweenness centrality scores in international trade in
manufactured goods between 1980 and 2018

Throughout the period, the United States and Germany struggle for
leadership (Figure 1.7). The hierarchies and the gaps between the highest
scores remain stable, with the noticeable exceptions of China and Mexico,
which joined the club of the 10 countries with the highest betweenness at
the beginning of 2000. China continues to make progress, while Mexico's
scores have stabilized. The main countries of the European Union and
the United Kingdom complete the ranking.

Some developing countries in East Asia are catching up: Malaysia,
Thailand, Vietnam and Indonesia (Figure 1.8). The situation in other
countries is improving only marginally. The ability of the four countries
mentioned above to integrate into the main international trade circuits is
still far from that of the Top 10 countries, with relative scores at the end
of the period about 2.5 times lower than those of Belgium, for example.
However, the current catching-up process of Thailand and Vietnam in
particular is spectacular.

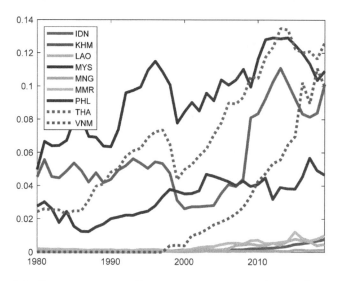

Figure 1.8: Betweenness centrality scores in international trade for nine East Asian developing countries between 1980 and 2018

Moving from absolute to relative terms (rankings), progress is more contrasted (Figure 1.9). Since 2000, the positions of the East Asian developing countries have remained stable (with a slight decline in the case of the Philippines), with the significant exception of Vietnam, which started the millennium above the 50th rank and less than twenty years later is approaching the world's Top 20. For Myanmar, Cambodia, Laos and Mongolia, the progression is also visible (starting from around the 100th world rank and approaching, for some, the 50th world rank), but the insertion remains so weak in absolute value that it does not seem significant to us. For the other countries, the increase in absolute terms and the stagnation in relative terms are the result of the densification of the international trade network, with many emerging and developing countries participating more actively in its main circuits, both in terms of supplies and outlets.

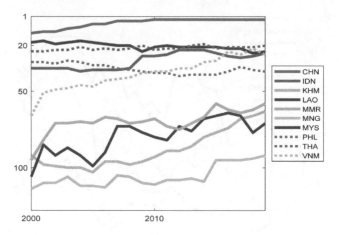

Figure 1.9: Relative position of betweenness centrality scores for East Asian developing countries between 2000 and 2018

Can we perceive through these dynamics a state and a transformation of the innovation systems of these countries? To do so, we need to look at the contributions of PGS, MPG and SSS products to their betweenness centrality scores. The contribution of a product group $k \in K$ is measured by the robustness of the overall structure to the elimination of inflows and outflows of this group for the country under study. Again, it corresponds to a ratio of determinants, with the elimination of flows mitigating or even destroying some circularities in the overall structure. The greater the difference between the determinant of the EDT matrix representing the partial graph (graph removed of flows) and that of the EDT matrix of the complete graph (this difference will necessarily be positive or zero), the more the betweenness centrality of the country will be affected by k. This difference will always be less than the betweenness centrality of the country, since only part of the flows are removed:

$$s_{i,t}^{k,exp} = \frac{d_{i,t}^{G-k,exp}}{d_t^{G,exp}} \geq 1 \qquad (7)$$

where $d_{i,t}^{G-k,exp}$ is the value of the diagonal cofactor when the flows in k to and from country i are removed. Figures 1.10 and 1.11 show the trajectories of $s_{i,t}^{k,exp}$ for the 10 East Asian developing countries over the period 1980–2018.

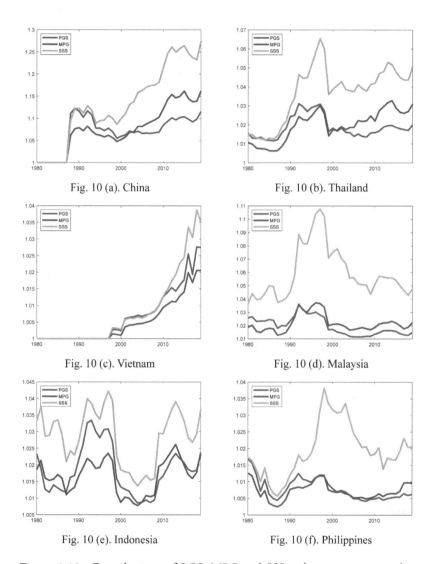

Fig. 10 (a). China

Fig. 10 (b). Thailand

Fig. 10 (c). Vietnam

Fig. 10 (d). Malaysia

Fig. 10 (e). Indonesia

Fig. 10 (f). Philippines

Figure 1.10: Contributions of PGS, MPG and SSS to betweenness centrality scores for the six major East Asian developing countries between 1980 and 2018

For the six major countries in the region (Figure 1.10), two config-urations seem to emerge. While SSS products (high technology inten-sity) currently dominate the dynamics of these economies' integration into world trade, for some this contribution has stagnated (Indonesia, Thailand) or even declined (Malaysia, Philippines) since the early 2000s. We have here another indication of the difficulty these countries are hav-ing in escaping the middle-income trap: a kind of inability to capitalize on a system of innovation that, since the 1980s, had allowed SSS prod-ucts to displace PGS and MPG products in their positioning within the product space.

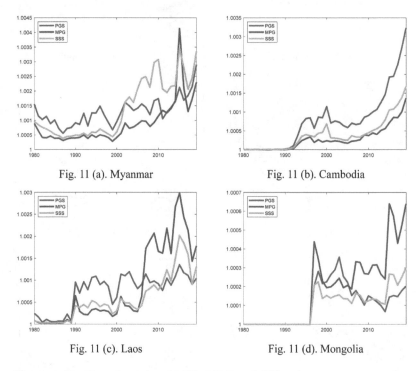

Fig. 11 (a). Myanmar   Fig. 11 (b). Cambodia

Fig. 11 (c). Laos   Fig. 11 (d). Mongolia

Figure 1.11: Contributions of PGS, MPG and SSS to betweenness centrality scores for the four worst-positioned East Asian developing countries between 1980 and 2018

From this point of view, this difficulty in renewing its innovation sys-tem does not seem to affect China or Vietnam, which are still increasingly relying on SSS to improve their absolute position in international trade circuits. However, each of these countries has its own peculiarities: while China continues to capitalize more on MPG products (including transport), Vietnam is giving pride of place to low-tech products (including agro-food and textiles) in order to strengthen its trade position. Vietnam's slower start than the other countries in Figure 1.10 may be a sign that it has not yet reached its own middle-income trap. For China, the EDT approach gives no indication that it will fall into this trap in 2018. In any case, the innovation systems of these countries generate a virtuous circle of integration into world trade through their actions in terms of absorbing, producing and disseminating new technological knowledge.

SSS products are not the main contributor to the position of the other four countries in the region (Figure 1.11). Cambodia stands out for its international insertion driven by low-tech products and Mongolia by MPG products. The other countries show no clear specialization between the main product categories. These countries do not seem to have an innovation system as such, *i.e.*, a set of actors working closely together to develop technological knowledge and products (Carlsson *et al.*, 2002).

4. Conclusion

To measure the performance of the innovation systems of East Asian developing countries, we favor a product space approach that considers both import and export flows linking each country to its trading partners over the long run (since 1980). We use economic dominance theory (Lantner & Lebert, 2015) to construct this space. Using an extension of Pavitt's taxonomy proposed by Castellacci (2008), we classify internationally traded manufactured goods into categories that differ in the technological intensity required for their development (absorption), production, and diffusion. We propose economic complexity indices, different from those used by Hidalgo and colleagues (2007), to position countries in relation to each other, identify significant developments, and infer the capacity of a national innovation system to deepen a country's insertion in the product space based on the mastery of complex technologies.

On this basis, the integration trajectories of East Asian developing countries are highly contrasted. Four countries (Cambodia, Laos, Mongolia, and Myanmar) do not appear to have an innovation system that promotes the mastery of complex production processes. Of the remaining six countries, some were able to develop a high-tech base in the 1980s and 1990s, enabling them to improve their position in the product space. Since the turn of the century, however, these same countries (Indonesia, Malaysia, the Philippines, and Thailand) have experienced difficulties in accentuating their specialization in these products, difficulties that we interpret as an essential marker of countries facing the middle-income trap. A more pronounced return to coordinated innovation policies could be the source of a fresh start to break out of this trap. Indeed, this is the explicit message sent by the World Bank (2021) in order to realize the "innovation imperative" that these countries must embrace in order to improve their total factor productivity and their positioning within a value chain that is in the midst of reconfiguration. Two countries seem to have been spared this difficulty in making their economies more complex: China and Vietnam. The former is pursuing a strategy of expanding and moving up the value chain, continuing its progress in controlling global trade flows and now challenging the US and Germany. The latter is rapidly catching up with the other countries in the region and does not yet seem to be experiencing the same slowdown in the complexity of its production system as the others. China and Vietnam now appear to be economically complex enough for decentralized coordination mechanisms to play a greater role in complementing the coordinated innovation policies that have driven their rise.

References

Agénor, P.-R. (2016). *Caught in the middle? The economics of middle-income traps.* FERDI Working Paper No. P142.

Archibugi, D. (2001). Pavitt's taxonomy sixteen years on: A review article. *Economics of Innovation and New Technology, 10*(5), 415–425.

Barigozzi, M., Fagiolo, G., & Garlaschelli, D. (2009). *The multi-network of international trade: A commodity-specific analysis.* Laboratory of Economics and Management (LEM) Working Paper No. 2009/09.

Brahmbhatt, M., & Hu, A. (2007). *Ideas and innovation in East Asia.* Policy Research Working Paper No. 4403, World Bank.

Britto, J. N. D. P., Ribeiro, L. C., & da Motta e Albuquerque, E. (2021). Global systems of innovation: Introductory notes on a new layer and a new hierarchy in innovation systems. *Innovation and Development*, *11*(2–3), 259–279.

Carlsson, B., Jacobsson, S., Holmén, M., & Rickne, A. (2002). Innovation systems: Analytical and methodological issues. *Research Policy*, *31*(2), 233–245.

Castellacci, F. (2008). Technological paradigms, regimes and trajectories: Manufacturing and service industries in a new taxonomy of sectoral patterns of innovation. *Research Policy*, *37*(6–7), 978–994.

Coe, D. T., & Helpman, E. (1995). International R&D spillovers. *European Economic Review*, *39*(5), 859–887.

De Benedictis, L., Nenci, S., Santoni, G., Tajoli, L., & Vicarelli, C. (2013). *Network analysis of world trade using the BACI-CEPII dataset*. CEPII Working Paper No. 2013–24.

Eichengreen, B., Park, D., & Shin, K. (2012). When fast-growing economies slow down: International evidence and implications for China. *Asian Economic Papers*, *11*(1), 42–87.

Eichengreen, B., Park, D., & Shin, K. (2014). Growth slowdowns redux. *Japan and the World Economy*, *32*, 65–84.

Felipe, J., Kumar, U., & Galope, R. (2017). Middle-income transitions: trap or myth?. *Journal of the Asia Pacific Economy*, *22*(3), 429–453.

Flaaen, A., Ghani, S. E., & Mishra, S. (2013). *How to avoid middle income traps? Evidence from Malaysia*. World Bank Policy Research Working Paper (6427).

Freeman, L. C. (2004). *The development of social network analysis: a study in the sociology of science*. Vancouver: Empirical Press.

Guerrieri, P. (1999). Patterns of national specialization in the global competitive environment. In Howells, J., Michie, J., & Archibugi, D. (Eds.), *Innovation policy in a global economy* (pp. 139–159). Cambridge: Cambridge University Press.

Hall, P. A., & Soskice, D. (2001). *Varieties of capitalism: The institutional foundations of comparative advantage*. Oxford University Press.

Hartmann, D., Guevara, M. R., Jara-Figueroa, C., Aristarán, M., & Hidalgo, C. A. (2017). Linking economic complexity, institutions, and income inequality. *World Development*, *93*, 75–93.

Hausmann, R., Hwang, J., & Rodrik, D. (2007). What you export matters. *Journal of Economic Growth*, *12*, 1–25.

Hidalgo, C. A. (2009). *The dynamics of economic complexity and the product space over a 42 years period.* CID Working Paper No. 189.

Hidalgo, C. A., & Hausmann, R. (2009). The building blocks of economic complexity. *Proceedings of the National Academy of Sciences, 106*(26), 10570–10575.

Hidalgo, C. A., Klinger, B., Barabási, A. L., & Hausmann, R. (2007). The product space conditions the development of nations. *Science, 317*(5837), 482–487.

Hill, H., Yean, T. S., & Ragayah, H. (2012), Malaysia: A success story stuck in the middle. *The World Economy, 35*(12), 1687–1711.

Jimenez, E., Nguyen, V., & Patrinos, H. A. (2012). *Stuck in the middle? Human capital development and economic growth in Malaysia and Thailand.* World Bank Policy Research Working Paper, No. 6283.

Keller, W. (2002). Trade and the transmission of technology. *Journal of Economic Growth, 7*, 5–24.

Kim, S., & Shin, E. H. (2002). A longitudinal analysis of globalization and regionalization in international trade: A social network approach. *Social Forces, 81*(2), 445–468.

Lantner, R. (1974). *Théorie de la dominance économique.* Dunod.

Lantner, R., & Lebert, D. (2015). Dominance et amplification des influences dans les structures linéaires. *Économie appliquée, 68*(3), 143–165.

Laverde-Rojas, H., & Correa, J. C. (2019). Can scientific productivity impact the economic complexity of countries?. *Scientometrics, 120*(1), 267–282.

Lebert, D. (2019). *Essais sur la théorie de la dominance économique.* HDR Thesis, Université du Littoral Côte d'Opale. ⟨tel-02977216⟩

Mahutga, M. C. (2006). The persistence of structural inequality? A network analysis of international trade, 1965–2000. *Social Forces, 84*(4), 1863–1889.

Malerba, F. (2002). Sectoral systems of innovation and production. *Research Policy, 31*(2), 247–264.

Mayer, T., Santoni, G., & Vicard, V. (2023). *The CEPII trade and production database.* CEPII Working Paper No. 2023–01.

Opsahl, T., Agneessens, F., & Skvoretz, J. (2010). Node centrality in weighted networks: Generalizing degree and shortest paths. *Social Networks, 32*(3), 245–251.

Pavitt, K. (1984). Sectoral patterns of technical change: Towards a taxonomy and a theory. *Research Policy, 13*(6), 343–373.

Qureshi, I., Park, D., Crespi, G. A., & Benavente, J. M. (2021). Trends and determinants of innovation in Asia and the Pacific vs. Latin America and the Caribbean. *Journal of Policy Modeling, 43*(6), 1287–1309.

Rodrik, D. (2003). *Growth strategies*. CEPR Discussion Papers No. 4100.

Wallerstein, I. (1985). *Le capitalisme historique*. Paris: La Découverte.

World Bank. (2012). *China 2030: Building a modern, harmonious, and creative high-income society*. Development Research Center of the World Bank.

World Bank. (2021). *The innovation imperative for developing East Asia*. World Bank East Asia and Pacific Regional Report.

Chapter 2

Endogenous R&D and innovation system across Chinese cities: New quasi-natural experiment evidence from innovative cities pilot policy

JIAYI SUN, YURUI LIU, PINGPING JIANG
AND XINGLE LONG

Abstract: Departing from previous studies on exogenous growth, this study mainly investigates how education impacts the innovation systems of 348 Chinese cities from the perspective of endogenous growth. The research also examined the impact of China's pilot policy of building innovative cities on innovation systems via Difference-in-Differences (DID) approach. The empirical DID analysis reveals that innovative cities pilot policy enhanced the innovation level across China's different regions, emphasizing the significance of policy interventions. Notably, endogenous research and development (R&D) emerges as the key driver, while certain industrial indicators display negative effects. Policy implementations for building innovative cities show substantial positive impacts. The findings underscore the need for enhanced funding in science and technology, industry-specific strategies, and tailored policies for innovative city construction. The importance of strategic investment in education is highlighted. These insights contribute to informed policy decisions, fostering sustainable regional innovation in China, aligning with the nation's innovation-driven development strategy.

Keywords: Economic Development, Technological Innovation, Quasi-Natural Experiment

1. Introduction

Schumpeter (1911) first proposed the concept of innovation. He pointed out that innovation is different from the input of external capital and labor, which is endogenous in the production process and is the essential regulation of economic development. Endogenous economic growth points out that long-term economic growth no longer depends on traditional factors such as material resources and labor, and innovation can promote the development of productivity and efficiency (Romer, 1986, 1990), the key factor of economic growth. Human capital stock is important to economic growth, and having a large population shortage is easy to generate growth (Lucas, 1988). The accumulation of knowledge has the property of increasing marginal utility, and its non-competitiveness and partial excludability enable it to produce positive spillover effect on the economy (Romer, 1986, 1990). At the 2019 Summit on Endogenous Growth of Enterprises, Romer also said that China has a population of more than one billion and sufficient endogenous factors supporting economic growth. How to stimulate the huge internal growth force contained in China's economy is the key issue.

Innovation-driven development strategy was proposed in 2012, it emphasizes that China's future development should be driven by innovation rather than traditional factors like labor, resources, and energy. The goal of innovation is to drive development, not just publish high-level papers. To transform from factor-driven to innovation-driven, the following points should be emphasized: refining strategic objectives, improving independent innovation capabilities, and accelerating reform and innovation in science and technology systems and mechanisms.

To achieve this goal, a circular on implementing documents that granted greater autonomy to scientific research institutions and personnel was issued in 2018. The Regulations on State Science and Technology Awards were revised in 2020. In 2021, the revised Law on Scientific and Technological Progress was adopted. A guideline on improving the evaluation mechanism of scientific and technological achievements was issued in 2021. Relevant documents also point out the need to "support the enhancement of scientific and technological innovation capacity" and "accelerate the promotion of digital transformation and technological transformation". In 2023, the Central Economic Work Conference emphasized science and technology finance, green finance, inclusive finance, pension finance, and digital finance. Among them, science and technology finance is the leading field in the "five major articles", indicating that one of the focuses of China's financial work in the future is to guide financial capital to invest more in the field of scientific and technological innovation, accelerate the formation of new quality productivity, and constantly promote economic development with high quality.

The 2023 Central Economic Work Conference emphasized the need for both proactive financial policy and prudent monetary policy to provide financial support for innovation. In recent years, the central bank and other financial regulatory authorities have established a comprehensive and multiple level financial service system for scientific and technological innovation, including bank loans, bond markets, stock markets, venture capital, insurance, and financing guarantees. This system has provided a variety of funding channels for technology company. One example is the rapid growth in loans to technology company. The central bank has also launched bond products to expand direct financing channels for science and technology enterprises. By using monetary policy tools like re-lending, the enthusiasm of banks to issue loans has been continuously enhanced. The "enterprise innovation point system" implemented in high-tech zones has provided an incentive for banks to lend to eligible enterprises. In 2022 alone, this system led to the issuance of 117.86 billion yuan in bank credit to enterprises with points. To further promote innovation, pilot zones for innovation will be built in Shanghai, Nanjing, Hangzhou, Hefei, and Jiaxing. In 2022, the state fiscal expenditure on it was 1112.84 billion yuan, reflecting a growth rate of 3.4 % compared to the preceding year. Over the years, China has introduced and updated various policies to provide support for innovation that will boost economic growth. These policies aim to encourage innovation, improve the business environment, and attract investment in science and technology enterprises.

As technologies advance and markets become increasingly globalized, the challenges facing intellectual property (IP) enforcement evolve, demanding agile and adaptive strategies. By understanding the nuances of IP enforcement, stakeholders can contribute to the development of effective strategies that encourage innovation while safeguarding the rights of creators and innovators.

IP enforcement plays a key role in safeguarding innovation, fostering economic development and fair competition in today's globalized knowledge-based economy. Intellectual property right (IPR), encompassing patents, trademarks, copyrights, and trade secrets, represent the lifeblood of innovation and creativity. Effective IP enforcement mechanisms are essential to ensure that innovators and creators receive due recognition and protection for their intellectual endeavors. Intellectual property enforcement involves a multifaceted approach, combining legal frameworks, regulatory measures, and law enforcement activities. The intricate nature of intellectual property disputes requires a sophisticated understanding of legal nuances and technological complexities. Governments and regulatory bodies worldwide strive to create robust legal frameworks that balance the interests of innovators, businesses, and the public (see Figure 2.1).

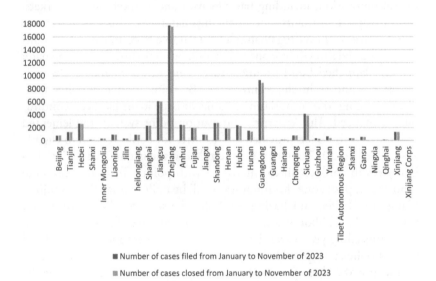

Figure 2.1: Analysis of administrative cases of patent infringement disputes from January to November of 2023
Source: National Intellectual Property Office of China

The Innovative City Pilot Policy is a key initiative implemented by the Chinese government to drive economic transformation, enhance competitiveness, and promote sustainable development. The core objectives include leveraging innovation and technology to lead urban development and boost economic competitiveness. The main components of the policy include: Support for Technological Innovation, Optimization of Industrial Structure, Talent Attraction and Development, Intellectual

Property Protection, Urban Planning and Construction and so on. The cities that have carried out pilot construction of innovative cities are shown in Table 2.1. Pilot innovation cities have continuously improved their innovation level through policy means such as talent subsidies and financial support. For example, in order to improve talent logistics support, Lianyungang has opened green channels or free policies for talent education and medical treatment. In respect of industry-university-research, rewards ranging from RMB80,000 to RMB500,000 will be given to those who carry out transfer and transformation of the introduced advanced technological achievements and hold large-scale industry-university-research cooperation and exchange activities; RMB100,000 to RMB1 million for the construction of industrial innovation platform; Incentives ranging from RMB30 million to RMB2 million will be given to new and high technology enterprises.

Table 2.1: List of innovative city pilot construction

Number	Province (district, city)	City (district)
1	Beijing	Haidian District
2	Tianjin	Binhai New District
3	Hebei	Shijiazhuang, Tangshan City, Qinhuangdao City
4	Shanxi	Taiyuan City
5	Inner Mongolia	Hohhot, Baotou City
6	Liaoning	Shenyang, Dalian City
7	Jilin	Changchun City
8	Heilongjiang	Harbin City
9	Shanghai	Yangpu district
10	Jiangsu	Nanjing, Changzhou, Lianyungang, Zhenjiang, Nantong, Taizhou, Yangzhou, Yancheng, Wuxi, Suzhou
11	Zhejiang	Ningbo, Jiaxing, Hangzhou, Huzhou
12	Anhui	Hefei City
13	Fujian Jiangxi	Fuzhou, Xiamen
14	Jiangxi	Nanchang, Jingdezhen, Pingxiang
15	Shandong	Jinan, Qingdao, Jining City, Yantai City
16	Henan	Zhengzhou, Luoyang, Nanyang City
17	Hubei	Wuhan, Xiangyang, Yichang

Continued

Table 2.1: Continued

Number	Province (district, city)	City (district)
18	Hunan	Changsha City
19	Guangdong	Guangzhou, Shenzhen
20	Guangxi	Nanning City
21	Hainan	Haikou City
22	Chongqing	Shapingba District
23	Sichuan	Chengdu city
24	Guizhou	Guiyang City, Zunyi City
25	Yunnan	Kunming City
26	Shanxi Gansu	Xi 'an, Baoji City
27	Gansu	Lanzhou City
28	Ningxia	Yinchuan City
29	Qinghai	Xining City
30	Xinjiang	Urumqi City, Changji City, Shihezi

Source: Ministry of Science and Technology of the People's Republic of China

In the realm of National Copyright Demonstration Cities, these cities are typically recognized for their significant achievements in copyright protection. This recognition is attributed to advancements in copyright laws and regulations, enhanced enforcement capabilities, and the development of cultural and creative industries. National Copyright Demonstration Cities serve as exemplars by exploring innovative copyright protection mechanisms, providing valuable experiences for other cities nationwide.

Table 2.2: Applications for the registration of intergrated circuit layout designs

Regions	2021	2022
Beijing	684	640
Tianjin	195	119
Hebei	114	68
Shanxi	68	54
Inner Mongolia	15	16
Liaoning	169	98
Jilin	102	18
Heilongjiang	266	80
Shanghai	2,499	1,766

Table 2.2: Continued

Regions	2021	2022
Jiangsu	3,585	2,777
Zhejiang	961	783
Anhui	616	479
Fujian	382	300
Jiangxi	56	21
Shandong	548	320
Henan	246	127
Hubei	443	520
Hunan	131	121
Guangdong	7,536	4,748
Guangxi	59	46
Hainan	61	21
Chongqing	319	137
Sichuan	621	649
Guizhou	89	56
Yunnan	14	31
Tibet	7	9
Shaanxi	228	178
Gansu	18	99
Qinghai	3	0
Ningxia	50	39
Xinjiang	14	8
Taiwan	6	6
Hong Kong	169	9
Macao	0	0
United States of America	78	60
United Kingdom	0	0
British Virgin Islands	0	0
Italy	1	0
Total	**20,353**	**14,403**

Firstly, the overall downward trend in the number of applications for integrated circuit layout design registrations from 2021 to 2022 may be attributed to several reasons (see Table 2.2). The maturing of the industry and the consequent stabilization of design innovations may have led to a decrease in the need for frequent new registrations. Secondly, the significant difference in application numbers across regions could be

explained by the varying levels of industrial development and technological advancement in different parts of the country. Regions with a higher
concentration of technology companies and research institutions, such
as Beijing, Shanghai, and Guangdong, tend to have higher application
volumes as these regions are more active in innovation and patent filings.
Thirdly, the relatively low number of applications from foreign entities
in China may reflect the challenges associated with navigating the local
patent registration process, which could discourage foreign applicants.
Additionally, the domestic market's increasing technological maturity
and self-sufficiency may have reduced the need for foreign entities to
file applications in China. Finally, the decline in application numbers in
certain regions like Beijing and Guangdong could be attributed to a variety of factors. In Beijing's case, the decline might be due to the relative
maturity of the technology sector and a shift towards more advanced and
specialized design innovations that require fewer overall registrations. In
Guangdong's case, it might reflect a combination of factors such as the
maturing of local industries, competition from other regions, and potential shifts in focus towards other emerging technologies or industries.

The overall trend indicates a growth in domestic patent applications
for inventions (see Table 2.3). This could be attributed to advancements
in technology and economic development, fostering an increased emphasis on intellectual property rights and, consequently, a rise in the number of patent applications. Regarding regional comparisons, areas such
as Beijing, Shanghai, Jiangsu, and Guangdong, situated at the forefront
of China's economic development, exhibit higher patent application
volumes. This can be attributed to well-developed technological infrastructure and innovation ecosystems in these regions. Conversely, certain western provinces and autonomous regions may face constraints due
to comparatively weaker innovation foundations and economic levels.
Differences in specific cities and regions may be linked to their distinctive
industrial characteristics. For instance, Guangdong's prowess in manufacturing and technology industries and Chengdu's notable progress in
technology innovation and entrepreneurship contribute to the observed
disparities in patent application volumes. Regional and industry disparities are likely intertwined, influenced by local policies, economic structures, and industrial layouts. Some areas may exhibit concentration in
specific industry domains, leading to variations in patent application
quantities across regions (see Figure 2.2).

Number of invention patent applications by Chinese provinces in 2022

Figure 2.2: Patent applications for invention originated from home by origin

The provided statistical table presents a comprehensive overview of trademark review cases for November 2023, categorized into application and adjudication cases. First and foremost, the breakdown of case types reveals that the majority of the cases pertain to application reviews. Among these, rejection after review and non-registration appeals constitute significant proportions, underscoring the substantial workload faced by the trademark review system in processing a multitude of applications. Moreover, the prevalence of invalidation declarations and rejection after review suggests a noteworthy share of cases involving disputes and regulatory compliance challenges. November stands out with higher application and adjudication case numbers. This could be indicative of heightened trademark activities, industry trends, or regulatory changes during that period. The monthly data provides insights into the short-term operational workload and the system's capacity to handle different case types efficiently. Secondly, examining the year-to-date accumulations affords a broader perspective on the trademark review system's overall performance throughout the year. The cumulative data allows an assessment of the system's ability to manage the increasing volume of cases and deliver timely resolutions. Stakeholders can use this information to gauge the system's efficiency and identify areas for improvement or resource allocation. Further analysis delves into the review outcomes, emphasizing rejection after review as a prevalent scenario. The substantial numbers in non-registration appeals and appeals for revoking registered trademarks warrant attention, reflecting complexities in the trademark registration process and potential shifts in regulatory landscapes. The distribution of case types, monthly variations, year-to-date accumulations, and review outcomes collectively provide stakeholders with valuable insights for informed decision-making and strategic trademark management. Understanding the intricacies of the data allows for targeted interventions to enhance the efficiency and effectiveness of the trademark review system (see Figure 2.3).

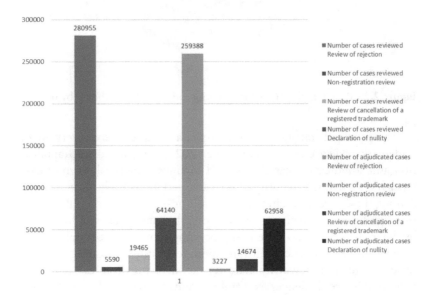

Figure 2.3: Status of trademark review cases from January to November 2023
Source: National Intellectual Property Office of China

The provided picture outlines the geographical indication (GI) business statistics for the period of January to November 2023. Firstly, with regard to the protection of GI products, there were 23 cases accepted for protection during the first eleven months of 2023. This signifies a recognition of the significance of GI and a proactive approach to safeguarding products associated with specific geographic origins. Moreover, the approval of GI product protection is highlighted with 10 cases approved during the same period. The approval process suggests a thorough evaluation of the criteria for granting protection, ensuring that the products meet the necessary standards to qualify for geographical indication status. Secondly, the registration of market entities authorized to use geographical indication special logos is a pivotal aspect of GI management. The data indicates that 5,662 market entities have been granted approval to utilize specific geographical indication logos. This signifies a widespread adoption of GIs among market participants, reflecting both the demand for such products and the effectiveness of the GI protection system in regulating their usage. Lastly, the registration of GIs as collective trademarks or certification trademarks is a noteworthy component. In the reported period, 182 cases involved the registration of GIs for these purposes. This reflects a strategic approach to not only protect individual products but also to collectively promote and certify products originating from specific geographical regions. In conclusion, the data underscores a commitment to preserving the authenticity and quality of such products while fostering a supportive environment for market entities to leverage GIs for commercial purposes. This approach contributes to the sustainable development and recognition of unique regional products in the marketplace (see Figure 2.4).

As of the conclusion of 2023, the cumulative number of effective invention patents in key regions-namely, the Yangtze River Delta, Beijing-Tianjin-Hebei region, and the Guangdong-Hong Kong-Macao Greater Bay Area–were 1.308 million, 703,000, and 672,000, respectively. Together, these regions represented 65.6 % of the total nationwide, exhibiting year-on-year growth rates of 21.1 %, 21.0 %, and 23.2 %, respectively. Primarily, the Yangtze River Delta stands out as a prominent player, registering the highest count of effective invention patents at 1.308 million, indicative of its robust innovation ecosystem. Subsequently, the Beijing-Tianjin-Hebei region, with 703,000 effective invention patents, also contributes substantially to the national total. Furthermore, the Guangdong-Hong Kong-Macao Greater Bay Area, with 672,000 effective invention patents, signifies a dynamic landscape in innovation. The impressive year-on-year growth of 23.2 % highlights the region's proactive efforts in cultivating a conducive environment for inventive activities. Collectively, these key regions play a pivotal role in

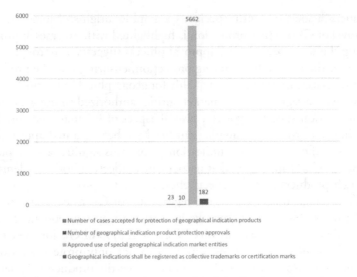

Figure 2.4: Business status of geographical indications from January to November 2023
Source: National Intellectual Property Office of China

driving national innovation, commanding a significant share of effective invention patents (see Figure 2.5).

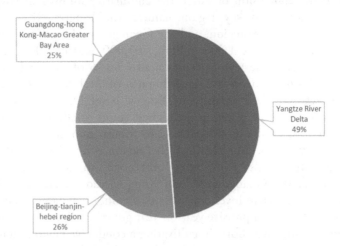

Figure 2.5: The number of effective invention patents in key areas
Source: National Intellectual Property Office of China

China's rapid economic transformation and its emphasis on innovation-driven development necessitate an in-depth examination of how innovation policies impact urban growth. The government's commitment to fostering innovation as a primary driver of economy underscores the urgency of understanding the practical implications of such policies on urban development. With the nation's strategic focus on transitioning from a manufacturing-centric economy to an innovation-driven one, the timing is critical for assessing the tangible effects of innovation-related initiatives on urban innovation.

The innovations are as follows: (1) This research excels in its detailed exploration of the specific impact of the pilot city Difference-in-Differences approach on innovation. It provides a granular analysis, unraveling the mechanisms propelling innovation in pilot cities. This detailed examination enhances the study's value, offering practical insights for policymakers and researchers engaged in the field of innovation. (2) This study compares and analyzes the level of Chinese innovation and the level of international innovation. This research provides a nuanced understanding of China's strengths and areas for improvement in the international context. This aspect adds a valuable dimension to the study, allowing for insights into China's position in the global innovation landscape.

2. China's innovation system

The 2023 Central Economic Work Conference underscored the imperative for innovation to spearhead the development of a contemporary industrial system. China's innovation capacity has significantly improved, and it is now at the forefront of innovative countries. China ranks 12th in the world, having risen 22 places in 20 years (according to Global Innovation Index (GII) reported by the World Intellectual Property Organization (WIPO)). The EU Industrial R&D Investment Scoreboard 2023 lists 20 Chinese companies (including Taiwan) among the top 100, with Huawei ranking first with 20.9 billion euros invested in R&D, fifth in the world. China's R&D investment has increased from 1.03 trillion yuan in 2012 to 2.79 trillion yuan in 2021, with the R&D investment intensity increasing from 1.91 % to 2.44 %. In 2022, China's total R&D investment exceeded RMB3 trillion for the first time, reaching 3,078.29 billion yuan, representing an increase of 282.66 billion yuan or 10.1 % over the previous year. Basic research funding in China reached 202.35 billion yuan in 2022, an increase of 11.4 % over the previous year, making it the second largest in the world. Additionally, Chinese enterprises are increasing their investment in innovation, with the number of valid patents held by Chinese enterprises increasing by 4.01 times since the 18th National Congress of the Communist Party of China, the number of invention patents increasing by 6.93 times, and the proportion of invention patents increasing by 14.83 percentage points. Data shows that in 2022, China's top 500 enterprises invested 1,447.467 billion yuan in R&D, accounting for 51.95 % of the total in 2021. This highlights the importance of large enterprises in innovation. Compared to the previous year's top 500, there was an increase of 140.82 billion yuan, or 10.78 %. When compared with other large companies of the same caliber, the increase in R&D was as high as 21.73 %. In terms of R&D intensity, the total R&D investment of China's top 500 enterprises in 2022 accounted for 1.81 % of their total operating revenue. This is a 0.04 percentage point increase compared to the preceding year. This is the fifth consecutive year that the R&D intensity of China's top 500 enterprises has increased since 2017, reaching a new high in the statistics. Among specific enterprises, Huawei, ZTE, Aerospace Science and Technology, China Information and Communication Technology and Aerospace Science and Technology had an R&D intensity exceeding 10 %. Huawei's R&D intensity reached 22.62 %, with an R&D expenditure of as much as 142.666 billion yuan, ranking first among all enterprises. There were 16 enterprises with an R&D intensity between 5 % and 10 %, including Glory Terminal, Meituan, Wentai Technology and Alibaba. The R&D investment of 105 enterprises was between 2 % and 5 %, with a corresponding total R&D expenditure of 672.009 billion yuan, accounting for 46.43 % of the total R&D investment. These 105 enterprises have become the key investment force for the R&D innovation of the top 500 enterprises.

In recent years, major countries worldwide have been continuously enhancing their scientific and technological innovation policies, leading to an increasingly fierce competition in the innovation environment. China, too, has been formulating and optimizing its scientific and technological policies, ensuring that effective, mature, and stable measures are elevated to laws. A comprehensive scientific and technological innovation policy system has been established.

China's national innovation index rose 28 places in 20 years, going from 38th in 2000 to 10th in 2023. Its score is 72.7. In 2020, China ranked 16th in the number of PCT (Patent Cooperation Treaty) patent applications per 10,000 enterprise scientific researchers. China is the only middle-income country in the top 20. Its Gross Domestic Product (GDP) per capita lags behind developed countries, but its innovation level is higher than countries with a similar GDP. China has an R&D intensity above 2 % and a leading overall ranking. Its national innovation index score is close to that of European countries with a GDP per capita of around $50,000.

The WIPO Report 2023 presents a visual representation of the global comparison and temporal evolution of patent applications and grants. It becomes evident that China holds a dominant position in this field, surpassing countries with similar economic development levels such as Russia, Mexico, Turkey, and Argentina. However, it is important to acknowledge that there still exists a certain disparity between China's innovation capacity and that of more advanced nations (see Figures 2.6 and 2.7).

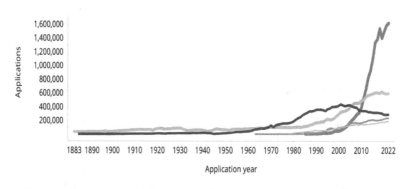

Figure 2.6: Trend in patent applications for the top five office, 1883–2022
Source: WIPO Statistics Database, August 2023

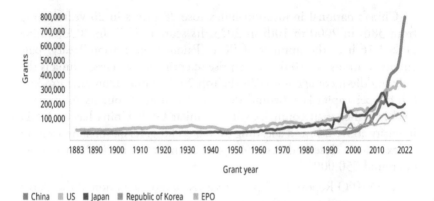

Figure 2.7: Trend in patent grants for the top five office, 1883–2022
Source: WIPO Statistics Database, August 2023

The initial proposal of the Tenth Five-Year Plan suggested the importance of "constructing a national innovation system" and "establishing a national knowledge innovation system to promote knowledge innovation projects". China's national innovation system comprises various elements such as innovation subjects, infrastructure, resources, environment, and external interaction. Related documents highlight that this social system is primarily governed by the government while leveraging market mechanisms for resource allocation. It emphasizes close connections and effective interactions among different entities involved in scientific and technological innovations. Currently, China has developed an innovative ecosystem involving government bodies, enterprises, research institutes, universities, as well as support systems for technological advancements. With a focus on integrating science and technology with the economy, China's scientific and technological reforms have achieved significant breakthroughs in strengthening innovation efforts. This includes promoting the transformation of scientific achievements into industrial applications through structural adjustments and transformative mechanisms. In 2012, the guidelines aimed at deepening reform within the science and technology sector while accelerating the construction of a national innovation system was issued. These measures aim to fully implement the goals outlined in related documents, thereby exert science and technology's effect in promoting economic growth effectively. According to the Evaluation Report on China's Regional Innovation

Capacity 2023, Guangdong Province will remain the first rank in the innovation ability field, ranking first in China for seven consecutive years. Beijing and Jiangsu ranked second and third respectively, while Zhejiang and Shanghai ranked fourth and fifth respectively. The top five rankings remained the same as in 2021 and 2022. The following figure shows that the top five provinces in regional innovation capability are all developed regions in eastern China, and there is a large gap between them and others (see Figure 2.8).

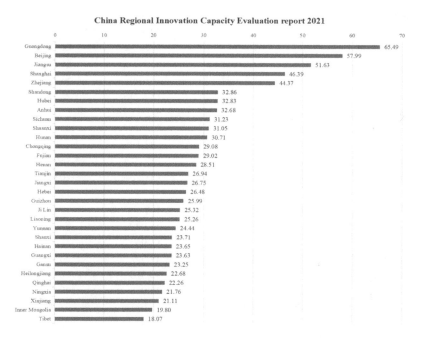

Figure 2.8: China Regional Innovation Capacity Evaluation report 2021
Source: https://zhuanlan.zhihu.com/p/507262896

Table 2.3: Patent applications originated from home by origin

Regions	Invention	Industrial Design	Utility Model	Total
Total	1,464,605	777,663	2,944,139	5,186,407
Beijing	189,198	25,075	92,902	307,175
Tianjin	21,466	4,648	58,221	84,335
Hebei	24,182	19,352	93,903	137,437
Shanxi	9,891	3,218	27,312	40,421
Inner Mongolia	6,676	2,208	24,037	32,921
Liaoning	23,080	5,319	68,893	97,292
Jilin	15,518	3,201	23,803	42,522
Heilongjiang	14,770	3,779	30,478	49,027
Shanghai	89,448	25,649	109,312	224,409
Jiangsu	194,983	47,101	420,425	662,509
Zhejiang	122,807	120,021	271,002	513,830
Anhui	65,368	16,760	138,935	221,063
Fujian	30,581	35,180	97,271	163,032
Jiangxi	20,625	24,486	46,704	91,815
Shandong	88,744	34,193	285,199	408,136
Henan	33,183	18,008	117,915	169,106
Hubei	55,207	15,125	131,786	202,118
Hunan	35,851	19,894	58,342	114,087
Guangdong	236,957	291,060	465,463	993,480
Guangxi	13,611	9,652	33,020	56,283
Hainan	4,402	1,828	11,043	17,273
Chongqing	28,907	8,247	49,597	86,751
Sichuan	48,283	20,903	96,313	165,499
Guizhou	10,732	5,727	24,096	40,555
Yunnan	12,036	3,982	36,981	52,999
Tibet	585	247	2,303	3,135
Shaanxi	38,569	6,497	63,030	108,096
Gansu	7,005	1,782	23,725	32,512
Qinghai	1,459	266	5,865	7,590
Ningxia	3,358	490	12,385	16,233
Xinjiang	4,951	1,520	19,324	25,795
Taiwan	10,941	1,073	3,787	15,801
Hong Kong	1,076	1,153	701	2,930
Macao	155	19	66	240

Source: National Intellectual Property Office of China

In recent years, China has continuously strengthened patent protection and incentives to maximize the use value of patents. In recent years, China's intellectual property pledge financing has developed well (see Table 2.4). It can alleviate the problem of "hard and costly financing" of enterprises to a certain extent, and obtain necessary capital replenishment with the "asset-light" intellectual property rights, which is conducive to helping technology-oriented small and medium enterprises (SMEs) solve the capital shortage caused by the lack of estate guarantee. In 2022, the scale of intellectual property pledge financing in China will continue to grow rapidly: In 2022, the amount of patent and trademark pledge financing nationwide will reach 486.88 billion yuan, with an increase of more than 40 % for three consecutive years. Among them, in 2022, the national registration project of inclusive loans with less than 10 million yuan of patent and trademark pledge will benefit 18,000 SMEs, exert the effect of inclusive loans in helping them rescue and development. Patent insurance is to point to policy-holder is the subject matter that authorizes patent to insure to insurance company, during insurance, the investigation cost that insurance company agrees according to the contract to policy-holder is patent safeguard and expense and legal cost undertake compensation. Since 2012, we have promoted pilot and practical exploration where conditions permit. The State Intellectual Property Office approved 44 regions to carry out pilot work of patent insurance. In that year, the patent insurance amount in the pilot areas of patent insurance nationwide reached 310 million yuan, and the number of projects was 1,702 items. By September 2022, it had been carried out in more than 22 provinces and 99 prefecture-level cities (see Figure 2.9). The intellectual property insurance business has accumulated more than 44,000 patents for more than 27,000 enterprises. Trademarks, geographical indications and IC layout-designs provide more than $110 billion in risk protection. The three-in-one intellectual property civil, administrative and criminal courts refers to the unified trial of IP in civil, administrative, and criminal cases by the intellectual property tribunal. It is an important measure to implement the national intellectual property strategy and innovation-driven development strategy, which is conducive to promoting the construction of working mechanism and judicial system in line with the characteristics and cost of intellectual property justice, and is beneficial to enhancing the overall efficiency of intellectual property judicial protection.

Table 2.4: **Annual intellectual property pledge financing situation**

Unit: 100 million RMB	Patent pledge financing amount	Trademark pledge financing amount	Total
2016	436	650	1,086
2017	720	370	1,090
2018	885	339	1,224
2019	1,105	410	1,515
2020	1,558	622	2,180
2021	2,199	899	3,098
2022	4,015	854	4,869

Source: China National Intellectual Property Administration 2022 ANNUAL REPORT[1]

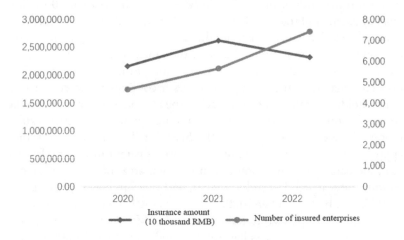

Figure 2.9: Changes in the amount of intellectual property insurance and the number of service enterprises since 2020
Source: White Paper on the development of intellectual property insurance in China[2]

---

[1]   https://www.cnipa.gov.cn/module/download/down.jsp?i_ID=185538&colID=3249

[2]   www.cnipa-ipdrc.org.cn.

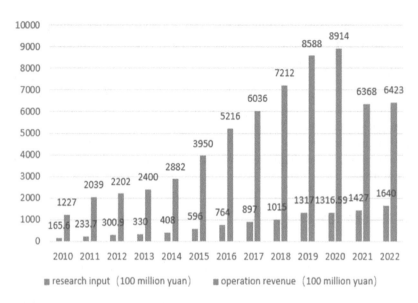

Figure 2.10: Huawei's operating revenue and R&D investment from 2010 to 2022

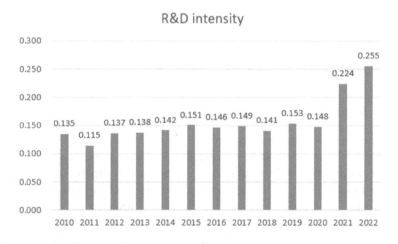

Figure 2.11: Huawei's R&D intensity from 2010 to 2022

As one of the enterprises that pay the most attention to R&D in China, as shown in the Figure 2.10 and 2.11, Huawei's R&D investment has been increasing. Huawei ranks fifth on a list of the world's

TOP50 companies investing in research and development published by the European Commission. The decline is also related to slow global economic growth, as well as Huawei's declining market share due to chip supply constraints and other factors. This also shows the importance of national innovation strength. Although Huawei's innovation ability is second to none among Chinese enterprises, there is also a shortcoming compared with other Western enterprises, so Huawei will be restricted by other countries. Therefore, China should vigorously support Chinese enterprises to develop innovation ability and promote China's innovation strength.

3. Literature research

The latecomer is always in the position of a follower if he follows the path of his predecessors. However, studies have shown that there is a kind of leapfrog catch-up, which can skip the old technology and bypass the large investment in the past technology to catch up with the developed countries (Hobday, 1995), especially in the current era of globalization and the rapid development of information technology. But under what conditions does this leapfrog catch up take place? Lee and Lim (2001) interpret the path-creating catching-up and path-skipping catching-up as a leapfrogging. This paper mainly reviews and summarizes domestic and foreign literature from the aspects of measurement and impact of innovation. Finally, the literature is reviewed.

3.1. Hypothesis

The essence of innovation-driven is talent-driven. The role of talents in promoting innovation is beyond doubt. Some research shows that master's education will benefit national innovation capability, and this effect mainly exists in the innovation leading countries and emerging countries; The positive impact of doctoral education on the innovation capability of leading countries, emerging countries and backward countries may take a long period of time to show (Li & Yang, 2021). It is gradually obvious that the talents in our country's graduate education gather in the top cities. For every 1 % increase in the cultivation and cumulative scale of postgraduate education, the city's innovation ability will increase by 0.15 % and 0.31 % respectively, and cities with higher innovation level will benefit most from the expansion of postgraduate education scale (Rousselière *et al.*, 2024). It is necessary to continuously strengthen the investment in graduate education, improve the efforts to cultivate, introduce and retain talents.

Therefore, Hypothesis 1 is proposed:

H1: When education expenditure increase, the city innovation will also improve.

The economic and social impact of innovation is not only reflected in promoting economic development, but also in improving living level, promoting social progress and reducing inequality. However, there is a positive interaction between innovation and economy: innovation promotes economy, while economic growth provides more resources, opportunities and talents for innovation. Economically developed regions have comparative advantages in innovation resource investment (Lu *et al.*, 2010), and increasing the intensity of innovation capital investment is conducive to improving the level of innovation (Shi, 2013).

Therefore, Hypothesis 2 is proposed:

H2: With the increase of economic development, the city innovation will also enhance.

Innovative cities are those with a sound innovation system, factors of agglomeration, good basic conditions, high efficiency, good benefits, strong support and leading role, and wide radiation demonstration scope. The establishment of innovative pilot cities not only strengthens government strategic guidance, promotes the agglomeration of talents and encourages enterprise investment, but also creates a good innovation ecological environment for the generation, implementation and promotion of innovative ideas. This helps to improve the urban innovation level. Numerous studies support this hypothesis. For instance, Li and Yang (2021) found that the innovative cities pilot policies improved the urban innovative ability. The agglomeration effect on talents and the incentive of enterprise investment were primary reasons for this improvement. Bai *et al.* (2022) also found that innovation-driven policies, benefits urban entrepreneurship activity. These policies had a positive impact on venture capital agglomeration, talent agglomeration, technology agglomeration, and policy agglomeration, all of which contributed to urban innovative ability. He and Ma (2021) discovered that the smart cities benefit the ability of city innovation. There is no delay in the impact of this development, and the effectiveness of pilot policies has grown over time. In cities which science and education are poor, as well as small and medium-sized cities, smart city pilots have had notable innovation effects. In conclusion, the establishment of innovative pilot cities can improve the urban innovative ability through various mechanisms such as government guidance, talent agglomeration, and enterprise investment.

Therefore, we propose Hypothesis 3:

> *H3: The innovative city pilot policy will positively impact the city innovation.*

The abundance of innovation factors has an important effect on innovation. Among them, the expenditure on science and technology can improve urban innovative ability by attracting talents, introducing advanced technology and equipment, and creating a good innovation environment. Relevant studies have proved that the competition of local government financial science and technology cost has an advantageous effect on regional innovation performance, and shows significant time characteristics. The competition of local governments' fiscal science and technology expenditure have an effect on the regional innovation gap and the evolution of its spatial pattern (Bian *et al.*, 2020). At the micro enterprise level, fiscal science and technology cost can promote the innovation output and efficiency of enterprises and improve the enterprises' innovative ability (Ma *et al.*, 2019).

Therefore, we propose Hypothesis 4:

> *H4: Science and technology expenditure will increase the city innovation.*

As the micro carriers of urban innovation, the level of enterprise innovation reflects the cities' innovative ability to a certain extent. According to the endogenous growth theory, economy and innovation have a positive interaction, and the economy predicts innovation to a certain extent. Therefore, the level of enterprise economic performance reflects the enterprise innovation to a certain extent, and is an effective predictor variable of urban innovation level. The current assets of enterprises can reflect the economic performance of enterprises, so the current assets of company can be used as a predictor variable of the innovation level of enterprises. The more current assets a firm has, the better its economic performance will be. Studies have shown that the policy of tax and fee reduction with continuous pertinency, cost reduction and long-term durability is conducive to reducing the burden of enterprises (Guo, 2019) and can effectively promote enterprise innovation (Deng *et al.*, 2020). Moreover, the more the tax burden decreases, the more the innovation output will be. Therefore, we propose Hypothesis 5, 6:

> *H5: The number of current assets of firms will increase the city innovation.*

> *H6: VAT payable by enterprises might reduce the city innovation.*

4. Data and methodology

This study examines the effect of policy of building innovative cities on China's innovation development. This paper deeply analyzes the data of 348 cities from 2001 to 2022. The "Guidelines for the Construction of Innovative Cities", which began in 2016 to build innovative cities, including 61 cities including Harbin, Nanjing, Changchun, Changsha and Guangzhou. The innovation index of Chinese cities, which comes from Kou Zonglai[3] (2017) and calculated the innovation index of various dimensions in China from 2001 to 2021. See Kou Zonglai (2017) for detailed calculation step one. The second step is the calculation of urban entrepreneurship index. The data of newly established enterprises in each city is used to measure other forms of innovation output. Considering the large differences in the size of different enterprises, it is imprecise to only use newly established enterprises to measure city entrepreneurship. For comparison purposes, the total registered capital of newly established enterprises in China in 2005 is normalized to 100 to calculate the city entrepreneurship index from 2005 to 2016. The third step is the index of city innovation and the index of industrial innovation. From the perspective of simplicity and practicality, this paper respectively ranks the innovation index and entrepreneurship index of each city, and then calculates the average of the two index rankings. Therefore, the index of urban innovation is a relative value, and the smaller the value is, the stronger the urban innovation is. Following this approach, this report calculates the innovation index for 348 cities across the country from 2001 to 2021 (see Table 2.5).

---

[3] China Urban and Industrial Innovation Report 2017.

We use Expenditure on science and technology as "endogenous R&D".

Table 2.5: Variables and sources

Variable	Explanation of variables	Data sources
innovation	Innovation index of different cities	China National Intellectual Property Administration
gdp	Gross regional domestic product	China City Statistical Yearbook
tax	Main financial indicators of industrial enterprises above designated size_VAT payable	China City Statistical Yearbook
mon	Assets status of industrial enterprises above designated size Total current assets	China City Statistical Yearbook
techno	Expenditure on science and technology	China City Statistical Yearbook
edu	Education expenditure	China City Statistical Yearbook

The descriptive analysis of each variable is shown in Table 2.6.

Table 2.6: Descriptive statistics

VARIABLE	No.	mean	S.t.d	min	max
innovation	6,888	13.09	82.11	0	2,908
lngdp	6,499	5.814	1.398	2.236	10.67
lntax	5,780	11.58	1.644	3.555	16.18
lnmon	6,479	14.38	1.662	8.452	19.66
lntechno	6,491	8.128	2.354	0	15.53
lnedu	6,500	11.10	1.495	4.248	16.26

4.1. Model construction

In order to study the effects of regional GDP, Value Added Tax payable by industrial company above designated size, total current assets of industrial company above designated size, expenditure on science and technology and expenditure on education on China's innovation level, the following model is set up:

$$Innovation_{it} = \alpha_0 + \alpha_1 lngdp_{it} + \alpha_2 lntax_{it} + \alpha_3 lnmon_{it} + \alpha_4 lntechno_{it}$$

$$+\alpha_5 lnedu_{it} + \sum \alpha_i X_{it} + \varepsilon_{it} \qquad (1)$$

In formula (1), *Innova* represents the innovation level in China, *Ingdp* represents the regional GDP, Intax represents the Value Added Tax payable by industrial company above a certain scale, Inmon represents the total current assets of industrial company above a certain scale, Intechno represents endogenous R&D, Inedu represents expenditure on education, and ε represents the random disturbance term.

4.2. Econometric specification

The correlative analysis is as follows (see Table 2.7), and the results show the relevant variables are positively correlated with the innovation indicators. Notably, the highest correlation coefficient is found between the current assets of sizable industrial enterprises and the innovation index, signifying a significant influence on urban innovation. With a correlation coefficient of 0.929, science and technology expenditure shows a robust positive relationship with the urban innovation index. Meanwhile, the impact of education expenditure on the urban innovation index, although slightly less than that of the current assets of sizable industrial enterprises, remains substantial.

Table 2.7: Correlation analysis

	Inovation	lngdp	lntax	lnmon	lntechno	lnedu
Inovation	1					
lngdp	0.377***	1				
lntax	0.284***	0.888***	1			
lnmon	0.337***	0.927***	0.929***	1		
lntechno	0.344***	0.882***	0.779***	0.833***	1	
lnedu	0.373***	0.923***	0.768***	0.830***	0.901***	1

Notes: ***, **, * denote the significance level of 1 %, 5 % and 10 %, respectively.

4.3. Results

The following table (see Table 2.8) reports the impact of innovative cities on city innovation. The results suggest that the urban innovation index has increased significantly in the policy pilot of innovative cities. The results show that the innovative cities contribute to the improvement of city innovation index.

Table 2.8: DID regression analysis

		Before	After	Total
	Control	4031	1691	5722
	Treated	830	336	1166
	Total	4861	2027	
Outcome var.				
	Innovation	S.Err	|t|	P>|t|
Before				
Control	2.506			
Treated	13.293			
Diff（T-C）	10.787	3.010	3.58	0.000***
After				
Control	19.525			
Treated	107.146			
Diff（T-C）	87.621	4.717	18.58	0.000***
Diff-in-diff	76.834	5.596	13.73	0.000***

Notes: ***, **, * denote the significance level of 1 %, 5 % and 10 %, respectively.

The DID model is used on the premise that parallel trends are satisfied, that is, when the experimental group and the control group are not impacted by the pilot policy, the urban innovation index has the same changing trend (see Figure 2.12). From the balance trend test, the difference between the innovation index of the experimental group and the control group is not very large before the pilot of the innovation city, but after the policy pilot, the difference between the innovation index of the experimental group and the control group becomes larger.

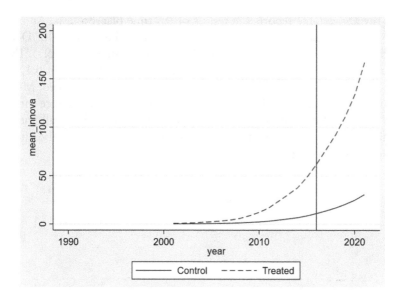

Figure 2.12: Parallel trend test

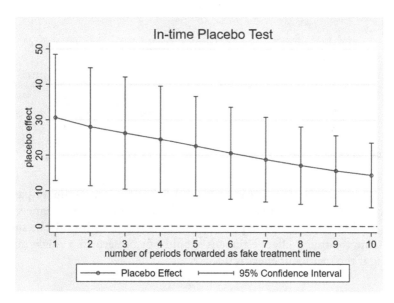

Figure 2.13: In-time Placebo test

The above table reports the results of ten time placebo tests. Among them, the standard error is the same as the standard error used for DID of the stored results (that is, both are cluster robust standard errors). The results show that the p values of all placebo effects are less than 0.1, so the null hypothesis that the placebo effect is 0 cannot be accepted. More intuitively, the command simultaneously draws 95 % confidence intervals for the placebo effect across time periods. Among them, all confidence intervals do not contain 0 values, indicating that the placebo effect is significant (see Figure 2.13).

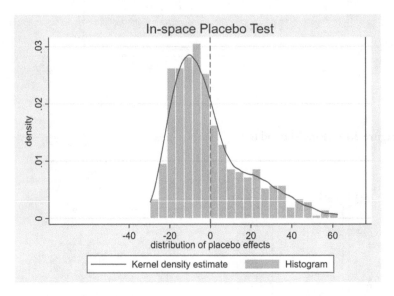

Figure 2.14: In-space Placebo test

The spatial placebo test is performed below, and in the upper panel (see Figure 2.14), the treatment effect estimates are at the extreme values in the right tail of the placebo effect distribution. Intuitively, such extreme treatment effect estimates should not be seen in a single sampling if the treatment effect is 0.

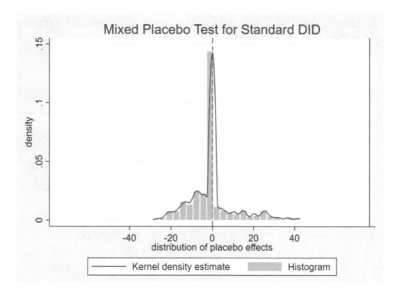

Figure 2.15: Mixed Placebo test for Standard DID

The above results show that the p-values of the two sides and the right side are less than 1 %, so the average treatment effect is significant at the level of 1 % (see Figure 2.15). More intuitively, this command also plots the distribution of the placebo effect, where the treatment effect estimate (the vertical solid line in the figure) is at the extreme value in the right tail of the placebo effect distribution.

5. An empirical analysis of the economic impact of innovation in China

The benchmark regression analysis is presented in the table below (see Table 2.9). The regression findings indicate that China's city innovation index is significantly influenced by regional GDP, Value Added Tax (VAT) payable of sizable industrial company, total current assets of such company, science and technology cost, and education cost. Notably, VAT payable, a key financial metric for large industrial enterprises, exhibits a negative impact on the city innovation index. Conversely, regional GDP, total current assets of sizable industrial company, science and technology cost, and education cost positively contribute to the city innovation index. Among them, the regional GDP is the most important to enhance the urban innovation capacity.

Table 2.9: Regression analysis

	(1)	(2)	(3)	(4)	(5)
Variables	Dependent variable: Innovation				
lngdp	24.162***	24.686***	22.616***	20.413***	15.834***
	(10.19)	(8.07)	(7.82)	(7.59)	(8.79)
lntax		-7.467***	-9.075***	-8.768***	-7.877***
		(-6.02)	(-6.38)	(-6.28)	(-6.41)
lnmon			3.317***	2.762***	3.122***
			(4.49)	(3.94)	(4.30)
lntechno				1.714***	0.279
				(4.71)	(0.73)
lnedu					5.610***
					(3.76)
Constant	-128.417***	-46.224***	-63.050***	-59.836***	-99.520***
	(-9.83)	(-9.98)	(-8.86)	(-8.86)	(-6.55)
Observations	5,994	5,264	5,260	5,245	5,243
R-squared	0.142	0.146	0.146	0.147	0.148
F test	0	0	0	0	0
r2_a	0.142	0.146	0.145	0.146	0.148
F	103.9	58.02	38.18	29.45	33.53

Notes: [a]Robust t-statistics in parentheses.[b]***, **, * denote the significance level of 1 %, 5 % and 10 %, respectively.

According to the regional division, the in-depth analysis of the urban innovation index shows that the results are basically parallel with the results in the above table (see Table 2.10).

Table 2.10: Comparative analysis of eastern, central and western regions

	(1)	(2)	(3)
Variables	Dependent variable: Innovation		
	Middle	East	West
lngdp	6.600***	31.655***	9.105***
	(6.46)	(5.50)	(5.87)
lntax	-2.802***	-20.121***	-1.840***

Table 2.10: Continued

	(1)	(2)	(3)
	(–6.47)	(–4.59)	(–3.30)
lnmon	1.832***	–0.279	0.224
	(4.72)	(–0.11)	(0.48)
lntechno	0.682***	4.904***	–0.560
	(2.98)	(3.59)	(–1.27)
lnedu	–0.814**	13.155***	–0.155
	(–2.24)	(2.75)	(–0.27)
Constant	–23.012***	–126.186***	–22.246***
	(–7.71)	(–4.60)	(–3.65)
Observations	1,838	1,853	1,552
R-squared	0.268	0.212	0.250
F test	0	0	0
r2_a	0.266	0.210	0.247
F	21.91	19.49	15.68

Notes: *"*Robust t-statistics in parentheses.*^b****, **, * denote the significance level of 1 %, 5 % and 10 %, respectively.

The following Tables 2.11, 2.12 and 2.13 provide an in-depth analysis of the impact of regional GDP, Value Added Tax payable by industrial company above designated size, total current assets of industrial company above designated size, science and technology expenditure, and education expenditure, and adds the impact of policy shocks.

Table 2.11: Comparative analysis of central regions

Variables	Dependent variable: Innovation (without the shock effect of innovation city pilot policy)				
lngdp	9.843***	8.492***	6.869***	6.060***	6.600***
	(9.26)	(8.05)	(7.12)	(6.24)	(6.46)
lntax		–2.060***	–2.939***	–2.700***	–2.802***
		(–5.68)	(–6.62)	(–6.53)	(–6.47)
lnmon			2.045***	1.814***	1.832***
			(5.04)	(4.71)	(4.72)
lntechno				0.463***	0.682***
				(2.73)	(2.98)
lnedu					–0.814**

Continued

Table 2.11: Continued

Variables	Dependent variable: Innovation (without the shock effect of innovation city pilot policy)				
					(-2.24)
Constant	-49.572***	-19.529***	-29.328***	-28.044***	-23.012***
	(-8.81)	(-7.16)	(-9.46)	(-9.32)	(-7.71)
Observations	2,095	1,840	1,839	1,838	1,838
R-squared	0.247	0.258	0.268	0.268	0.268
F test	0	0	0	0	0
r2_a	0.247	0.258	0.267	0.266	0.266
F	85.81	36.75	34.93	25.87	21.91

Variables	Dependent variable: Innovation (with the shock effect of innovation city pilot policy)					
did	70.867***	56.068***	38.274***	34.962***	33.623***	33.589***
	(7.73)	(6.93)	(4.91)	(4.79)	(4.58)	(4.58)
lngdp		6.125***	5.832***	4.797***	4.245***	4.656***
		(11.52)	(10.87)	(8.56)	(7.04)	(7.33)
lntax			-1.158***	-1.885***	-1.748***	-1.827***
			(-6.21)	(-6.57)	(-6.37)	(-6.32)
lnmon				1.536***	1.376***	1.390***
				(4.10)	(3.79)	(3.80)
lntechno					0.374**	0.539***
					(2.54)	(2.72)
lnedu						-0.617*
						(-1.96)
Constant	3.206***	-30.777***	-16.128***	-23.670***	-22.876***	-19.069***
	(17.40)	(-10.62)	(-7.84)	(-9.62)	(-9.53)	(-7.82)
Observations	2,186	2,095	1,840	1,839	1,838	1,838
R-squared	0.354	0.433	0.414	0.414	0.405	0.405
F test	0	0	0	0	0	0
r2_a	0.353	0.433	0.414	0.412	0.403	0.403
F	59.82	69.68	40.98	38.96	30.57	27.57

Notes: [a]Robust t-statistics in parentheses.[b]***, **, * denote the significance level of 1 %, 5 % and 10 %, respectively.

Table 2.12: Comparative analysis of eastern regions

Variables	Dependent variable: Innovation (without the shock effect of innovation city pilot policy)				
lngdp	45.533***	54.073***	52.552***	40.366***	31.655***
	(8.54)	(6.29)	(5.83)	(5.05)	(5.50)
lntax		-22.948***	-23.764***	-21.171***	-20.121***
		(-4.64)	(-4.89)	(-4.56)	(-4.59)
lnmon			2.172	0.048	-0.279
			(0.94)	(0.02)	(-0.11)
lntechno				8.620***	4.904***
				(6.39)	(3.59)
lnedu					13.155***
					(2.75)
Constant	-267.974***	-41.299***	-54.227**	-54.672**	-126.186***
	(-8.24)	(-2.72)	(-2.38)	(-2.29)	(-4.60)
Observations	2,104	1,860	1,858	1,853	1,853
R-squared	0.192	0.202	0.202	0.210	0.212
F test	0	0	0	0	0
r2_a	0.192	0.201	0.201	0.208	0.210
F	73.01	40.53	27.04	20.13	19.49

Variables	Dependent variable: Innovation (with the shock effect of innovation city pilot policy)					
did	129.751***	48.663**	35.135*	34.856*	32.792*	32.652*
	(7.38)	(2.51)	(1.83)	(1.82)	(1.72)	(1.70)
lngdp		41.864***	49.865***	49.049***	37.507***	28.879***
		(6.91)	(5.08)	(4.83)	(4.13)	(4.35)
lntax			-20.433***	-20.924***	-18.580***	-17.550***
			(-3.58)	(-3.73)	(-3.43)	(-3.43)
lnmon				1.238	-0.745	-1.066
				(0.63)	(-0.36)	(-0.50)
lntechno					8.296***	4.612***
					(6.15)	(3.74)
lnedu						13.048***
						(2.70)
Constant	21.474***	-247.730***	-47.272***	-54.612**	-55.182**	-126.112***
	(7.43)	(-6.79)	(-2.90)	(-2.43)	(-2.34)	(-4.64)
Observations	2,130	2,104	1,860	1,858	1,853	1,853
R-squared	0.060	0.199	0.207	0.207	0.214	0.217
F test	0	0	0	0	0	0
r2_a	0.0598	0.199	0.206	0.206	0.212	0.214
F	54.49	56.70	32.20	24.82	20.26	18.22

Notes: [a]Robust t-statistics in parentheses. [b]***, **, * denote the significance level of 1 %, 5 % and 10 %, respectively.

Table 2.13: Comparative analysis of western regions

Variables	Dependent variable: Innovation (without the shock effect of innovation city pilot policy)				
lngdp	8.674***	8.157***	8.063***	8.976***	9.105***
	(7.93)	(6.91)	(7.13)	(6.04)	(5.87)
lntax		-1.667***	-1.765***	-1.819***	-1.840***
		(-4.37)	(-3.42)	(-3.34)	(-3.30)
lnmon			0.180	0.249	0.224
			(0.43)	(0.55)	(0.48)
lntechno				-0.605*	-0.560
				(-1.67)	(-1.27)
lnedu					-0.155
					(-0.27)
Constant	-42.275***	-21.645***	-22.529***	-23.483***	-22.246***
	(-7.61)	(-7.96)	(-6.46)	(-6.12)	(-3.65)
Observations	1,795	1,564	1,563	1,554	1,552
R-squared	0.226	0.247	0.247	0.250	0.250
F test	0	0	0	0	0
r2_a	0.226	0.246	0.246	0.248	0.247
F	62.88	35.92	23.91	19.25	15.68

Variables	Dependent variable: Innovation (with the shock effect of innovation city pilot policy)					
did	34.341***	34.303***	34.473***	34.476***	37.874***	49.937***
	(4.23)	(4.22)	(4.22)	(4.22)	(4.73)	(6.00)
lngdp	5.949***	6.218***	5.511***	5.606***	6.237***	
	(5.81)	(5.64)	(6.52)	(6.94)	(7.34)	
lntax	-0.950***	-0.995***	-0.954***	-0.857***		
	(-2.64)	(-2.75)	(-2.83)	(-3.68)		
lnmon	0.287	0.234	0.178			
	(0.67)	(0.56)	(0.45)			
lntechno	-0.545	-0.464				
	(-1.42)	(-1.55)				
lnedu	0.301					
	(0.61)					
Constant	-22.018***	-19.570***	-18.772***	-17.897***	-30.564***	2.122***
	(-3.84)	(-6.46)	(-6.78)	(-7.34)	(-7.03)	(9.59)
Observations	1,552	1,554	1,563	1,564	1,795	2,572
R-squared	0.360	0.359	0.358	0.358	0.318	0.204
F test	0	0	0	0	0	2.19e-09
r2_a	0.357	0.357	0.356	0.357	0.317	0.204
F	15.00	18.02	20.56	27.40	35.30	36.06

Notes: [a]Robust t-statistics in parentheses.[b]***, **, * denote the significance level of 1 %, 5 % and 10 %, respectively.

In order to further analyze the changes of urban innovation index, this paper divides four time periods into 5 and 6 years for dynamic comparison. It can be seen from the results that it is basically similar to the previous regression results. In addition, we can see that with the development of time, each variable has a more significant impact on the city innovation index (see Table 2.14).

Table 2.14: Regression analysis of different years

Variables	Dependent variable: Innovation			
	2001–2005	2006–2010	2011–2015	2015–2021
lngdp	0.121	2.673***	6.532***	15.810***
	(0.63)	(5.81)	(3.53)	(3.07)
lntax	–0.291***	–1.662***	–7.804***	–23.947***
	(–4.31)	(–4.90)	(–5.16)	(–4.71)
lnmon	0.080	0.144	2.872**	16.901***
	(0.93)	(0.52)	(2.52)	(4.08)
lntechno	0.183**	–0.074	2.256***	–2.481
	(2.29)	(–0.40)	(2.83)	(–1.35)
lnedu	1.300***	5.109***	20.240***	60.174***
	(3.45)	(3.78)	(4.00)	(3.72)
Constant	–11.650***	–50.021***	–238.250***	–752.126***
	(–4.28)	(–4.63)	(–5.18)	(–4.85)
Observations	1,366	1,411	1,425	1,041
R-squared	0.246	0.259	0.301	0.317
F test	0	0	0	0
r2_a	0.244	0.256	0.298	0.314
F	22.73	16.42	22.49	24.31

Notes: [a]Robust t-statistics in parentheses.[b]***, **, * denote the significance level of 1 %, 5 % and 10 %, respectively.

6. Conclusions and policy implications

6.1. Theoretical contribution

This study constructs a theoretical model to explore the influencing factors of city innovative level. We use the DID model to empirically analyze the effect of innovative city pilot policies on city innovative level from 2001 to 2021. The theoretical contributions are as follows: Firstly, departing from previous literature, this study mainly investigates the endogenous R&D on the innovation of different cities. We also compare the differences for patents, trademarks, integrated circuit layout designs, geographic indicators among different regions in China. Secondly, this paper also compares the different effects of innovative city pilot policies on innovation across China's different regions. Furthermore, we compare how R&D expenditure and education expenditure impact innovation of different cities. We also explore how enterprise VAT payable impact urban innovation level. Moreover, the different effects of the five influencing factors on city innovation in different periods are compared. Finally, the DID model is used to identify the relationship between innovative cities pilot policy and city innovation level. We find through empirical analysis that urban economic development level, enterprise current assets, city's science and technology cost, city's education cost all have an advantageous effect on city innovation. VAT payable by firms has a negative impact on city innovation. The DID analysis reveal that innovative pilot cities are beneficial to the urban innovation.

6.2. Findings

6.2.1. R&D expenditure enhanced city's innovation

The study finds that science and technology expenditure has the most beneficial effect on China's city innovation index. The emphasis on science and technology cost in policies positively correlates with city's innovation. Increased investment in research and development contributes to technological advancements and fosters an innovative environment. The results suggest that prioritizing science and technology funding is crucial for enhancing urban innovation capabilities.

6.2.2. Innovative cities pilot policy improved urban innovation

The results suggest a notable rise in the city innovation index following the implementation of policies aimed at fostering innovative cities. The positive policy impact underscores the effectiveness of innovative city policies in fostering urban innovation. The policies likely include incentives, infrastructure development, and support mechanisms that create a conducive environment for innovation. This suggests that targeted and well-designed policy interventions play a vital role in driving urban innovation.

6.2.3. Education expenditure enhanced urban innovation

The study highlights the substantial impact of education expenditure on the urban innovation index, indicating its significance in promoting innovation. Education expenditure's strong positive correlation suggests that a well-educated workforce contributes significantly to urban innovation. Investments in education enhance human capital, fostering a skilled and innovative workforce. This finding emphasizes the need for comprehensive strategies that prioritize educational development to fuel long-term urban innovation.

In conclusion, this research provides valuable insights into the factors influencing urban innovation in China. The prioritization of science and technology expenditure, the careful consideration of financial indicators in certain industries, the positive impacts of well-crafted policies, and the crucial role of education expenditure collectively contribute to shaping urban innovation capabilities. The findings offer actionable implications for policymakers, urging a holistic approach that addresses these factors to foster sustainable and impactful urban innovation in China.

6.3. Policy implications

6.3.1. It is important to increase R&D expenditure for science and technology initiatives

The paper underscores the pivotal role of science and technology cost in driving city's innovation. It is important to increase government funding for science and technology initiatives. This can be achieved through strategic allocation of resources, incentivizing private sector investment in research and development, and supporting collaborative efforts between research institutions and industries. A robust ecosystem for innovation requires sustained financial backing to fuel technological advancements and foster a culture of innovation.

6.3.2. It is significant to provide tax incentives for research and development firms

The negative impact of certain industrial financial indicators on urban innovation suggests the need for targeted strategies. Develop industry-specific innovation strategies that align with the goals of sustainable development. It is better to provide tax incentives for research and development firms, such as Value Added Tax exemption or reduction. Additionally, sustainable practices in the retail and wholesale sectors should be promoted to mitigate negative impacts on urban innovation. Policymakers should strive for a balance between economic growth and environmental and social responsibility.

6.3.3. It is crucial to expand policies that support innovative city construction

The study indicates a significant positive impact of policies for building innovative cities on urban innovation. It is crucial to continue and expand policies that support innovative city construction. It is important to tailor these policies to address the specific needs of different urban environments, considering factors such as existing infrastructure, economic specialization, and demographic characteristics. It is essential to implement supportive measures, including tax breaks, regulatory flexibility, and funding incentives, to create a favorable environment for innovation. It is vital to regular evaluation and adjustments to these policies will ensure their continued effectiveness.

6.3.4. It is highly significant to prioritize education as a critical component of urban innovation strategies

The study highlights the substantial impact of education expenditure on urban innovation. It is highly significant to prioritize education as a critical component of urban innovation strategies. It is vital to increase investment in educational infrastructure, teacher training, and curriculum development to cultivate a skilled and innovative workforce. It is essential to promote STEM (science, technology, engineering, and mathematics) education to align with the demands of a technology-driven economy. Collaboration between educational institutions and industries can bridge the gap between academic knowledge and practical skills, nurturing a talent pool essential for urban innovation.

Acknowledgments

This study is supported by National Natural Science Foundation of China (Nos.71911540483, 7160310), Copyright Protection Center of China (No. BQ2022002), National Social Science Fund of China (Nos. 22BGL093, 21AZD067).

References

Bai, J., Zhang, Y., & Bian, Y. (2022). Whether innovation-driven policies promote urban entrepreneurial activity: Empirical evidence from the national innovative city pilot policy. *China Industrial Economics*, (06), 61–78.

Bian, Y., Wu, L., & Bai, J. (2020). Does the competition of fiscal S&T expenditure improve the regional innovation performance? – Based on the perspective of R&D factor flow. *Public Finance Research*, *1*, 45–58.

Deng, L. P., He, Q., & Wang, Z. (2020). The impact of corporate tax burden on innovation under the background of tax and fee reduction. *Review of Economy and Management*, *36*(06), 101–111.

Guo, Q. (2019). Potential fiscal impact and risk prevention of tax and fee reductions. *Management World*, *35*(06), 1–10.

He, L. Y., & Ma, Q. S. (2021). Can smart city pilots promote level of urban innovation? Empirical evidence based on multi-period DID. *Finance and Trade Research*, *32*(3), 28–40.

Hobday, M. (1995). *Innovation in East Asia: The challenge to Japan*. Aldershot, Hants: Edward Elgar.

Lee, K., & Lim, C. (2001). Technological regimes, catching-up and leapfrogging: Findings from the Korean industries. *Research Policy*, *30*(3), 459–483.

Li, Z., & Yang, S. (2021). Has the innovative city pilot policy improved the level of urban innovation?. *China Political Economy*, *4*(1), 56–85.

Lu, N., Li, G., & Liu, G. (2010). China's independent innovation and regional economic growth: an empirical study based on provincial panel data from 1998 to 2007. *Journal of Quantitative & Technological*, *27*(01), 3–18.

Lucas Jr, R. E. (1988). On the mechanics of economic development. *Journal of Monetary Economics*, *22*(1), 3–42.

Ma, H., Cai, Y., & Hao, X. (2019). Does fiscal expenditure on science and technology promote the innovation of Chinese industrial enterprises?. *Review of Economy and Management*, *35*(05), 43–57.

Romer, P. M. (1986). Increasing returns and long-run growth. *Journal of Political Economy*, *94*(5), 1002–1037.

Romer, P. M. (1990). Endogenous technological change. *Journal of Political Economy*, *98*(5, Part 2), S71–S102.

Rousselière, D., Bouchard, M. J., & Rousselière, S. (2024). How does the social economy contribute to social and environmental innovation? Evidence of direct and indirect effects from a European survey. *Research Policy, 53*(5), 104991.

Schumpeter, J. A. (1911). *Theorie der wirtschaftlichen entwicklung (The theory of economic development)*. Leipzig: Duncker Humdoldt.

Shi, Z. (2013). Empirical research on the relationship between regional innovation ability and economic growth quality. *Journal of Chongqing University (Social Science Edition), 19*(06), 1–8.

Chapter 3

Research on the national innovation performance: China and the rest of the world

Jin Chen and Shuo Yang

Abstract: Innovation is the first driving force to lead development, and national innovation performance is an important indicator to improve the development level of national innovation. This study comprehensively considers the whole chain process of innovation input, innovation intermediate output and innovation economic benefit, and constructs the national innovation performance evaluation index system from the dimensions of innovation input, innovation achievement and innovation benefit, in order to accurately analyze the level of China's innovation performance and indicate future directions for performance enhancement. It is found that with the support of numerous science and technology policies, China's innovation performance has soared rapidly and surpassed Switzerland in 2016, becoming the second-largest innovation country after the United States. China has made great progress in innovation input, results and efficiency in the past decade, but the low intensity of research and development (R&D) investment, insufficient number of high-level innovative talents and lack of top science and technology awards are the key problems restricting the further improvement of China's innovation performance. In order to build China into the world's scientific and technological power at an early date, China should strengthen innovation resources, strengthen innovation entities, and optimize the innovation environment to enhance innovation momentum and improve China's innovation performance.

Keywords: Innovation Performance, Evaluation Index System, Innovation Input, Innovation Achievement, The World's Scientific and Technological Power

1. Introduction

The CPC Central Committee has attached great importance to scientific and technological innovation since the 18th National Congress of the CPC, adhering to innovation as the primary driving force for development, and placing scientific and technological innovation at the core of the overall development of the country. China has made remarkable achievements in innovation development in recent years, ranking 12th in the 2023 Global Innovation Index (GII), which is the only middle-income economy among the global top 30. However, with the continuous increase of China's innovation resource input, the allocation and utilization performance of innovation resources has attracted great attention from the academic community (Chen & Guan, 2012; Guan & Liu, 2005; Wu *et al.*, 2010). Existing studies mainly focus on provincial regions in China. Based on the measurement of innovation performance, positive discussions have been conducted on how to allocate innovation resources, reduce redundancy and improve efficiency. However, there are shortcomings in the articles analyzing innovation performance from a national perspective. Based on this, it is undoubtedly of important reference value to scientifically construct a national innovation performance evaluation index system, effectively measure the level of national innovation performance, and thus locate China's innovation status in the world and the direction of future innovation performance improvement.

The innovation evaluation based on the national perspective generally adopts the index synthesis method to construct the index system, such as the Global Innovation Index (GII) and the EU Innovation Scoreboard (IUS). The advantage of synthetic index method is that it can intuitively give the overall ranking of different countries. Most of the existing studies use the index synthesis method to evaluate national innovation, focusing on the total amount of innovation, treating each country as a "black box" system, and only synthesizing the input-output index of innovation resources into an innovation performance index. It is difficult to accurately reflect the direct results of countries' innovation performance when some intermediate outputs of innovation are not translated into economic output without in-depth consideration.

The evaluation index system of innovation performance in academia is not mature at present. To fill the gaps, the final market value and process realized by innovation are combined to evaluate national innovation performance in this paper. Innovation input is the most direct and effective way for the government to support innovation activities (Lee, 2011), which mainly measures innovation talents and innovation funding input. Some scholars believe that government investment in science and technology has a positive spillover effect on innovation performance (Szczygielski *et al.*, 2017), especially on patent output (Sanyal, 2003). Innovation intermediate output refers to knowledge output, including papers, awards and patents, which reflect the results of innovation intermediate output. Economic output is a measure of the transformation of innovation results, mainly the economic value of innovation results generated by innovation activities. This study will fully consider the three aspects of innovation input, innovation achievement and innovation benefit, and synthesize the whole chain process of input, intermediate output and economic output into a national innovation performance evaluation index system, so as to scientifically evaluate the level of innovation performance of major economies in the world, and explore the current level and existing gaps of China. Targeted policy recommendations to improve China's innovation performance.

2. Design of national innovation performance evaluation index system

2.1. Principles of innovation performance index system construction

The design of innovation performance indicator system is a comprehensive, comprehensive and complex issue. This study strives to build a scientific and effective evaluation system to objectively reflect the development status and evolution trend of global innovation performance. Based on a full review of the current literature and available public data, this paper makes a comprehensive evaluation of the innovation performance of countries from multiple dimensions. First of all, the core indicators of innovation performance are selected reasonably according to the principle of index system construction, so as to build an evaluation index system that can reflect the level of national innovation performance. To construct the innovation performance development indicator system, we must follow the following guiding principles.

Scientific principle. Evaluation index system design should be based on the existing theoretical research and practical experience, adopt appropriate theories and design methods, so that the index system can fully reflect the characteristics of innovation performance development ability. The adopted evaluation index of innovation performance should reflect the connotation and internal function relationship of innovation performance development ability scientifically and reasonably on the basis of full scientific investigation.

Principle of representativeness. Since it is difficult to exhaust all the indicators that can quantify the development ability of innovation performance, this paper mainly selects representative innovation performance evaluation indicators in the process of constructing the index system. The index system should objectively reflect the level and development trend of a country's innovation performance, and use fewer indicators to fully reflect the performance content of the evaluation object, so as to avoid the inefficiency caused by the complexity of the index system, and avoid the evaluation content that is easy to be ignored in the selection of indicators.

Principle of comparability. The purpose of constructing the innovation performance index is to comprehensively evaluate the level of a country's innovation performance, which requires a horizontal and vertical comparative analysis. In order to make countries with different degrees of development and different levels of scientific and technological development comparable, the focus should be on the ratio index and the intensity index when designing the innovation performance index system. At the same time, the influence of scale effect should be taken into account, and a certain proportion of scale indicators should be selected to measure innovation performance. Based on this, the evaluation index system should be established to ensure that the index data obey the principle of comparability.

Operability principle. The ultimate purpose of index system design is to evaluate and measure. In order to measure the innovation performance level of major countries in the world more objectively, the operability of the selected indicators should be fully considered. In the process of index selection, the key is to take into account the availability of data. The data source should have the characteristics of easy access and reliable source, and the index system should also have the effectiveness and applicability.

2.2. Innovation performance evaluation index system

Establishing a scientific and reasonable evaluation index system is the basis for effective evaluation of national innovation performance. Many scholars have studied the evaluation index system of national innovation performance, but the selection of these indicators is too few and not comprehensive enough. Based on the existing statistical indicators and the classical indicators of authoritative institutions at home and abroad such as the European Innovation Report and the China Science and Technology Evaluation (European Commission, 2014; World Economic Forum, 2013), this study combined with the definition of innovation performance, and based on the principles of scientificity, comprehensiveness and data availability, conducted a study on national innovation performance from three dimensions: innovation input, innovation achievement and innovation benefit.

Innovation input is the resource input in the process of national innovation activities, which mainly includes the input of innovative talents and R&D funds. In terms of innovative talents, the total number of researchers, the number of highly cited scientists, the number of R&D researchers per 10,000 employed people and other indicators reflect the scale of innovative talents. Moreover, the proportion of STEM (science, technology, engineering, and mathematics) undergraduate and doctoral graduates and the number of graduates reflect the reserve of innovative talents. As for R&D expenditure, the ratio of R&D expenditure to gross domestic product (GDP) and R&D expenditure per 10,000 people are two indicators that reflect the intensity and intensity of R&D expenditure.

Innovation results refer to the academic research results produced in innovation activities and the exclusive rights enjoyed by knowledge invention and creation results, mainly including knowledge results and technical results. Previous studies have found that increasing the number of patent applications and promoting product innovation will improve innovation performance (Soh, 2014). In terms of the selection of indicators, patents are usually selected as a measure of innovation performance in the literature (Acs et al., 2002; Bettencourt et al., 2007). Patents have certain advantages in representing technological achievements. On the one hand, patents contain a large amount of information about technologies and inventions; on the other hand, patent data is relatively easy to obtain, and the system and regulations of patent application, examination and authorization in different regions are basically consistent within a country, making patent data of different countries comparable. In addition, scientific papers and scientific awards can reflect innovative knowledge achievements. Knowledge achievements are mainly composed of the number of scientific and technological papers, the proportion of highly cited scientific and technological papers and the number of top scientific and technological awards. The technical achievements mainly include the number of PCT (Patent Cooperation Treaty) international patents, the number of valid patents, the number of patent applications per thousand R&D personnel, the number of applications per hundred billion dollars of GDP and other indicators.

Innovation benefit refers to the economic value generated by innovation activities. Some scholars use the income of knowledge products as a measure of innovation performance, which can better reflect the application and commercialization level of innovation achievements (Pellegrino *et al.*, 2012). In this study, intellectual property income, information and communication technology (ICT) service exports, creative products exports, intellectual property income as a proportion of total trade, ICT service exports as a proportion of total trade, creative products exports as a proportion of total trade, and high-tech products exports as a proportion of exports were measured.

The comprehensive evaluation index system of national innovation performance is composed of 3 first-level indicators, 6 second-level indicators and 22 third-level indicators. The specific national innovation performance evaluation index system is shown in Table 3.1.

Table 3.1: **National innovation performance evaluation index system**

First-level index	Secondary indicators	Tertiary indicators
Innovation input	Innovative talent scale	Total number of researchers
		High number of cited scientists
		Number of R&D researchers per 10,000 employed people
		Proportion of undergraduate graduates in STEM majors
	Stock up on innovative talent	The proportion of STEM doctoral graduates
		Number of STEM graduates
	Research and development funding input	R&D expenditure as a proportion of GDP
		R&D expenditure per 10,000 people

Table 3.1: Continued

First-level index	Secondary indicators	Tertiary indicators
Innovations	Knowledge outcomes	The number of scientific and technological papers included in the main search tools
		High proportion of cited scientific and technological papers
		Number of top tech awards won
	Technical achievements	Number of PCT international patents
		Number of patents in force
		Patent applications per 10,000 R&D personnel
		Patent applications per $100 billion of GDP
Innovation benefits	Economic benefits	Proportion of high-tech exports
		Intellectual property income
		Exports of information and communications technology (ICT) services
		Creative products exports
		Income from intellectual property as a share of total trade
		ICT services exports as a share of total trade
		Share of creative exports in total trade

3. Measurement models and quantitative sources of national innovation performance

3.1. Measurement model

Index comprehensive evaluation methods can be broadly divided into subjective weighting method and objective weighting method. The entropy method is an objective weighting method, which can scientifically and objectively assign weights to indicators according to the degree of dispersion of indicators, so as to reduce the subjective arbitrariness of subjective weighting method. This paper uses the entropy method to measure the innovation performance level of 17 countries. The specific calculation steps are as follows.

First, the original data of 22 three-level indicators are processed without dimension. In order to make the national innovation performance evaluation index have annual comparability, this study processed the data of each index based on the efficiency coefficient method.

$$y_{ij}\left(t_k\right) = \frac{x_{ij}\left(t_k\right) - \min\left[x_j\left(t_1\right)\right]}{\max\left[x_j\left(t_1\right)\right] - \min\left[x_j\left(t_1\right)\right]}. \tag{1}$$

Where $x_{ij}\left(t_k\right)$ and $y_{ij}\left(t_k\right)$ represent the original and standard data values of the j indicator in the i country in the t_k year respectively, $\max\left[x_j\left(t_1\right)\right]$ and $\min\left[x_j\left(t_1\right)\right]$ represent the maximum and minimum values of the index of each country respectively.

Secondly, each indicator is standardized and the weight coefficient value of the i country in the j indicator is calculated:

$$P_{ij} = \frac{s_{ij}}{\sum_{i=1}^{n} s_{ij}}. \tag{2}$$

Where P_{ij} represents the standardized value of the j indicator of the i country, n indicates the year.

Then, the entropy value $\left(e_j\right)$ of the j indicator is obtained:

$$e_j = -k\sum_{i=1}^{n} P_{ij} ln P_{ij}. \tag{3}$$

Where $k = 1/ln\left(n\right)$, e_j range is $[0,1]$.

Further, the weight ω_j of the j indicator is calculated.

$$\omega_j = \frac{1-e_j}{\sum_{j=1}^{m}\left(1-e_j\right)}. \tag{4}$$

Where m represents the number of countries.

Finally, the comprehensive evaluation index $S_i\left(t_k\right)$ of the national innovation performance of the i country in the year t_k is calculated by using the linear weighting method. The specific formula is as follows:

$$S_i\left(t_k\right)=\sum_{j=1}^{m}\omega_j P_{ij}\left(t_k\right).\qquad(5)$$

3.2. Sample selection and data sources

Based on the principles of data availability and representativeness, this study selected two countries in North America (the United States and Canada), four countries in Asia (South Korea, China, Japan and Turkey), and 11 European countries such as the United Kingdom, France, Switzerland, Germany and Sweden as research objects, totaling 17 countries. This study focuses on the innovation performance status and evolution trend of different economies from 2010 to 2022. The data is obtained mainly from international organizations such as the Organization for Economic Cooperation and Development (OECD), the US National Science Foundation (NSF), and the World Intellectual Property Organization (WIPO). There are some individual missing values in some index data due to the long research period, and the missing data is reasonably estimated by interpolation method in this paper.

As for the specific data sources of the indicator system, the total number of researchers and R&D researchers per 10,000 people are obtained from the official website of OECD, and the data of highly cited scientists is derived from Clarivate; The proportion of undergraduate graduates in STEM majors, the proportion of doctoral graduates in STEM majors and the total number of STEM majors graduates are derived from NSF database. R&D expenditure as a share of GDP and R&D expenditure per 10,000 people are derived from the OECD database.

The number of scientific papers included in the main search tool refers to the selected journal papers and conference papers in the Scopus database, assigned according to the author's country and the proportion of the number of participating authors; The proportion of highly cited scientific and technological papers refers to the proportion of papers in the R&E field whose citation rate is in the top 1 %, and the data comes from the NSF database. The number of top science and technology awards awarded is mainly measured by the Nobel Prize, Fields Medal and Abel Prize, and the data is obtained mainly from the official website of the Nobel Prize and the International Mathematical Union (IMU).

Data for the PCT indicator of the number of international patents and patent applications per thousand people are obtained from the

OECD database, while indicators such as the number of patents in force and the number of applications per billion dollars of GDP are derived from the WIPO database. The export proportion of high-tech products is measured by the proportion of high-tech products in the export of manufactured products. The income of intellectual property is measured based on the cost of using the country's intellectual property in foreign countries. The data of the export proportion of high-tech products, intellectual property income and ICT service export are obtained from the WIND database. The exports of creative products are derived from the UNCTAD database, and the three indicators of intellectual property income as a share of total trade, ICT services exports as a share of total trade and creative products exports as a share of total trade are derived from the WIPO database.

4. National Innovation Performance Index and comparative analysis

4.1. Overall situation of national innovation performance

Based on the comprehensive evaluation system of national innovation performance, this study measures the innovation performance index, innovation input, innovation achievement and innovation benefit of 17 countries during 2010–2022. Table 3.2 shows the development level and evolution trend of innovation performance of each country. The results indicated that the United States ranks the first place in the innovation performance index. China's innovation efficiency is soaring, and the gap with the US is narrowing. Furthermore, the performance of South Korea's innovation efficiency index is stable, showing a steady upward trend and jumping to the third place in the world in 2020. Switzerland, Japan and Sweden show a steady and fluctuating trend in innovation performance. From the perspective of the growth rate of the innovation performance index, China occupies a dominant position with a high growth rate of 6.40 %. China's innovation performance has entered a fast-rising channel in the past decade, rising all the way from the sixth place in the world in 2010, and surpassing Switzerland to become the second-largest country in the world after the United States in 2016. China's innovation performance has made great progress.

Table 3.2: The level and growth rate of innovation efficiency of major countries

Innovation performance	2010	2011	2012	2013	2014	2015	2016	2017	2018	2019	2020	2021	2022	Growth Rate
U.S.	0.468	0.501	0.503	0.533	0.538	0.525	0.514	0.560	0.588	0.599	0.618	0.608	0.624	2.66 %
China	0.267	0.279	0.314	0.322	0.330	0.359	0.373	0.393	0.419	0.441	0.473	0.511	0.529	6.40 %
South Korea	0.257	0.266	0.281	0.291	0.298	0.309	0.314	0.325	0.345	0.351	0.370	0.386	0.394	3.97 %
Swiss	0.329	0.348	0.354	0.364	0.364	0.360	0.366	0.353	0.359	0.372	0.360	0.363	0.363	0.90 %
Japan	0.339	0.342	0.353	0.348	0.363	0.342	0.343	0.347	0.334	0.353	0.351	0.352	0.353	0.37 %
Sweden	0.319	0.323	0.326	0.329	0.331	0.340	0.341	0.330	0.330	0.331	0.337	0.344	0.348	0.80 %
Germany	0.253	0.263	0.273	0.280	0.290	0.282	0.289	0.306	0.318	0.314	0.314	0.342	0.333	2.52 %
Britain	0.277	0.263	0.274	0.274	0.272	0.276	0.319	0.293	0.299	0.305	0.311	0.312	0.332	1.65 %
France	0.247	0.241	0.249	0.248	0.274	0.256	0.268	0.269	0.271	0.270	0.264	0.260	0.276	1.03 %
Denmark	0.225	0.238	0.239	0.234	0.232	0.238	0.252	0.240	0.241	0.240	0.242	0.240	0.249	0.92 %
Belgium	0.192	0.193	0.199	0.221	0.213	0.207	0.218	0.214	0.219	0.224	0.236	0.239	0.244	2.23 %
Austria	0.192	0.202	0.205	0.207	0.227	0.216	0.227	0.220	0.221	0.229	0.226	0.234	0.239	2.00 %
Czech Republic	0.155	0.161	0.164	0.171	0.174	0.173	0.169	0.175	0.185	0.192	0.200	0.210	0.210	2.78 %
Canada	0.190	0.201	0.196	0.197	0.197	0.201	0.184	0.186	0.203	0.194	0.195	0.197	0.198	0.38 %
Italy	0.140	0.141	0.140	0.143	0.151	0.150	0.156	0.158	0.170	0.167	0.173	0.181	0.176	2.10 %
Russia	0.096	0.083	0.085	0.095	0.103	0.107	0.110	0.114	0.111	0.116	0.115	0.126	0.122	2.16 %
Türkiye	0.067	0.064	0.064	0.047	0.066	0.073	0.076	0.071	0.075	0.079	0.087	0.092	0.098	3.59 %

4.2. The fractal dimension of national innovation performance

Figure 3.1 shows the evolution trend of innovation performance level, innovation input, innovation outcome and innovation efficiency for each country during 2010–2022, with significant differences among different economies in each dimension. From the dimension of innovation input, the world's major economies showed a steady improvement trend during the study period, with the United States rising rapidly and maintaining the first place in the world. Japan, which had been ranked second in the world until 2014, showed a downward trend from 2015 and dropped out of the top 10 in 2020. The level of innovation investment in China and South Korea showed rapid improvement during the study period, entering the top three in the world since 2015. From the dimension of innovation achievements, the United States showed a large fluctuation trend, maintaining the world's first place in the decade 2010–2021, but was surpassed by China in 2022. China showed a steady rise in the innovation achievements index compared with the United States, jumping from the 11th place in 2010 to the first place in the world in 2022, achieving earth-shaking changes. The rest of the countries are relatively stable in the innovation Achievement Index, and the change in the ranking is not significant. In terms of innovation effectiveness, the United States ranked first, China steadily improved to second globally, the United Kingdom ranked third, and Sweden and Switzerland fell out of the top three after 2017, to fourth and fifth place in 2022. China's innovation performance index, innovation input, innovation achievement and innovation efficiency all showed a rapid rise, indicating that China's scientific and technological innovation had been greatly improved during the study period. In particular, the total number of researchers, the number of highly cited scientists, the number of STEM graduates, the number of scientific and technological papers, the number of PCT international patents and other scale indicators rose rapidly. Although China's performance is relatively good in terms of scale indicators, there is still a large room for growth in structural indicators such as the number of R&D researchers per 10,000 employees, the proportion of R&D expenditure in GDP, the proportion of R&D expenditure per 10,000 people, the number of patent applications per 1,000 R&D personnel, and the proportion of intellectual property income in total trade volume.

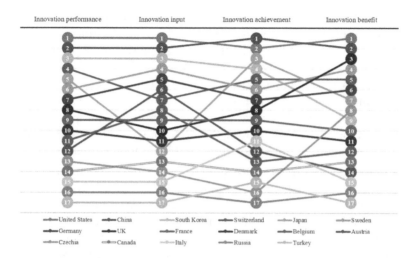

Figure 3.1: Development trends of innovation performance in different dimensions and countries

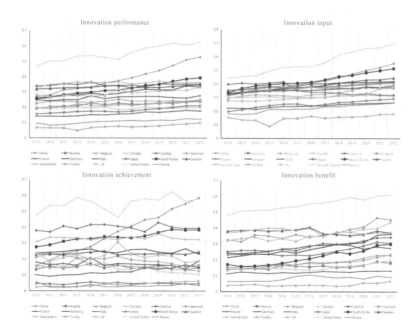

Figure 3.2: Ranking of countries by dimension and innovation performance in 2022

In order to improve the level of innovation performance, China should not only focus on its own development, but also understand the gap between China and the world's innovation powers and learn from the development path of the world's innovation powers. As can be seen from Figure 3.2, China has made great progress in terms of innovation input, achievements and benefits, especially in the dimension of innovation achievements, which has achieved a qualitative leap in the past decade. However, there is still a certain gap between China and the United States in the dimensions of innovation input and innovation efficiency.

The innovation performance of the United States is much better than that of other countries in the world, mainly because the United States has established an efficient modern science and technology system after the Second World War, and the improvement of innovation performance cannot be achieved without a large amount of innovation investment. Whether in military, economy or science and technology, the United States can become the world's number one power, which is closely related to its continuous investment in research and development funds in the field of scientific innovation. The United States ranks first in the world in R&D investment for a long time, accounting for 35.6 % of the world's total in 2021. The US R&D investment rose from US $72.75 billion in 1981 to US $806 billion in 2021, an increase of more than 10 times in four decades. In terms of R&D intensity, the proportion of US R&D input to GDP rose from 2.27 % to 3.46 % in 1981–2021. Although China's R&D investment shows an increasing trend year by year, in 2021, the R&D expenditure will be 668 trillion yuan, and the proportion of R&D expenditure in GDP will only be 2.43 %, which is still a big gap compared with the US. In addition, in terms of the number of highly cited talents and the number of researchers per 10,000 people, China still has a lot of room for improvement compared with the US. On the one hand, the US encourages foreign high-level scientific and technological talents to immigrate to the US, promotes the free and beautiful living environment in the US, and provides generous welfare benefits. On the other hand, the US research universities are an important force for scientific and technological innovation in the US, cultivating a large number of high-level innovative talents for the US. The immigration policy and the high level of higher education have provided the United States with a steady stream of talent resources.

In terms of innovation benefits, the United States has increased policy support for scientific and technological innovation and concentrated on the development of low-energy and technology-intensive industries. The United States far exceeds other countries in terms of intellectual property income and export of creative products. The high income of technical products and services is a key feature of the United States to become a strong country in innovation performance. In 2021, China's intellectual property exports will be only US $11.76 billion, with a net payment of US $35.14 billion. The US intellectual property exports will be more than ten times that of China (US $128.35 billion), with a net income of US $82.28 billion. In terms of export of creative products, China's export value is less than one third of that of the US.

In addition, in terms of innovation achievements, although China surpassed the US in 2022 and ranked first in the world, it lagged behind in the number of top international science and technology awards and the number of patents per 10,000 R&D personnel. According to statistics, the US has ranked first in both the number of international science and technology awards and the number of patents per 10,000 R&D personnel since the Second World War. According to the study, the US has undoubtedly become the global innovation highland with 46.4 % of the talents who won the international top science and technology awards from 2010 to 2020[1]. In contrast, China is obviously not enough to win the Nobel Prize, the Fields Medal and the Abel Prize. The lack of international science and technology awards will inevitably restrict the development of China's science and technology, and hinder the process of China's construction of a world science and technology power. In addition, China is lower than the global average in the number of PCT patent applications per 1,000 people, and the number of PCT patent applications per 1,000 people is only 1/4 of that of the US. China should strengthen its efforts in the development of key core technologies, disruptive technologies and leading-edge technologies.

5. Research conclusions and recommendations

As an important participant in innovation activities, the state is not only the promoter and policy supporter of innovation activities, but

---

[1]   The United States has won the Nobel Prize, the Fields Medal and the Abel Prize and other top international science and technology awards 58 talents, and the world's top science and technology awards 125 talents.

also an important investor in innovation activities and an organizer of major innovation. National innovation performance is the core factor of national economic development and comprehensive competitiveness improvement. This study constructs a national innovation performance evaluation index system from the dimensions of innovative talents, innovation achievements and innovation benefits, and finds that China has made all-round progress. However, there is a big gap between China and the United States in such indicators as R&D investment intensity, high-level innovative talents, high-tech product and service income, and the number of top science and technology awards awarded. It is urgent for China to build on its innovation endowment, pool innovation resources, strengthen innovation entities and improve the innovation environment, so as to enhance its independent innovation capacity and continuously narrow the innovation performance gap with the US.

Innovation resources are the basic guarantee factor for driving innovation performance, and governments should prioritize ensuring adequate supply of human resources and research and development funding. In terms of the development of innovative talents, a multi-level system for training innovative talents should be established, a platform for sharing talent information should be established, and the talent management system should be optimized. At the same time, the talent market service system should be improved, and the talent incentive mechanism should be innovated to ensure the high-level development of talents. In terms of funding input, innovation entities are encouraged to rely on industrial alliances and other innovation ecological platforms to jointly raise R&D funds. At the same time, actively promote capital market financing, vigorously expand indirect financing channels, and build a multi-level technology financial service platform system to create a good financing ecology for innovation entities.

Innovation entities are the basic carriers to drive innovation performance. On the basis of effective protection of innovation resources, China should choose the "subject-resource" dual driving strategy. Efforts should be made to support the synchronous development of technological innovation entities and knowledge innovation entities. On the one hand, it has promoted the development of Chinese universities and actively cooperated with foreign universities, providing China with knowledge resources and scientific and technological talents. On the other hand, we will further promote industry-university-research cooperation, promote coordinated development among innovation subjects in an all-round way, further increase investment in science and technology education, and strengthen the production, transformation and application of knowledge in the field of innovation. We should strengthen the building of China's industry-university-research community and enhance the openness of all entities.

The innovation environment is the accelerator and stabilizer that drives innovation performance. The Chinese government should foster a competitive innovation environment to ensure the sustainable development of innovation in China. In terms of the market environment, China should improve the fair competition system, further promote the reform of "deregulation", implement the negative list of market access, actively integrate with the international industrial chain, supply chain and value chain, and provide a fair and open environment for innovation activities. In terms of promoting the transformation of scientific and technological achievements, we should improve the incentive mechanism for the transfer and transformation of scientific and technological achievements, clearly define the important contributors to the transformation of scientific and technological achievements, rationally distinguish the contributions of researchers and related transfer and transformation service personnel, and fully mobilize the enthusiasm of all transformation entities. In addition, the Chinese government should set up a guiding fund for the transformation of achievements of major scientific and technological projects, and build a "green channel" for major independent innovation products to enter the market.

References

Acs, Z. J., Anselin, L., & Varga, A. (2002). Patents and innovation counts as measures of regional production of new knowledge. *Research Policy*, *31*(7), 1069–1085.

Bettencourt, L. M., Lobo, J., & Strumsky, D. (2007). Invention in the city: Increasing returns to patenting as a scaling function of metropolitan size. *Research Policy*, *36*(1), 107–120.

Chen, K., & Guan, J. (2012). Measuring the efficiency of China's regional innovation systems: application of network data envelopment analysis (DEA). *Regional Studies*, *46*(3), 355–377.

European Commission. (2014). *Innovation union scoreboard 2014*. Report of European Commission.

Guan, J., & Liu, S. (2005). Comparing regional innovative capacities of PR China based on data analysis of the national patents. *International Journal of Technology Management, 32*(3–4), 225–245.

Lee, C. Y. (2011). The differential effects of public R&D support on firm R&D: Theory and evidence from multi-country data. *Technovation, 31*(5–6), 256–269.

Pellegrino, G., Piva, M., & Vivarelli, M. (2012). Young firms and innovation: A microeconometric analysis. *Structural Change and Economic Dynamics, 23*(4), 329–340.

Sanyal, P. (2003). Understanding patents: The role of R&D funding sources and the patent office. *Economics of Innovation and New Technology, 12*(6), 507–529.

Soh, P. H., & Subramanian, A. M. (2014). When do firms benefit from university–industry R&D collaborations? The implications of firm R&D focus on scientific research and technological recombination. *Journal of Business Venturing, 29*(6), 807–821.

Szczygielski, K., Grabowski, W., Pamukcu, M. T., & Tandogan, V. S. (2017). Does government support for private innovation matter? Firm-level evidence from two catching-up countries. *Research Policy, 46*(1), 219–237.

World Economic Forum (WEF). (2013). *The global competitiveness index 2013–2014: Country profile highlights.* Report of World Economic Forum.

Wu, J., Zhou, Z., & Liang, L. (2010). Measuring the performance of Chinese regional innovation systems with two-stage DEA-based model. *International Journal of Sustainable Society, 2*(1), 85–99.

Chapter 4

The innovation model in South Korea

YEN VU, LIEN P. NGUYEN AND DIEU ANH N. LE

Abstract: This study analyzes the distinctive features of the Korean Innovation Model, unraveling the unique blend of government interventions, industry dynamics, and societal factors that have propelled South Korea into a global innovation powerhouse. By studying the evolution of the innovation model through the improvement of policies over the historical timeline of Korea, the development of the innovation management system from the grassroots level to the national level, and some typical success case studies, this research sheds light on the adaptability and resilience associated with Korea's innovation model. Through a comparative analysis, this study aims to distill valuable lessons and principles that can inform innovation strategies and policy frameworks for other countries worldwide.

Keywords: Korean Innovation Model, Korean National Innovation System, Regional Innovation System, Innovation Development Management System, Creative Economy.

1. Regional, industrial and national innovation systems of Korea

1.1. Regional and national innovation systems

Since the 1980s, the National Innovation System (NIS) of South Korea (hereafter Korea) has undergone a transition not far removed from its remarkable economic growth model. However, sector-specific growth across the country has left imbalances in Korea's geographical distribution of research and development (R&D) activities (Shapiro *et al.*, 2010). Since the 2000s, South Korea has been actively working towards establishing the NIS to foster technological innovation, which in turn is expected to bolster economic growth on a national scale. The administration under

Roh Moo-hyun (2003–2008) laid the foundation for the South Korean National Innovation System (KNIS) (Kim *et al.*, 2020).

Since the mid-1980s, the Korean government has focused on promoting the development of high-tech industries such as the semiconductor industry. By the 1990s, high-tech industries had transformed into knowledge-intensive sectors. During this time, the Korean government invested heavily in industrial cities and science and technology (S&T) parks. The national R&D program is implemented along with initiatives to help private companies develop high technologies.

Entering the 21st century, the Korean economy has faced many challenges as the rapid economic growth ended, with Gross Domestic product (GDP) per capita growth continuously stagnating since 2007. The economic growth rate is forecast to decrease from 3.5 % in 2010 to 2.1 % in 2020, and the employment rate has only been about 59 % since 2007. Besides, the population is aging rapidly, and the need for new growth-boosting technologies is clouding South Korea's economic development prospects. Therefore, in 2013, President Park Geun-hye's administration launched the "Innovation Economy" initiative as a core philosophy to address the above challenges (Cirera *et al.*, 2021).

South Korea's transition from an economy driven by low-wage coefficients to an economy driven by average-wage efficiency and an economy driven by high-wage innovation in recent decades has been impressive. Korea has implemented appropriate innovation policies, especially fiscal and monetary policies, focusing on investment in people and infrastructure and expanding abroad to increase the proportion of world trade.

1.1.1. Korean National Innovation Systems (NIS)

The expansive interpretation covers every interconnected institutional entity involved in generating, disseminating, and utilizing innovations. Conversely, the specific interpretation focuses on organizations and institutions directly engaged in seeking and advancing technological innovations, such as research and development departments, universities, and public institutes (Chung, 2002; Dodgson, 2009).

We understand innovation to mean technological innovation and define a NIS as a complex of innovation actors and institutions directly related to the generation, diffusion, and appropriation of technological innovation and the interrelationship between innovation actors (Kina, 1993).

A NIS consists of three comprehensive innovation actor groups, *i.e.*, public research institutes, academia, and industry. They are actual research producers who carry out R&D activities. In addition, there are governments, *i.e.*, the central and regional governments, which act as coordinators among research producers regarding their policy instruments, visions, and perspectives for the future (Lee & Lee, 2018) (see Figure 4.1).

The central government has undertaken multilateral measures to support balanced regional development and promote numerous research- and development-based policies.

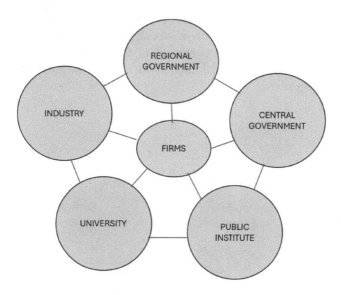

Figure 4.1: National innovation systems of Korea
Source: Chung (2002), Nelson (2013), Lee and Lee (2018)

Central and local governments act as supporters and assistants to activate innovation clusters based on administrative districts.

The NIS can be depicted as a regional and sectoral innovation system matrix. The concept of Regional Innovation System (RIS) is an excellent tool to generate effective sectoral innovation systems. Therefore, by generating different but competent Spatial Innovation Systems (SISs) in different regions, RISs can build an effective NIS (Chung, 2002).

The Korean national innovation system is relatively weak, with only three advanced regional innovation systems. However, it shows that six fast-developing regional innovation systems and seven less-developed regional innovation systems exist. They should be refined and further developed based on the active support of the central government, a number of policy measures aimed at activating interactive learning between innovation actors, and the close cooperation between the central and regional governments (Chung, 2002).

1.1.2. Korean Regional Innovation Systems (RIS)

RIS is a complex of innovation actors and institutions in a region that are directly related to technological innovation's generation, diffusion, and appropriation and an interrelationship between these innovation actors. Like a NIS, a RIS is composed of three main innovation actor groups: universities, industrial enterprises, and public research institutions (see Figure 4.2).

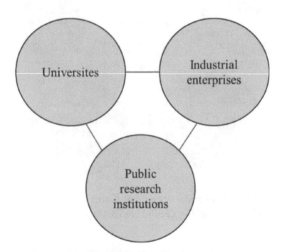

Figure 4.2: Regional innovation systems of Korea
Source: Chung (2002), Kim *et al.* (2020)

Only when Korea introduced a regional political system for the first time in 1995, did it begin to recognize the importance of regional innovation activities? Since then, the Korean central and regional governments have made a great effort to develop their regional economies in terms of technological innovation (Chung, 2002).

(1) The regional governments are emphasized in effectively directing and coordinating innovation activities in each region: Promote efficient region-led growth by establishing systematic governance between existing innovation institutions; Identify R&D issues necessary in the region; Promote and support specialized regional R&D planning organization; Reinforce regional R&D competence; Share R&D know-how between local and central government (Development & Act, 2015).

(2) Public research institutes, private companies, and universities are the actors in innovation activities. They are placed differently in innovation and significantly enhance regional and national technological competitiveness.

(3) Korean universities are heavily focusing on education, and university research institutes are included for the measurement of the innovation potential of the university sector (Sohn *et al.*, 2009).

Creating an innovation ecosystem for regional innovation clusters in differentiated domains under the leadership of innovative regional stakeholders. Innovation environments are ones in which many clusters coexist due to the environment's industries, size, and cooperating agencies centered around science belts, special R&D districts, and local universities.

2. Innovation, technology policy, and Intellectual property laws

2.1. Innovation, technology policy

Korea's innovation policy through stages of development is as follows (see Table 4.1):

Table 4.1: Korea's innovation policy through stages of development

Period from 1960 to 1990	Period from 1991 to 2012	Period from 2012 to present
– Nationalize banks to provide scarce capital for large family-run industrial corporations (Chaebol), prioritizing privileges for Chaebol to grow strongly. – Shift from light industry to heavy industry and high technology, promote the building of domestic science and technology capacity by establishing science and technology research institutes. These research institutes conduct research and development in key technology areas, supporting the technology upgrading strategy. – Create a science and technology system capable of absorbing and adapting foreign technologies – Public financial investment supports science and technology research and development; the private sector is also encouraged to actively absorb and improve technology from technologically pioneering countries such as the US and Japan.	– In 2008, the Korean government issued "Initiative 577" – The private sector enjoys government R&D tax incentives and is supported in importing foreign technology. – Develop national strategic science and technology. – Strengthen basis: promote basic research, develop human resources – Globalization and regionalization: build R&D hub in Asia, promote regional innovation – Improve R&D efficiency: support technology commercialization for small and medium enterprises (SMEs) – Extend public participation From 2008 to 2013: – Foster top 7 technology areas – Cultivate world-class human resources – Promote basic research	– Strengthen links between public research institutes and the private sector and improve the legal environment for innovative entrepreneurs. In addition, small businesses are also encouraged to apply information and communications technology (ICT) to seize the opportunities of the digital economy. – The Korean government has transformed the traditional economic model into a growth model led by innovation. – Future promising technologies such as 5G mobile communications and realistic media will be selected and developed. – New generation network industries such as 10Gbps Internet and new generation Wi-Fi targeting foreign markets will be promoted.

Table 4.1: Continued

Period from 1960 to 1990	Period from 1991 to 2012	Period from 2012 to present
– Innovation policy in the internalization stage was based on implementing functional incentives, such as tax-based incentives for R&D, rather than sectoral incentives. These incentives enhanced the private firm's capacity for innovation and accumulating in-house R&D capabilities and were coupled with public R&D investments under the National R&D Program (NRDP) of the Ministry of Science and Technology (MOST). – Universities and private firms could participate in such a program, competing against Government Research Institutes (GRIs) for R&D project funding. These policies targeted balanced development of research capabilities within universities, GRIs, and private firms, and the fostering of networks among researchers, but decentralization policy from the early 1980s was primarily focused on expanding the Seoul macro-cluster to include proximate regions (Sohn et al., 2009)	– Support technology innovation of SMEs: promote commercialization – Globalization: reinforce joint research with other countries – Strengthen regional science & technology – Spread science and technology culture (Kim et al., 2020)	– Transition to an innovation economy: Transforming Korea's economic model to a creativity-based growth model. – The Korean government focuses on supporting the fields of healthcare research, bioscience, ICT, and new materials – Develop national strategic technologies – Promote basic research – Foster human resources with diverse abilities – Build regional innovation systems – Support SME venture companies: promote technology transfers and commercialization – Create jobs in science & technology – Spread creative culture (Kim et al., 2020)

2.2. Intellectual property laws

Intellectual property (IP) refers to a brand, invention, design, or other creations over which a person or business has legal rights. Almost all businesses own some forms of IP, which could be a business asset (Cho, 2019).

Classification of intellectual property laws may vary subject to legal scholars or countries and may change over time. A common way of classifying intellectual property laws could be as follows (see Table 4.2):

Table 4.2: Structure of intellectual property laws in South Korea

Categorize	Contents
Laws on Industrial property and industrial designs	– Patent Act – Utility Model Act – Design Protection Act – Act on the Design of semiconductor integrated circuits
Laws on Copyright and neighboring rights	– Copyright – Computer Programs Protection Act
Laws on Trademarks and other distinctive signs	– Trademark Act – Internet Address Resource Act
Laws on Plant variety protection	– Act on the Protection of new varieties of plants

Source: Hyung-Gun (2015)

- Copyright safeguards written or published materials, including books, music, films, online content, and artistic creations;
- Patents protect commercial innovations, such as new products or processes for businesses;
- Designs protect visual designs like drawings or digital models;
- Trademarks protect symbols, logos, words, or sounds that distinguish your products or services from competitors.

Since 1995, the Republic of Korea has been a member of the World Trade Organization (WTO), mandating member nations to establish intellectual property laws under minimum standards. Consequently, there should be minimal discrepancies between the intellectual property laws of South Korea and those of other developed count.

2.2.1. Copyright

The Republic of Korea is a participant in the Berne Convention regarding copyright protection. Its copyright laws are rooted in the Copyright Act of 1957, known as the Korean Copyright Act. Copyright is an inherent intellectual property right in South Korea, meaning registration isn't mandatory, although advisable for potential disputes. Registration for all copyright forms, except computer software, is conducted through the Ministry of Culture, Sports, and Tourism. In contrast, software requires registration with the Ministry of Information and Communications. Given South Korea's significant online presence, particular copyright concerns involve internet piracy, with books, especially textbooks, frequently subject to unauthorized copying. Additionally, there's a market for hardware circumvention tools, such as modified chips and game copiers, designed to evade technological protection measures.

2.2.2. Patents, utility models, and industrial designs

South Korea's patent regulations are outlined in the Patent Act and the Utility Model Act. The Republic of Korea distinguishes between two types of patents: patents, also known as "invention patents," and utility models, referred to as "minor patents." A utility model can be granted for any device defined as "the creation of technical ideas using the rules of nature." In contrast, an invention patent can be granted for more advanced devices and inventions. Invention patents protect for up to 20 years. South Korean patent law adheres to the "first to file" principle, meaning if two individuals apply for a patent for the same invention, the first applicant will receive the patent. Industrial designs are covered under the Design Act, which grants protection for a maximum of 15 years. The Korean Intellectual Property Office oversees all aspects of patents, utility models, and industrial designs.

2.2.3. Trademarks

Trademark regulation in the Republic of Korea is governed by the Trademark Act. The process is identical to that in the UK, which protects designs, symbols, colors, or other elements employed to distinguish a company's goods or services. Registration typically spans seven to ten months, and a trademark remains valid for ten years, renewable indefinitely in ten-year increments thereafter. The Korean script presents challenges for foreign rights holders during registration and enforcement due to the potential for various renditions of the same word's sound. Given the intricacies involved, seeking local guidance is advisable when selecting Korean brands or trade names.

2.2.4. Customs record

You have the option to register your marks with the Korean Customs Service, commonly referred to as "customs records". This enables local Customs offices to monitor and intercept counterfeit goods. Typically, applying for records is facilitated by a lawyer or local attorney and entails a fee of approximately £250.

2.2.5. Unfair competition

In addition to the legislation governing specific forms of intellectual property, such as patents and trademarks, the Unfair Competition Prevention and Trade Secrets Protection Act safeguards rights holders against unfair practices. This encompasses activities such as "cybersquatting" and infringements involving unauthorized copies of designs, commonly known as "dead copies."

3. Korean innovation and innovation development management system

3.1. Korean innovation development management organisational apparatus

The management of the innovation development system in Korea is organized around a complex infrastructure, consultancies, and many other institutions involved in formulating, implementing, and evaluating the technology and innovation policy portfolio (see Figure 4.3).

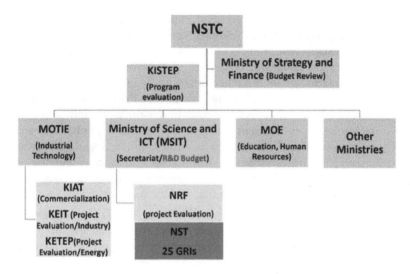

Figure 4.3: Korean innovation development management organizational apparatus
Source: MSIT

- National Science and Technology Council (NSTC) was established in 1999. This committee includes 13 ministers involved in science, technology, and innovation policy and 9 experts in the Science and Technology community. NSTC is an inter-ministerial organization expected to play a vital role in policy coordination between ministries, chaired by the president himself. The tasks of NSTC are:
  + Coordinate policies and plans to promote science and technology;
  + Develop a Basic Plan for Science and Technology;
  + Allocation and coordination of national R&D budget;
  + Investigate, analyze, and evaluate national R&D programs;
  + Coordinate policies for developing science and technology and human resources.

MSIP (Ministry of Science, ICT and Future Planning) and MOTIE (Ministry of Trade, Industry and Energy) are the central ministries. Other departments with primary responsibility for the study include the Defense Acquisition Program Administration (DAPA), The Small and Medium Business Administration (SMBA), and the Ministry of Land, Infrastructure, and Transport (MOLIT).

- The Ministry of Science, ICT, and Future Planning (MSIP) was responsible for developing the creative economy through S&T, established in February 2013. MSIP's primary functions include: Building and coordinating creative economy strategies; Coordinating national science and technology strategy; Developing, implementing, and evaluating basic science R&D policy; Planning, encouraging, and supporting core, future-oriented, and large-scale technology development; Supporting basic and applied research conducted at public research institutes, universities, and private research institutes; Achieving technological autonomy and safe use of nuclear technology; Enhancing general awareness of science and technology; Improving IT infrastructure and industry.

- Ministry of Trade, Industry and Energy (MOTIE) is responsible for developing, transferring, and commercializing industrial technology and supporting business innovation. MOTIE's main tasks in technology and innovation include: Developing, implementing, and evaluating R&D policy; Promoting the transfer and commercialization of industrial technology and industrial standards; Promoting the regional innovation system; Strengthening the internal innovation capacity of companies; Supporting private investment for R&D; Strengthening global cooperation on technology development coordination; Developing technology policies according to needs.

- The Ministry of Economy and Finance (MOSF) also participates in technology and innovation policy in budget allocation. MOSF allocates the total budget for R&D to ministries based on technology and innovation programs in the form of ordinary capital after being approved by the National Assembly in December each year.

- The Korea Institute of S&T Evaluation and Planning (KISTEP) is Korea's main S&T planning agency. Specific functions of the Institute include: Building, coordinating, and supporting central science and technology policies, including forecasting 11 science and technology development trends; Analyzing and evaluating S&T-related programs implemented by all government ministries and supporting the coordination and allocation of R&D budgets; Conducting research on planning, evaluation, and research management systems at home and abroad; Disseminating information and data on R&D policy.

- The Ministry of Education (MOE) is the government agency responsible for education policy and management in the country.

Its mission is to ensure the provision of quality education that meets the needs of all learners and contributes to national development.

In addition, public organizations in technology and innovation in Korea, such as:

- The National Research Foundation of Korea (NRF) is responsible for managing and evaluating basic R&D projects, spending budget to operate academic research organizations, supporting domestic/international academic exchanges, providing facilities and equipment to prepare for academic activities, providing scholarships or educational loans, conduct surveys, analyzes and evaluations, and collect statistical information on the support and management of research carried out in university.

- National Research Council of Science & Technology (NST). Its mission is to support national research projects and policy and drive the development of the knowledge industry by supporting and managing 25 GRIs in science and technology. Its strategies are strengthening the leading type of research system, forming a research cooperation ecosystem, disseminating tangible research accomplishments, improving the research-centered management system, and activating an S&T policy-think tank.

- Korea Institute of Advancement of Technology (KIAT). KIAT's primary functions include assessing and managing regional industrial support projects, upgrading innovation capacity through joint R&D and international cooperation, and promoting the transfer and commercialization of developed technology.

- Korea Planning & Evaluation Institute of Industrial Technology (KEIT) supports the planning, evaluation, and management of industrial R&D projects. Also, it conducts technology needs surveys and technology forecasts in manufacturing.

- Korea Institute of Energy Technology Evaluation and Planning (KETEP) supports MOTIE in developing industrial technology policy. KETEP also evaluates and manages national R&D projects in the energy sector.

- The Science and Technology Policy Institute (STEPI) is a specialized agency on science and technology policy. STEPI conducts research and analysis on S&T-related issues, providing ministries and public agencies with policy ideas and recommendations for policy to promote technology and innovation.

3.2. Management of innovation development

3.2.1. National level

Korea has coordinated a policy consisting of three mechanisms: promulgating national laws and plans, institutionalizing horizontal coordination, and evaluating 12 public R&D programs.

✓ Promulgate national laws and plans (see Table 4.3)

**Table 4.3: Korean innovation development policy
for the period 1962–2023**

Period	Policy

1962–1996	– 1st Five-Year Plans (FYP) for Technology Development (1962–1966)
	– 2nd FYP for S & T Development (1967–1971)
	  + Science and Technology Promotion Act (1967)
	  + Science Education Act (1967) 3rd FYP for S & T Development (No Materials)
	– S & T Section Plan of 4th FYP for Economic & Social Development (ESD) (1977–1981)
	– The first national R&D program initiated by the Ministry of Science and Technology was implemented in 1982
	– S & T Section Plan of 5th FYP for ESD (1982–1986)
	– S & T Section Plan of 6th FYP for ESD (1987–1991)
	– Creation of the Presidential Advisory Council on S & T (PACST) (1991)
	– S & T Section Plan of 7th FYP for ESD (1992–1996)
	– Technological Strategy Section Plan of FYP for New Economy (1993–1997)

1997–2012	– FYP for S & T Innovation (1997–2002) – Framework Act on Science and Technology (2001) Provisions on NSTI System Promotion and S & T Basic (Master) Plan – The Complementary FYP for S & T Innovation (2000 -2002) – S & T Basic Plan (2002–2006) – S & T Basic Plan in Participatory Government (2003–2007) – 2nd S & T Basic Plan (2008–2012) – "577 Initiative" (2008)
2013– present	– Created MISP (2013) – The Creative Economy Plan (2013) – S & T Section Plan of 3rd FYP for ESD (2013–2017) – S & T Section Plan of 4th FYP for ESD (2018–2022)

Source: The authors

Framework Act on Science and Technology 2001 was developed to promote science and technology development systematically. This legal framework includes regulations for developing mid- and long-term policies and implementation plans. It is also the legal basis for inter-ministerial cooperation in coordination with science and technology policies. The law also provides an overall framework supporting R&D activities, science and technology agencies, and the legal basis for promoting an innovation-oriented culture.

In 2008, the Government announced the "577 Initiative" with ambitious targets focusing upon seven critical areas of R&D and seven support systems. Seven key technology areas (50 Critical technologies, 40 Candidate technologies): (1) Key industrial technologies, (2) Emerging industrial technologies, (3) Knowledge-based service technologies, (4) State-led technologies, (5) National Issues-related technologies, (6) Global Issues-related technologies, and (7) Basic & Convergent technologies. Seven support systems such as (1) World-class human resources, (2) Basic and fundamental research, (3) SME innovation, (4) Science and technology globalization, (5) Regional innovation, (6) Science and technology infrastructure, and (7) Science and technology culture – to become one of the world's seven central science and technology powers.

In 2010, the government enacted a "Long-Term Vision for Science and Technology Development and a Future Vision for S&T: Towards 2040" which aimed to shift the locus of the "national innovation system from government to the private sector, enhancing the efficiency of R&D investments, upgrading R&D to world standards, and harvest the opportunities presented by new technologies" (Ministry of Education, Science and Technology, 2008, 2010).

After the implementation of the Creative Economy Plan in 2013, the goal is to merge Korean creativity and imagination with science, technology, and ICT to foster the development of new industries and markets, as well as to fortify existing industries, ultimately leading to the creation of quality employment opportunities. This is outlined with three overarching objectives and six strategies. There are three goals: (1) Create new jobs and markets through creativity and innovation, (2) Strengthen Korea's global leadership through a creative economy, and (3) Create a society where creativity is respected and manifested. Six Strategies: (1) Properly compensate creativity and develop an ecosystem that promotes start-ups; (2) Strengthen the role of venture companies and SMEs in the creative economy and support entry in global markets; (3) Growth engines to pioneer new markets and new industries; (4) Fostering global creative human resources; (5) Strengthening the innovation capacity of science, technology, and ICT; (6) Building a creative economy culture. Other Basic Plans followed in 2013 and 2018, and the Future Vision was updated in 2017 (UNESCO, 2020). For instance, the current Master Plan (2018–2022) aims to expand national STI capacity, enhance the S&T ecosystem, and help to create new industries.

✓ Institutionalize links

The Korean government coordinates cooperation between many ministries and agencies related to innovation. The scale of this coordination task in Korea is complicated by the many ministries and public implementation agencies involved in technology and innovation policy and programming. The National Science and Technology Commission (NSTC) is critical in policy coordination between ministries. MSIP funds universities and public research institutes related to basic and applied research and IT R&D support. However, MOTIE emphasizes support for SMEs related to research and implementation at the pre-commercial stage. Other ministries support universities, research institutes, and businesses in their fields.

✓ Evaluate the R&D program and budget allocation

The evaluation of R&D programs, as part of the R&D budget allocation process, also plays a vital role in coordinating Korea's technology and innovation policies.

Post-evaluation of R&D programs is carried out in three forms:

+ Self-assessment: Self-assessment work is carried out by relevant Ministries or agencies (for example, MOTIE evaluates industrial technology programs; Public research institutes, under the supervision of MSIP, conduct a management review once a year). The main evaluation criteria include compatibility with program objectives, relevance of action goals, program management system quality, plan completion, and use of assessment results.

+ Comprehensive assessment: conducted by MSIP with support from KISTEP. Integrated evaluation is used for budget allocation decisions and appraisal of evaluation results and processes for each Ministry.

+ Specific assessments (focused, in-depth assessments) are carried out by MSIP for (1) programs that require significant support from the state budget over a long period; (2) programs that require inter-ministerial or inter-program coordination; (3) programs need to be streamlined as well as require close links to achieve synergistic effects, or (4) programs with content related to critical socioeconomic issues of national significance.

3.2.2. Local level

In 2003, the Government initiated an extensive innovation-oriented drive in all sectors of the economy. It looked to the subnational regions – which are underdeveloped relative to the capital area – as a new source of growth. Four significant policies for regional innovation:

- Providing the basis for establishing RIS
- Enhancing the innovation capabilities of provincial universities
- Encouraging the advancement of science and technology in provincial areas
- Establishing industry-university-research institution network

The focal point shifted towards the convergence and integration of technologies and industries for the growth of the next generation, with future economic productivity relying more on technology convergence.

- In 2003, the policy focused on next-generation growth engine industries, particularly the development of high technologies (6 T): information, bio-, nano-, space, environment, and cultural technologies.
- These industries encompassed digital TV and displays, intelligent robots, future cars, next-generation semiconductors, next-generation mobile communication, intelligent home networks, digital content and software solutions, next-generation batteries, and biomedical product.

In 2004, the Industrial Complex Cluster Program (ICCP) was introduced as part of the nation's balanced development policies. This initiative fosters collaboration, mutual learning, and information exchange among regional innovation stakeholders, including large corporations, SMEs, universities, research institutions, support organizations, and local government entities. The objective is to establish a cooperative and inclusive network involving industry, academia, government, and research institutions, bolstering corporate R&D capabilities, improving living and working conditions for highly skilled technical professionals, creating open clusters with both domestic and international ties, and enhancing the alignment between government policies and regional innovation initiatives.

3.2.3. Enterprise level

In 2010, the Government reformed the ICCP into the Pan Regional Cluster Program with the policy of a 5+2 Regional Economic Area (REA) and also launched a so-called "win-win" strategy between SMEs and large companies.

Since 2015, the Korean Government has established 17 Regional Centers for Creative Economy and Innovation (CCEI) with 18 offices in localities to support start-up businesses in connecting with local and foreign corporations. The CCEI model focuses on supporting the development of a specific field by connecting local authorities with a large enterprise, which is often the leading enterprise in a particular field in the locality. Each major corporation (Samsung, Hyundai Motor Group, LG, SK, Lotte, Hyundai Heavy Industry, Hanwha and GS) is required to participate in one of these 17 centers and focus on its area of expertise.

Each CCEI operates a direct support system for each subject, cooperating with local/central governments and large corporations. Each center is a non-profit operating unit, selected from affiliated organizations or in cooperation with state agencies, economic organizations, universities, and research institutes... based on consultation with the Minister of Science, Information and Communications and Future Planning of Korea; leaders of large enterprises; and city mayor or governor.

CCEIs have about $1.8 billion annually to operate through investments, guarantees, and loans. Because they operate on the basis of in-depth knowledge, experience, and simple investment and cooperation mechanisms, CCEIs effectively support start-up businesses in accessing modern technology and equipment and in all business activities, from design to product export.

In 2023, the Ministry of SMEs and Startups (MSS) announced the "Manufacturing Innovation and DX Acceleration Strategy (MIDAS 2027)". This strategy includes direction for the digital transformation of the small and medium-sized manufacturing industry and the action plan of the Yoon administration. The strategy prioritizes the digital advancement of small and medium-sized manufacturing sectors. Government efforts are being made to encourage larger corporations to partner with SMEs. A proposed manufacturing innovation portal will facilitate and simplify these collaborative efforts.

4. A case study of the innovation models in Korea

4.1. Case study 1: Creative economy in Korea

4.1.1. Introduction and background

South Korea has been actively promoting the concept of a "creative economy" as part of its economic development strategy. Since the 1990s, the local government has implemented policies to create creative cities (Cha, 2015). However, Korea ended its significant economic growth era in the 21st century; the country has faced several crises, including a reduction in the economic growth rate from 6.8 % in 2010 to 2.6 % in 2022 (World Bank, 2023) and a decline in the employment rate. In addition, the rapidly aging population from around 11 million people in 2011 to 16.7 million people in 2022 (Statista, 2021), the lowest birth rate in 2022 at 0.78 births per woman (Statista, 2022) and the lack of next-generation technology growth contribute to clouding over the economic outlook. To cope with these problems, in 2013, the Korean government started a new creative economy policy concept under the Park Geun-Hye administration called "job-centered creative economy". The policy aimed to promote deep collaboration between businesses, education, and the government to create an environment that fosters innovation and economic development. It created an innovation ecosystem consisting of research centers, startup companies, and educational institutions (Yoon & Park, 2017).

4.1.2. Objectives (Cha & Yu, 2013)

➢ Connecting industries: The program emphasizes combining traditional and innovative industries to create added value.

➢ Encouraging startups and businesses: It focuses on supporting and fostering the development of startups and innovative businesses to create new jobs and markets.

➢ Developing creative economic communities: The program aims to build creative economic communities where collaboration between businesses, the government, and local communities is emphasized.

➢ Connecting the industry and academic sector: The program encourages a great collaboration between industries and academic organizations to fill the gap between theoretical knowledge and practical applications.

➢ Sustainable economic development: Contribute to sustainable economic development by developing and using environment-friendly initiatives in business practices and promoting corporate social responsibility.

4.1.3. Action plan

The government had set up six strategies and developed 24 promotion tasks to reach its objectives (see Table 4.4).

Table 4.4: The action plan for the new model of creativity economy

Strategy 1 • Creation of the ecosystem in which creativity is rewarded fairly and it is easy to start a new company
Promotional Task 1-1 • To expand investment in creative idea and technology
Promotional Task 1-2 • To create an environment where it is easy to establish a start-up
Promotional Task 1-3 • To convert ideas and technologies into intellectual properties and to protect, utilize, and promote the same
Promotional Task 1-4 • To vitalize the commercialization of creative property
Promotional Task 1-5 • To construct a start-up safety network with which it may be possible to try again
Strategy 2 • Strengthen the competitiveness of the venture and small & medium-sized company as a key player
Promotional Task 2-1 • To establish the foundation for the growth of venture business as well as small and medium-sized businesses
Promotional Task 2-2 • To support the global market development of venture business as well as small and medium-sized businesses
Promotional Task 2-3 • To promote the coexistence and cooperation among large businesses as well as small and medium-sized business-
Promotional Task 2-4 • To solve difficulties, such as labor shortage, etc., of venture businesses as well as small and medium-sized business-
Strategy 3 • Creation of the new growth engine to develop new products and new markets
Promotional Task 3-1 • To create a new growth engine of the existing industry through the convergence of scientific technology and ICT
Promotional Task 3-2 • To develop software and Internet-based new industry and high-value contents industry
Promotional Task 3-3 • To create a new market through human-centered technology innovation
Promotional Task 3-4 • To develop a new market through the discovery and promotion of a new promising industry
Promotional Task 3-5 • To promote industrial convergence and market creation through regulation rationalization
Strategy 4 • Training of creative global talent
Promotional Task 4-1 • To reinforce the convergence and creative talents training
Promotional Task 4-2 • To expand education in order to infuse competitiveness and entrepreneurship
Promotional Task 4-3 • To vitalize the overseas expansion and domestic inflow of creative talents
Strategy 5 • Strengthen the Innovation Competitiveness of S&T and ICT as the basis of the creative economy
Promotional Task 5-1 • To improve the R&D system to expand potential and strengthen commercialization
Promotional Task 5-2 • To reinforce ICT innovation competency and to accelerate the creative economy
Promotional Task 5-3 • To reinforce the cooperation of industry, academy, research institution, and local government in order to create jobs
Promotional Task 5-4 • To reinforce the roles of scientific technology and ICT to solve global problems
Strategy 6 • Development of the creative economy culture in which people and government work together
Promotional Task 6-1 • To develop an environment of creativity and imagination
Promotional Task 6-2 • To fuse public resources and national ideas through Government 3.0
Promotional Task 6-3 • To innovate methods with which the government operates to realize the creative economy

Source: MSIP (2013)

The government also emphasized in the plan the importance of creative economy innovation centers, which would be placed for each of the 17 local governments by 2015. Each center is a nonprofit institution that is selected from local organizations such as public organizations, universities, and research organizations under the direction and consultation of the government and the Ministry of Science. The purposes of these centers are to support the local creative economy and improve the development of local society, which is towards realizing the goals of policy in general (Ministry of Science, ICT and Future Planning, 2014). In particular, the center uses a diversity of methods and models to build a specialized local industry by connecting and matching a local government with a large enterprise (see Figure 4.4).

In addition to the creative economy centers, the government established the online creative economy town in 2013. This online platform aimed to create an online community that supports a variety of economic actors to collaborate and create a platform for them to share ideas online, support each other, and connect with experts in the fields.

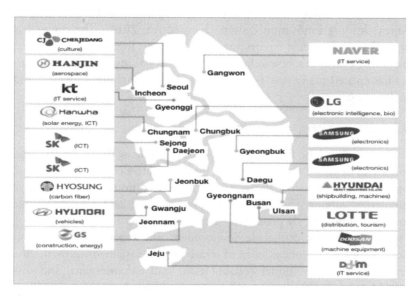

Figure 4.4: Connection of creative economy innovation centres by government and businesses
Source: MSIP (http://www.msip.go.kr)

4.1.4. Achievements

The creative economy program has also achieved many remarkable achievements. After three years of implementation, the program has created over 2 million jobs for residents and increased the nation's employment rate. Besides, it also creates 13 new growth engine industries (focused on technology) such as 5G mobile communications, renewable energy hybrid systems, big data, intelligent internet of things, and so on (Lee, 2013).

In addition, with creative economy towns, 17 CCEIs have been established in cities and provinces across South Korea (Kim & An, 2014). The Korea Institute of Startup and Entrepreneurship Development (KISED) operates and controls all these centers. CCEIs have supported over 1,200 startups in Korea to increase their sales revenue, creating over 1,400 employments (John, 2023). The companies in these centers have made significant contributions to the Korean economy by creating competitive products and services.

One of the notable successes of the policy is the Daejeon Innovation Center. The center was established in 2013 and has become one of Korea's leading innovation centers (Kim & An, 2014). The center has created an innovation environment by bringing together stakeholders, including businesses, researchers, and educational institutions. The center has created many new products and services, including medical and high-tech products.

4.1.5. Conclusion

In summary, the Creative Economy programs in Korea are strategic initiatives designed to create vibrant and innovative communities. These programs prioritize collaboration between traditional and innovative industries, support startups and small businesses, and actively engage local communities. By promoting a culture of innovation and providing crucial support for economic development, the programs aim to position designated regions as hubs of creativity and sustainable growth. The emphasis on international collaboration, skill enhancement, and sustainable practices further contributes to building dynamic and resilient communities that thrive in the global creative economy. Through ongoing monitoring and adaptability, these programs demonstrate a commitment to remaining responsive to changes in economic and technological landscapes, ensuring long-term success and prosperity for the designated areas in South Korea.

Despite the great success of economic development, the program also faces a number of long-term challenges, including financial sustainability, integration technology, talent retention, and attraction.

- Financial sustainability: Like many other long-term programs, maintaining financial sustainability is always a major challenge for the authorities. Maintaining consistent and sufficient funding for the creative economy program requires long-term financial commitment and the efforts of all stakeholders.
- Integration technology: Rapid technological change requires continuous adaptation within programs. The challenge is to integrate emerging technologies effectively and keep pace with industry trends. Creating the frameworks for technology integration, encouraging collaboration, and providing technical training to the workforce would be possible solutions to this problem.
- Talent retention and attraction: Ensuring a vibrant program ecosystem depends on a professional and skillful workforce. Therefore, retaining and attracting more skilled professionals, entrepreneurs, and researchers to participate in programs can be challenging. Developing comprehensive programs, offering incentives, and promoting the program's success stories could be the way to fix problems.

4.2 Case study 2: The Free Semester Program and the SMART initiative in Korea

4.2.1. Overview

The technology-driven world holds great promise but raises public concern as jobs across all industries become increasingly automated, generating enormous opportunities and potential risks. A report by the McKinsey Global Institute (2017) suggests that around 50 % of all work activities worldwide have the potential to be automated by adapting current technologies. The report also estimated that by 2030, 75 to 375 million workers (3 % to 14 % of the global workforce) will need to change jobs. According to prediction by the World Economic Forum (2016a), 65 % of children entering primary school today will eventually work in jobs that do not exist today. These transformations provide changes for people worldwide to take advantage of technologies to accelerate economic growth and foster an inclusive and creative future. These technological advancements are forcing governments to reconsider how to generate new values while workers must adapt to novel work methodologies.

Adapting to these changes will involve engaging in diverse activities that necessitate social and emotional skills, creativity, high-level cognitive abilities, and other skills that are relatively difficult to automate. This is closely connected to an increased demand for education systems (World Economic Forum's prediction, 2016b). Therefore, many countries are developing their national education competency framework and reforming educational systems to effectively address these advancements.

Korea's impressive economic growth over the last forty years has been well documented. A key factor propelling this progress has been the government's investment in human capital. Consequently, Korea has ensured a proficient workforce through vocational education and training (Ministry of Education, 2015a). Moreover, Korea is currently addressing challenges posed by the Fourth Industrial Revolution and the innovation economy in preparation for the future. To this end, the Korean government has introduced and executed two notable educational policies: The Free Semester Program (FSP) and the SMART Initiative. Through these efforts, Korea seeks to meet the industrial demands and promote the development of a creative economy.

4.2.2. The Free Semester Program (FSP)

The Free Semester Program, introduced by the Korean government, represents a paradigm shift in the traditional education system. Launched to encourage creative thinking, interdisciplinary learning, and a deeper understanding of practical skills, the program allows students to choose courses freely for one semester.

First announced in 2013, FSP aimed to develop competencies for the 4th industrial revolution, such as creativity, problem-solving, higher-order thinking, and social-emotional skills (Ministry of Education, 2015b). There are four objectives in this program: providing students with opportunities to discover their dreams and talents and encouraging continuous self-reflection and development through experiences in exploring and designing their aptitudes and futures; transforming knowledge and competition-centric education into a framework that facilitates self-directed creative learning and the cultivation of creativity, personality, and social skills; fostering a positive school environment that instills confidence in public education policy direction for a joyful student life; providing focused career and experiential education across different educational stages (recognition at primary level, exploration at middle level, determination at high school level) and enhancing school autonomy in curriculum design to facilitate the effective implementation of programs aimed at nurturing dreams and talents.

The FSP was initially implemented in 43 schools and then further expanded to all 3,204 middle schools (all public middle schools) as its overall positive impact was recognized. The FSP is implemented for one semester in the first year (Grade 7) across all public middle schools. During this period, students can choose a more interactive curriculum and participate in extracurricular activities that align with their interests and passions (Park, 2016). The FSP is characterized by a student-centered approach to teaching and learning, moving away from traditional lecture-based classes. Instead, students solve complex problems through project-based learning and debates. Extracurricular activities within the FSP encompass field trips to regional career centers, aiding students in exploring and navigating their career interests. These opportunities extend to other activities, including student club involvement, arts, and sports. Each school can choose one of four tracks, determined by considerations such as capacity, infrastructure, and the specific needs of students and parents.

Several studies have aimed to assess the effects and influence of the FSP on classrooms, with early findings indicating positive outcomes. Recent survey findings indicate that the FSP is fulfilling its intended objectives. According to research conducted by the Korean Educational Development Institute (Choi & Lee, 2014), 81.1 % of students engaged in the FSP reported an enhancement in their ability for self-expression, 74.6 % noted an improvement in their relationships with teachers, 63.5 % experienced an increase in their enjoyment of learning, and 50.4 % observed a stress reduction related to studying.

Participants in the FSP improved their social skills and ability to collaborate with others (Park, 2016). Teachers also observed the positive influence of the FSP. Teachers noted that students were more active in teamwork and self-organization. Furthermore, some students acquired skills in using design software and employed 3D printers to create new products. As a result, academic achievements improved more significantly among students who participated in the FSP compared to those who did not, as reported by the Korean Educational Development Institute (KEDI, 2018).

The FSP goes beyond being merely an innovative education program; it entails coordinated efforts among policymakers, teachers, parents, and students. The government plays a vital role by offering comprehensive guidelines, conducting teacher training programs, and providing a web-based platform (http://www.ggoomggi.go.kr/) to assist schools in implementing FSP. This platform ensures that students, parents, and teachers can access valuable resources and exchange the latest information.

The FSP significantly transforms Korea's education system and equips students with essential skills for the future. The lessons learned from FSP could potentially have implications for other education programs aimed at enhancing students' non-cognitive skills to meet the requirements of a creative economy.

4.2.3. SMART initiative

In 2011, Korea introduced its SMART Education initiative, which stands for Self-directed, Motivated, Adaptive, Resource-enriched, and Technology-embedded education. The primary objective of this initiative is to customize educational systems, bridging the divide between emerging sectors and the education sector to fulfill the workforce requirements of an innovative economy through the utilization of digital educational materials.

There are five main features (Chun, 2018):

(1) Enhancing the use of digital textbooks based on intelligent learning model.
(2) Organizing online classes in all education levels and setting up an online assessment system.
(3) Creating a free and safe education environment and developing an ecosystem for sharing content.
(4) Promoting teacher training.
(5) Developing the foundational infrastructure for cloud educational services in schools.

The SMART Education initiative is a comprehensive effort that involves building infrastructure, introducing new teaching methods, establishing relevant policies and legal frameworks, and fostering a cultural shift to support ICT education. The overarching objective is to redefine the concept of education, moving away from traditional classroom lectures to a more interactive format. Establishing an online platform for sharing educational materials is a crucial factor contributing to the success of the SMART Education initiative.

Various assessments have been conducted to evaluate the impact of the SMART Education initiative, focusing on the use of online platforms and digital textbooks in education. These findings show positive changes in students, especially in problem-solving and communication skills, creativity and innovation abilities, and critical thinking. Besides, teachers also become more active and effective when using digital platforms in teaching (Kye *et al.*, 2016).

Many mixed opinions about using digital platforms in education are primarily related to their downside effects, including exposure to harmful online content and health-related problems (UNESCO, 2019). Also, there are concerns about the weak relationship between teachers and students and their peers due to the use of digital technology in education (Chun, 2018).

In summary, despite some weaknesses of adopting the SMART education initiative in Korea, the program has achieved meaningful outcomes, including free high-quality materials, the creation of a digital learning environment and ecosystem, the application of new teaching methods for innovative education, and improved collaboration between school, public, local government and businesses.

4.2.4. Conclusion

The Free Semester Program and the SMART Initiative exemplify South Korea's commitment to innovative and technology-driven education. By fostering creativity, interdisciplinary learning, and digital literacy, these policies contribute to shaping a new generation of students equipped with the skills needed to succeed in an increasingly digital and interconnected world.

References

Cha, D. W. (2015). The creative economy of the Park Geun-hye administration. *Korea's Economy*, *30*, 34–46.

Cha, D. W., & You, J. Y. (2013). The concept of creative economy and analysis policies of leading countries. *Korea Institute of Science & Technology Evaluation and Planning, ISSUE PAPER, 1.*

Cho, Y. (2019). *Intellectual property law in South Korea.* Kluwer Law International.

Choi, S., & Lee, S. (2014). *Second semester free semester program satisfaction survey results.*

Chun, S. (2018). Birth and major strategies of smart education initiative in South Korea and its challenges. In *Smart education and e-Learning 2017 4* (pp. 439–449). Springer International Publishing.

Chung, S. (2002). Building a national innovation system through regional innovation systems. *Technovation, 22*(8), 485–491.

Cirera, X., Mason, A. D., De Nicola, F., Kuriakose, S., & Tran, T. T. (2021). *The innovation imperative for developing East Asia.* World Bank Publications.

Development & Act. (2015). *Basic research promotion and technology development support Act. 13211.*

Dodgson, M. (2009). Asia's national innovation systems: Institutional adaptability and rigidity in the face of global innovation challenges. *Asia Pacific Journal of Management, 26*, 589–609.

Hyung-Gun, K. (2015). *Overview and historical development of intellectual property laws in South Korea.* Retrieved from: https://klri.re.kr:9443/bitstream/2017.oak/4631/1/61625.pdf

John. (2023, May). *Center for creative economy and innovation in South Korea – CCEI.* Retrieved from: https://www.seoulz.com/center-for-creative-economy-innovation-in-south-korea-ccei/ on 28 December 2023.

KEDI (Korea Education Development Institute). (2018). *The analysis of free semester programs.* Sejong: KEDI.

Kim, E. S., Bae, K. J., & Byun, J. (2020). The history and evolution: A big data analysis of the national innovation systems in South Korea. *Sustainability, 12*(3), 1266.

Kim, Y.-J., & An, S.-G. (2014). Government R&D medium- and long-term investment strategies for the realization of the creative economy. *KISTEP Inside and Insight, 5*, 45.

Kina, L. I. N. S. U. (1993). National system of industrial innovation: Dynamics of capability building in Korea. *National Innovation Systems: A Comparative Analysis*, 357–383.

KISTEP. (2023). Retrieved from: https://www.kistep.re.kr/eng/ on 24 December 2023.

Kye, B., Kim, H., Shin, A., & Jeong, G. H. (2016). *The impact of the implementation fidelity of research schools on the effectiveness of digital textbook.* Daegu: Korea Education and Research Information Service. [In Korean]

Lee, J.-J. (2013). *The creative economy and roles of government* (p. 32). Science and Technology.

Lee, K., & Lee, J. (2018). *The National Innovation System (NIS) and readiness for the 4th industrial revolution: South Korea compared with four European countries.*

Mckinsey Global Institute. (2017). *Jobs lost, jobs gained: Workforce transitions in a time of automation.* New York: Mckinsey Global Institute.

Ministry of Education. (2015a). *Education, the driving force for the development of Korea.* Sejong: Ministry of Education in Korea.

Ministry of Education. (2015b). Plans to start the middle school free semester program confirmed (in Korean). *The Ministry of Education of the Republic of Korea Blog.* 2015. (Press Release), Retrieved from: https://ifblog.tistory.com

Ministry of Education, Science and Technology. (2008). *The second science and technology master plan.* Seoul, Republic of Korea: Ministry of Education, Science and Technology.

Ministry of Education, Science and Technology. (2010). *2040 future vision for science and technology.* Seoul, Republic of Korea: Ministry of Education, Science and Technology.

Ministry of Science, ICT and Future Planning. (2014). *Rules of installation and operation of the creative economy people and government conference,* Presidential Decree No. 25820 (December 2014).

Ministry of Science, ICT and Future Planning and related authorities. (2013). Action plan for the creative economy—Creation plan for creative economy ecosystem (June 2013).

MOTIE. (2023). Retrieved from: https://english.motie.go.kr/www/main.do on 23 December 2023.

MSIT. (2023). Retrieved from: https://www.msit.go.kr/eng/index.do on 24 December 2023.

Nelson, R. R. (2013). National innovation systems. In *Regional innovation, knowledge and global change* (pp. 11–26). Routledge.

NST. (2023). Retrieved from: https://www.nst.re.kr/eng/index.do on 25 December 2023.

NRF. (2023). Retrieved from: https://www.nrf.re.kr/eng/main on 28 December 2023.

NSTC. (2023). Retrieved from: https://www.nstc.gov.tw/?l=en on 24 December 2023.

Park, R. K. E. (2016). *Preparing students for South Korea's creative economy: The successes and challenges of educational reform.* Asia Pacific Foundation of Canada.

Shapiro, M. A., So, M., & Woo Park, H. (2010). Quantifying the national innovation system: inter-regional collaboration networks in South Korea. *Technology Analysis & Strategic Management, 22*(7), 845–857.

Sohn, D. W., Kim, H., & Lee, J. H. (2009). Policy-driven university–industry linkages and regional innovation networks in Korea. *Environment and Planning C: Government and Policy, 27*(4), 647–664.

Statista. (2021). *How Korea is aging.* Retrieved from: https://www.statista.com/chart/24275/population-of-korea-by-age-group/ on 27 December 2023.

Statista. (2022). *The average number of births per woman in South Korea from 1970 to 2022.* Retrieved from: https://www.statista.com/statistics/1403684/south-korea-birth-rate/#:~:text=In%202022%2C%20the%20birth%20rate%20in%20South,Korea%20lay%20at%200.78%20births%20per%20woman on 27 December 2023.

UNESCO. (2019). *Classroom revolution through SMART education in the Republic of Korea: A case study by the UNESCO-Fazheng project on best practices in mobile learning.* Paris: UNESCO.

UNESCO. (2020). *UNESCO science report.* Paris: UNESCO.

WEF (World Economic Forum). (2016a). *The future of jobs: Employment, skills and workforce strategy for the fourth industrial revolution.* Geneva: World Economic Forum. Retrieved from: https://www3.weforum.org/docs/WEF_Future_of_Jobs.pdf

WEF (World Economic Forum). (2016b). *New vision for education: Fostering social and emotional learning through technology.* Geneva: World Economic Forum. Retrieved from: https://www3.weforum.org/docs/WEF_New_Vision_for_Education.pdf

World Bank. (2023). *GDP growth (annual %)*. Retrieved from: https://data.worldbank.org/indicator/NY.GDP.MKTP.KD.ZG on 28 December 2023.

Yoon, J., & Park, H. W. (2017). Triple helix dynamics of South Korea's innovation system: a network analysis of inter-regional technological collaborations. *Quality & Quantity, 51*(3), 989–1007.

Chapter 5

Effects of patents on economic performance of Korean firms

Keunyeob Oh and Yun Bai

Abstract: This chapter provides an empirical analysis of how technology development, through innovation activities such as R&D investment by Korean companies, affects their economic performance. Patent applications are used as a proxy variable for technology development. The study examines the impact of patent applications on the corporate performance of the Korean manufacturing industry over the past 21 years, from 1999 to 2019. The analysis differentiates between overseas and domestic patents and assesses their respective effects on the entire manufacturing industry, the Information and Communications Technology (ICT) industry, and non-ICT industries. The main findings are as follows: First, patents have a positive effect on both exports and sales of Korean manufacturing firms. Second, overseas patents have a greater impact on corporate performance than domestic patents. Third, patents have a more positive effect on the ICT industry than on non-ICT industries. These results indicate that patents play a significant role in enhancing exports and sales across the manufacturing sector.

Keywords: Technology Development, Patent Application, Corporate Performance, ICT Industry.

* This chapter is a revised version based on the authors' paper in Korean titled "Patenting abroad and its effects on exports and sales in Korean Manufacturing firms" published in *Korea Trade Review*, 2022.

1. Introduction

The South Korean economy has transitioned from a period of high growth to a phase of low growth. During the high growth period, Korea achieved economic development through what is commonly known as export-led growth, with a focus on exports. However, in the current era of the Fourth Industrial Revolution, continuous growth and development require enhanced productivity through technological innovation. Long ago, Solow (1956) argued that 7/8 of economic growth is attributed to productivity improvement, emphasizing that such improvement arises from technological advancements fueled by research and development (R&D) investments. Subsequently, Romer (1986) introduced the theory of endogenous economic growth, highlighting that sustained economic growth is achieved through the accumulation of knowledge within the economy, leading to technological innovation. In either case, technological innovation or advancement remains a common source of economic growth.

Since Pakes and Griliches (1980), numerous studies analyzing the relationship between technology and the economy have utilized patents as an indicator representing the technological level of firms, empirically examining the impact of patents on economic growth. This may be attributed to the convenience of using patent data, which is well-documented and readily available, unlike the challenging quantification of technology levels. In this context, this study empirically analyzes the economic effects of patents, considering patents as a proxy for technology development.

Examining the stages of economic growth in Korea, it is evident that while factors such as labor and capital played a central role in driving economic growth during the early stages, recent growth is more reliant on productivity improvement (Wu *et al.*, 2019). Continuous productivity improvement is achievable through constant R&D investments, and South Korea has dedicated efforts to technological development through substantial R&D investments. In terms of R&D spending, Korea is one of the leading countries globally, following the United States, China, Japan, and Germany. In terms of R&D intensity, Korea competes closely with Israel, ranking among the top two worldwide. Technologies developed through such R&D investments are protected by intellectual property rights, particularly patents. Ultimately, the existence of a patent protection system promotes the development of new technologies.

However, patents are protected only in the country where they are applied and registered. If companies intending to export do not apply for patents in the target export country, the technology used in their products or services remains unprotected in the international market, posing significant obstacles to exports. Consequently, to gain recognition for the technological exclusivity of their products in export markets, patent applications in the respective countries are essential. For this reason, companies worldwide actively seek patent applications in foreign countries.

Like its commitment to R&D investment, Korea is also one of the top five countries globally in terms of patent applications, along with the United States, China, Japan, and Germany. However, in the Korean manufacturing sector, about 90 % of patents are filed by large enterprises, with 57 % focusing on the Information and Communications Technology (ICT) industry. The ICT industry forms the foundation of advanced technologies driving the Fourth Industrial Revolution, encompassing technologies such as the Internet of Things, big data, and artificial intelligence. The emergence of new technologies resulting from the convergence of ICT with other industries is increasingly recognized as a key factor influencing the competitiveness of nations and companies.

Against this backdrop, this study analyzes the impact of patent applications by Korean manufacturing firms as a proxy for technological development on exports and sales over the period from 1999 to 2019. Through this analysis, it is anticipated that the economic impact of innovation activities, specifically technological development, can be empirically validated. This research particularly focuses on the ICT industry, a core sector of the Fourth Industrial Revolution. Additionally, recognizing that overseas patents include relatively higher technological capabilities compared to domestic patents, the study classifies patent applications into two types – overseas and domestic patents – and compares their effects. Finally, considering that corporate performance may be influenced not only by patents filed in the current year but also by those accumulated in the past, the study analyzes both the flow and stock of patents.

2. Theoretical background, previous literature, and research distinctiveness

2.1. R&D, knowledge accumulation, patents and economic performance

Neoclassical economic growth theory argued that as the economy grows and income increases, the economic growth rate gradually decreases due to the diminishing marginal productivity of labor and capital, and that technological progress is necessary for sustainable economic growth. In this theory, technological progress is considered to be given externally, so it is called exogenous growth theory. Afterwards, Romer

(1986) developed the endogenous growth theory, which emphasized that technological progress occurs through knowledge accumulation, which is an endogenous result within the economy, and that continuous economic growth is possible. According to endogenous growth theory, as the productivity of labor and capital improves as knowledge accumulates, continuous economic growth can be achieved by escaping from the law of diminishing marginal production in the long run. Knowledge accumulation can be seen as an output of R&D investment, and many studies use patents as a proxy variable for knowledge accumulation (Griliches *et al.*, 1986; Cockburn & Griliches, 1987).

Before delving into the analysis of the economic effects of patents in this study, let's visually represent the theoretical relationship as depicted in Figure 5.1. Economic Output refers to a company's economic performance, such as productivity, sales, and exports. The amount of knowledge accumulated in the center of the picture is a variable that cannot be measured quantitatively, and is determined by the amount of R&D input, and the patent is determined by the amount of knowledge accumulated. Therefore, there is a positive relationship between R&D and patents. Output is also influenced by other variables that affect knowledge accumulation and productivity. At this time, because patents grant monopoly power to the technology holder in the market, a company's performance is directly affected by the number of patents themselves. This study measures the relationship between patents and corporate performance that appears in this theoretical relationship through multiple regression analysis.

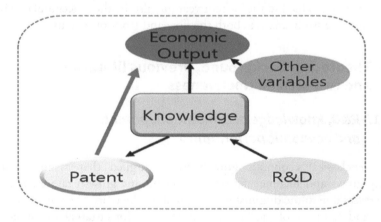

Figure 5.1: Relationship among R&D, knowledge accumulation, and patents
Source: Pakes and Griliches (1980)

Since patents have territorial characteristics that are protected only within the country in which they are registered, you must apply for a patent in the country in which you wish to obtain patent rights in that country to secure exclusive rights. However, because there are significant costs involved in filing overseas patent applications, it is advantageous for companies to only apply overseas for patents with high competitiveness and technology. Therefore, overseas patents are more likely to have higher technological and economic value than patents filed only domestically (Putnam, 1996; Harhoff *et al.*, 2003).

In the modern economy, the development of ICT has made it possible for economic entities separated in time and space to collaborate at low cost. And as overseas investment and accompanying ideas, knowledge, and technology spread, production stages are subdivided geographically, resulting in the development of Global Value Chain (GVC) (Choi, 2022). ICT technology is a special technology that affects various economic activities and improves the productivity of other sectors (Kretschmer, 2012), and is a basic technology across industries that creates new value-added and affects the productivity of other industries (Ji *et al.*, 2019). The 4th Industrial Revolution is the next-generation industrial revolution that consists of the convergence of ICT, and the key is to converge various technologies based on ICT technology. However, the ICT industry, which operates on the premise of interoperability, differs from traditional industries in that it forms close relationships across various fields through convergence. Therefore, in the ICT industry, technology leadership and market dominance through domestic and international standardization activities hold even greater significance compared to other industries (Chung & Jeong, 2014). In particular, standard essential patents (SEPs) in the ICT industry are of utmost importance because all companies manufacturing products according to the standard specifications must necessarily use them. Therefore, it is crucial to proactively develop technologies with a high likelihood of being adopted as domestic and international standards and file patents for the core aspects of these technologies. This proactive approach ensures a competitive advantage in future standardization activities.

2.2. Previous research

Since Romer (1986) and Lucas (1988) raised the importance of R&D in endogenous growth theory, the relationship between R&D and the economy has been studied extensively. Grossman and Helpman (1993) find that product differentiation through R&D has a positive effect on exports, and Wakelin (2001) argues that R&D has played an important role in the productivity growth of British firms. Long ago, Gruber *et al.* (1967) found that U.S. exports are dominated by R&D-intensive industries, and Lee and Habte-Giorgis (2004) found that R&D investment has a positive effect on firm exports in U.S. manufacturing. In addition, numerous studies have confirmed the positive effects of R&D on the economy, and in recent years, the importance of patents, which are the product of R&D, has become increasingly important as the competition for technological hegemony has spread around the world, and research on patents continues.

Now, we discuss studies that directly analyze the relationship between patents, exports, and sales. Blind and Jungmittag (2005) analyzed the effect of patents using industry-level data for Germany for the period 1980–1995 and found a significant positive effect of patent applications on exports. Madsen (2008) found that for 16 OECD countries over the period 1883–2004, an increase in overseas patents increased annualized manufacturing export growth by 1.8 %. Kim *et al.* (2012) found that patent applications have a positive effect on the sales growth rate of Korean firms over the period 1970–1995, with the effect of patents in the period 1987–1995 being larger than for the entire period. Mun and Choe (2017) found that overseas patent applications have a positive effect on the export intensity of pharmaceutical firms during 1998–2010, and studies using country-level data by Frietsch *et al.* (2014) and Brunel and Zylkin (2022) also confirmed the positive effect of patent applications on exports. In the ICT industry, von Laer *et al.* (2022) found that standardized patents have a positive effect on exports on a value-added basis.

Next, we look at studies that analyze the relationship between patents and productivity. Lach (1995) found that R&D and patents in the United States over the period 1958–1983 have a positive effect on productivity growth in manufacturing, with the effect of patents being larger than that of R&D. Ulku (2004) conducted various analyzes using R&D and patent data for 20 OECD countries and 10 non-OECD countries over the period 1981–1997. He found a positive relationship between R&D and gross domestic product (GDP) per capita in OECD and non-OECD countries, and found that patents have a positive effect on total factor productivity in non-OECD countries. Xu and Chiang (2005) analyzed the effect of patents using data for 48 countries over the period 1980–2000 and found that foreign patents had a positive effect on low- and middle-income countries' total factor productivity, and foreign patent inflows also had a significant positive effect on low- and middle-income countries' total factor productivity. Crass and Peters (2014) found that patents have a positive effect on productivity in Germany, and Sudsawasd and Chaisrisawatsuk (2014) found that patents do not have a significant effect on the growth rate of total factor productivity in 57 countries whereas the level of IPR protection has a positive effect on productivity.

Oh and Kim (2005) analyzed the effect of patents on total factor productivity in the Korean information and communication industry, and Kim *et al.* (2009, 2014) found that the effect of patents is positive for the entire manufacturing industry. On the other hand, Kim and Kim (2017) found that the effect of Korean patents on total factor productivity was not significant, and Lee *et al.* (2022) analyzed the effect of design and patents by dividing the period 1971–2010 into three periods, and found that design and patents had a positive effect on sales growth only in the period after the 1997 Asian foreign exchange crisis.

In addition to studies analyzing the relationships between patents, exports, sales, and productivity, you can also find studies analyzing patents, growth rates, value-added, and GVC. Lee and Park (2019) found that patents did not have a significant effect on value-added in Korea's non-patent-intensive industries, but had a significant effect on value-added in patent-intensive industries. Josheski and Koteski (2011) found that the increase in patents in G7 countries had a negative impact on the growth rate of GDP in the short term, but had a positive impact in the long term. Tajoli and Felice (2018) found that increased participation in GVCs has a positive effect on patents per capita, arguing that this means that there is a technology ripple effect through GVC participation. Reddy *et al.* (2021) argued that corporate innovation is a driving force for GVC participation, and Lema *et al.* (2021) found that patent applications decreased GVC participation in the hardware sector and increased GVC participation in the software sector.

While many of the existing studies mentioned above mainly analyzed the effects of patents using country-level data, this study analyzes the economic performance of Korean manufacturing companies using firm-level patent data. Specifically, it has the following characteristics. First, considering the importance of the ICT industry, we conduct a focused analysis on it. Second, we compare and analyze the differences in the effects of overseas and domestic patents on exports and sales. Third, we analyze both patent flow (PF) and patent stock (PS).

3. Trend of patent applications and performance of Korean companies

3.1. Building data for analysis

The patent application data for this study was extracted from the Document Database (DOCDB) of the Korea Intellectual Property Office (KIPO) and the European Patent Office (EPO). In the case of domestic patent data, information such as applicant code, application date, and application number is recorded for each applied patent. We first calculated the number of applications per applicant by year. Next, using the linkage data between the applicant code received from the KIPO and business registration number, domestic patents and corporate financial data were constructed into one integrated data.

In the case of overseas patents, data from all the patent offices around the world are collected in DOCDB. First, patents filed by Korean in each country's patent office were extracted, and then patents filed in Korea were excluded. For analysis, it is necessary to construct overseas patent application data by applicant and year. In DOCDB, the applicant's name is in English, and in reality, the same applicant's name is often recorded in various forms. For example, although it is the same company, SAMSUNG ELECTRONICS CO. LTD., SAMSUNG ELECTRONICS LTD, SAMSUNG ELECTRONICS INC, SAMSUNG ELECTRONIC, SAMSUNG ELECTRONICS CO LTD, etc. Since they all represent the same company, they should be standardized into a consistent format. Lastly, we linked the overseas patent data constructed above with corporate financial data using the English names of companies in FN Guide and KIS Value, Korea's corporate financial databases.

3.2. Trend in patent applications

Figure 5.2 displays the patent application status of South Korean manufacturing companies. The number of patents applied for by industry and year is presented in Appendix Table A. In the figure, the patent application count represents the flow of patents. Patent applications in the manufacturing industry have generally been on the rise, with the total number of patents and overseas patents showing a similar trend. It is evident that from 2007 to 2009 and from 2015 to 2017, both total and overseas patents experienced two periods of decline, but they have been increasing again since 2018. Over the past 21 years, total patents have increased approximately three-fold, and overseas patents have increased approximately eight-fold, and overseas patents have surpassed domestic patent applications since 2013. In the case of domestic patents, it has steadily increased since 2000, but experienced a decline from 2006 to 2009, and has shown an increasing trend since then. Domestic patents have approximately doubled in 21 years.

In the ICT industry, both total patents and overseas patents experienced a sharp increase from 2000 to 2005, followed by two periods of decline, but they have been showing an overall increasing trend. However, domestic patents in the ICT industry have been consistently declining. Over 21 years, total patents doubled, overseas patents increased sixfold, and domestic patents decreased to about 70 % of their initial count. In the case of non-ICT industries, both total patents, overseas patents, and domestic patents have consistently increased over the entire 21-year period. However, domestic patents have shown relatively little change in the number of applications since 2015. On the other hand, overseas patents experienced substantial growth, with 15,459 applications in 2019, representing approximately a 24-fold increase compared to 1999. It is noteworthy that in both ICT and non-ICT industries, overseas patents have seen a significant surge compared to domestic patents.

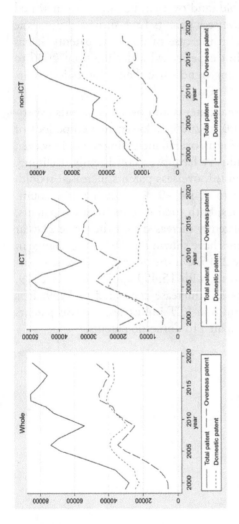

Figure 5.2: Trend of patent flow

3.3. Patent stock trends

Patents represent newly developed technologies, and technology can impact a company's performance not only in the current year but also over several subsequent years. Therefore, the economic effects of patents extend beyond the year they are granted and can have a lasting impact. In addition, in light of the general use of capital stock in the production function, it is necessary to consider the concept of patent stock in the number of patents indicating the level of technology.

Therefore, we calculated the patent stock using the patent flow, which is defined as the annual number of patent applications, and analyzed its influence on corporate performance. The patent stock is calculated using the perpetual inventory method, a widely used approach for estimating capital stock in typical research studies. The formula for calculating patent stock is as follows:

$$PS_{i,t} = PF_{i,t} + (1 - \delta) \times PS_{i,t-1}, \quad t = 2000, \cdots, 2019, \tag{1}$$

$$PS_{i,1999} = PF_{i,1999} / (\gamma_i + \delta), \tag{2}$$

where PS represents the patent stock, PF represents the patent flow, γ represents the average annual growth rate of the patent flow (sample average growth rate of the patent flow during the estimation period), and δ represents the patent depreciation rate. Many studies including Lach (1995), Hall $et\ al.$ (2005), Crass and Peters (2014), and Dechezleprêtre $et\ al.$ (2021) assumed a depreciation rate of 15 %, and this study also applied the same value accordingly. The initial patent stock is calculated by formula (2), and the patent stock of subsequent periods is calculated using formula (1).

Figure 5.3 shows the trend of patent stock by industry. In the entire manufacturing industry, total patents, overseas patents, and domestic patents are all steadily increasing, and the growth rate of overseas patents is greater than that of domestic patents. In the case of the ICT industry, total patents and overseas patents are steadily increasing, but domestic patents have been decreasing since 2007, and the growth rate of overseas patents is shown to be much greater than that of the entire manufacturing industry. In the case of non-ICT industries, total patents, overseas patents, and domestic patents are all steadily increasing.

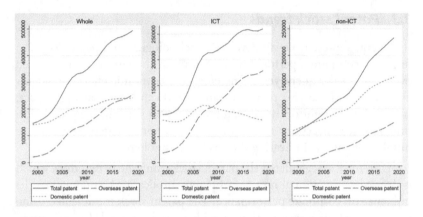

Figure 5.3: Patent stock trend by industry

3.4. Corporate performance

Figure 5.4 shows trends in exports and sales by industry of Korean manufacturing companies. As seen in the figure, exports and sales are increasing overall. Exports in the ICT industry steadily increased until 2014, but then faced two declines and increased approximately 6.8 times over 21 years. In the case of the non-ICT industry, it shows a similar trend to the entire manufacturing industry, steadily increasing since 1999 and decreasing since 2013. Since then, it has increased again since 2017, but has not recovered to the previous level. This can be seen as reflecting the deglobalization situation that has emerged due to neo-protectionism and Brexit. Sales are steadily increasing in the entire manufacturing industry, ICT industry, and non-ICT industry. In non-ICT industries, sales were growing faster in the period before the global financial crisis, and ICT industry has recently shown a decreasing trend. Over 21 years, sales in the ICT industry increased approximately 11 times and in non-ICT industries approximately 5 times.

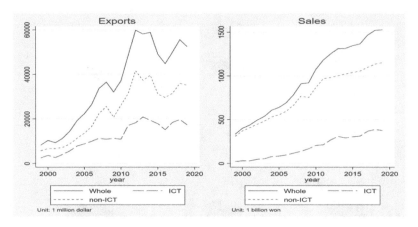

Figure 5.4: Trend of corporate performance by industry

4. Models, data, and empirical analysis

4.1. Relationship between patents and corporate performance

Prior to regression analysis, we present scatterplots of the relationship between patent flow and corporate performance. Figure 5.5 shows the relationship between patent flow and exports by industry of Korean manufacturing companies. Both overseas patents (PF) and domestic patents (KPF) exhibit a clearly positive correlation with exports. Among them, the relationship between overseas patents and exports in the ICT industry appears to be the strongest, while the relationship between domestic patents and exports in the ICT industry appears to be the weakest.

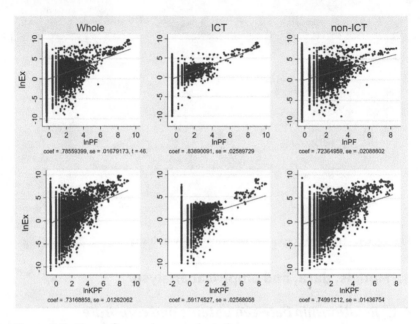

Figure 5.5: Patent flow and exports by industry

The relationship between patent flow and sales is shown in Figure 5.6. Similar to exports, there is a clear positive correlation between patents and sales. Overseas patents, once again, exhibit the strongest relationship with sales in the ICT industry, while the relationship between domestic patents and sales in the ICT industry appears to be the weakest.

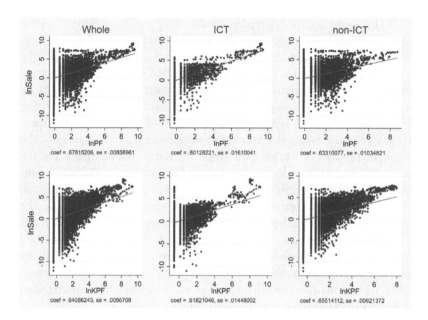

Figure 5.6: Patent flow and sales by industry

Based on the scatterplots above, it seems that overseas patents have the most significant impact on exports and revenue in the ICT industry. However, because these analyzes show a simple relationship between two variables, we intend to conduct an empirical analysis through multiple regression analysis that adds control variables, and also take into account endogeneity problems which may arise from issues such as the omission of explanatory variables.

4.2. Regression model and data description

This study established the following dynamic panel model to examine the impact of patents on companies' exports and sales over the 21-year period from 1999 to 2019.

$$lnEx_{i,t} = \beta_0 + \beta_1 lnEx_{i,t-1} + \beta_2 lnPAT_{i,t-1} + \beta_3 lnLab_{i,t-1} + \beta_4 lnAge_{i,t-1} + \mu_i + u_t + \varepsilon_{i,t}, \quad (3)$$

$$lnSale_{i,t} = \beta_0 + \beta_1 lnSale_{i,t-1} + \beta_2 lnPAT_{i,t-1} + \beta_3 lnLab_{i,t-1} + \beta_4 lnAge_{i,t-1} + \mu_i + u_t + \varepsilon_{i,t}, \quad (4)$$

In the above equation, i represents the company, t represents the year, $EX_{i,t}$, $Sale_{i,t}$ and represents exports and sales, respectively. Exports were converted to dollars, and sales were converted to constant prices using the producer price index for each industry provided by ISTANS (Industrial Statistics Analysis System). $PAT_{i,t-1}$ is an indicator representing the number of patent applications in year t-1, and this variable was analyzed using $PF_{i,t-1}$, and $PS_{i,t-1}$ which represent the patent flow and patent stock, respectively. $Lab_{i,t-1}$ represents the number of workers in year t-1. Generally, the larger the number of workers, the larger the size of the company and the increase in exports or sales, so this was used as a control variable for company size. $Age_{i,t-1}$ represents the age of company i in year t-1. Because you learn about your own experience and abilities accumulated over time, the longer the business has been in business, the more positive impact it has on corporate performance (Evans, 1987). Lastly, lagged values were used for patents, number of workers, and company's age in order to address reverse causality between these variables and corporate performance. Table 5.1 summarizes the explanation of each variable, the expected sign of the empirical analysis, and the data source.

Table 5.1: Variable description and data source

Variable	Description	Expected sign	Source
$Ex_{i,t}$	Exports of company i in year t		KIS Value
$Sale_{i,t}$	Sales of company i in year t		
$Ex_{i,t-1}$	Exports of company i in year $t-1$	(+)	
$Sale_{i,t-1}$	Sales of company i in year $t-1$	(+)	
$PAT_{i,t-1}$ $(PF_{i,t-1}, KPF_{i,t-1},$ $PS_{i,t-1}, KPS_{i,t-1})$	Indicators of the number of patent applications filed by company i in year $t-1$ (overseas patent flow, domestic patent flow, overseas patent stock, domestic patent stock)	(+)	DOCDB
$Lab_{i,t-1}$	Number of workers in company i in year $t-1$	(+)	KIS Value
$Age_{i,t-1}$	Age of company i in year $t-1$	(+)	

4.3. Regression results

Since the data in this study consists of panel data, a model including fixed effect variables was used to remove the effects of time and individual. However, when the lagged value of the dependent variable is included as an explanatory variable in this fixed effect model, there could be an endogeneity problem due to the correlation between the error term and the explanatory variable. In dynamic panel models, to address endogeneity issues, instrumental variables are employed, which typically include past values of the dependent variable or lagged difference variables. In this study, we adopted the System GMM (generalized method of moments) estimation method, utilizing both past values and lagged difference variables of the dependent variable as instrumental variables to overcome endogeneity concerns.

As explained previously, this study is interested in the impact of patents on exports and sales of ICT and non-ICT industries according to patent type. In the modern economy, production is based on ICT technology in most manufacturing industries, so patents in the ICT industry play a very important role in improving the productivity of companies in other industries. In particular, the number of ICT standard patents is a very important factor in evaluating and utilizing technology level. Accordingly, in the following, we present and explain not only the analysis of the entire manufacturing industry, but also the results of a regression analysis performed by separating the ICT industry and non-ICT industry and using patents.

Tables 5.2 and 5.3 present the estimation results of the relationship between patent flow and exports, as well as the relationship between patent flow and sales, respectively. Columns (1), (3), and (5) are the analysis results for overseas patents, and columns (2), (4), (6) are the analysis results for domestic patents. In the table, overseas patents and domestic patents were found to have a significant positive effect on exports and sales of the entire manufacturing industry, ICT industry, and non-ICT industry. In addition, in all industries, overseas patents appear to have a greater effect on exports and sales than domestic patents. When overseas patents increase by 1 %, exports increase by 0.047 %~0.108 % and sales increase by 0.032 %~0.063 %. However, when domestic patents increase by 1 %, exports increase by 0.026 %~0.041 % and sales increase by 0.024 %~0.031 %. In addition, in both overseas and domestic patents, the effect on the ICT industry appears to be greater than the effect on the entire manufacturing industry or non-ICT industries. 1 % increase in overseas patents, exports and sales in the ICT industry increased by 0.108 % and 0.063 %, respectively, while in the non-ICT industry, exports and sales increased by 0.047 % and 0.032 %, respectively. The number of workers, as expected, has a positive relationship with a company's exports and sales. The company's age has a significant or insignificant negative effect on exports and sales. It seems to suggest that younger companies, due to their flexibility and dynamism in decision-making, experience faster growth in their performance.

Table 5.2: Estimation results for patent flow and exports

	Whole		ICT		non-ICT	
	(1)	(2)	(3)	(4)	(5)	(6)
L.lnEx	0.510***	0.506***	0.554***	0.558***	0.505***	0.503***
	(0.044)	(0.044)	(0.089)	(0.092)	(0.048)	(0.048)
L.lnPF	0.065***		0.108***		0.047***	
	(0.013)		(0.023)		(0.016)	
L.lnLab	0.597***	0.601***	0.446***	0.486***	0.617***	0.617***
	(0.056)	(0.057)	(0.098)	(0.108)	(0.063)	(0.064)
L.lnAge	−0.114***	−0.117***	−0.004	−0.037	−0.114***	−0.114***
	(0.024)	(0.024)	(0.053)	(0.051)	(0.026)	(0.026)
L.lnKPF		0.036***		0.041**		0.026*
		(0.013)		(0.017)		(0.015)
Constant	7.613***	7.665***	7.288***	7.125***	7.572***	7.616***
	(0.651)	(0.659)	(1.395)	(1.408)	(0.706)	(0.719)
Obs	19,675	19,675	3,296	3,296	16,379	16,379
AR(2)	0.184	0.208	0.134	0.147	0.459	0.488
Hansen test	0.596	0.113	0.524	0.197	0.609	0.270

Notes: 1. $*p <0.1$, $**p <0.05$, $***p <0.001$.
            2. Standard errors in parentheses.
            3. The p-values reported by the AR(2)/AR(3) and Hansen tests are to verify the null hypothesis that no second/third-order autocorrelation exists and the null hypothesis that the set of instruments is appropriate, respectively.
            4. Notes 1, 2, and 3 are applied to all the tables below.

Table 5.3: Estimation results for patent flow and sales

	Whole		ICT		non-ICT	
	(1)	(2)	(3)	(4)	(5)	(6)
L.lnSale	0.711***	0.712***	0.686***	0.679***	0.706***	0.706***
	(0.027)	(0.027)	(0.065)	(0.066)	(0.032)	(0.032)
L.lnPF	0.037*		0.063***		0.032***	
	(0.004)		(0.010)		(0.005)	
L.lnLab	0.247***	0.244***	0.256***	0.279***	0.255***	0.251***
	(0.026)	(0.026)	(0.062)	(0.066)	(0.030)	(0.030)
L.lnAge	−0.067***	−0.067***	−0.083***	−0.094***	−0.066***	−0.065***
	(0.006)	(0.006)	(0.018)	(0.017)	(0.007)	(0.007)
L.lnKPF		0.024***		0.031***		0.025***
		(0.004)		(0.009)		(0.004)
Constant	6.152***	6.131***	6.755***	6.858***	6.231***	6.232***
	(0.542)	(0.542)	(1.265)	(1.288)	(0.625)	(0.626)
Obs	69,053	69,053	8,386	8,386	60,667	60,667
AR(2)	0.033	0.028	0.457	0.391	0.050	0.047
AR(3)	0.315	0.303			0.220	0.220
Hansentest	0.133	0.116	0.422	0.439	0.484	0.351

Tables 5.4 and 5.5 present the analysis results regarding the impact of patent stock on exports and sales, respectively. Examining the results for exports in Table 5.4, it is evident that overseas patents have a significant positive effect on exports across all industries, while the effect of domestic patents is not statistically significant. Furthermore, the impact of overseas patents on exports is most pronounced in the ICT industry compared to the non-ICT industry. An increase of 1 % in overseas patents results in a 0.091 % increase in exports for the ICT industry, while the exports of the overall manufacturing sector and non-ICT industry increase by 0.052 % and 0.037 %, respectively.

Table 5.4: Estimation results for patent stock and exports

	Whole		ICT		non-ICT	
	(1)	(2)	(3)	(4)	(5)	(6)
L.lnEx	0.510***	0.507***	0.561***	0.559***	0.505***	0.503***
	(0.044)	(0.044)	(0.088)	(0.092)	(0.048)	(0.048)

Continued

Table 5.4: Continued

	Whole		ICT		non-ICT	
L.lnPS	0.052***		0.091***		0.037***	
	(0.012)		(0.021)		(0.014)	
L.lnLab	0.593***	0.611***	0.436***	0.507***	0.614***	0.624***
	(0.055)	(0.057)	(0.095)	(0.110)	(0.063)	(0.065)
L.lnAge	−0.113***	−0.123***	−0.004	−0.035	−0.113***	−0.119***
	(0.024)	(0.024)	(0.053)	(0.051)	(0.026)	(0.026)
L.lnKPS		0.015		−0.001		0.008
		(0.010)		(0.016)		(0.012)
Constant	7.588***	7.627***	7.136***	7.043***	7.566***	7.587***
	(0.651)	(0.656)	(1.373)	(1.406)	(0.707)	(0.714)
Obs	19,675	19,675	3,296	3,296	16,379	16,379
AR(2)	0.190	0.206	0.144	0.153	0.465	0.481
Hansen test	0.529	0.112	0.426	0.170	0.582	0.277

Table 5.5 shows the analysis results for sales similar to the estimated results for patent flow. Overseas patents and domestic patents were found to have a positive effect on sales in whole industries. The effect of overseas patents was greater than that of domestic patents, and the effect of patents in the ICT industry was the largest. When overseas patents increase by 1 %, sales in the ICT industry increase by 0.043 %, and sales in the entire manufacturing industry and non-ICT industries increase by 0.025 % and 0.022 %, respectively. In the case of domestic patents, when patents increase by 1 %, sales increase by 0.006 %, 0.014 %, and 0.006 % in the entire manufacturing industry, ICT industry, and non-ICT industry, respectively. The number of workers and company's age were found to have positive and negative effects on exports and sales, respectively, consistent with the estimation results for patent flow.

Table 5.5: Estimation results for patent stock and sales

	Whole		ICT		non-ICT	
	(1)	(2)	(3)	(4)	(5)	(6)
L.lnSale	0.715***	0.712***	0.685***	0.687***	0.710***	0.707***
	(0.027)	(0.027)	(0.065)	(0.066)	(0.032)	(0.032)
L.lnPS	0.025***		0.043***		0.022***	
	(0.003)		(0.008)		(0.003)	

Table 5.5: Continued

	Whole		ICT		non-ICT	
L.lnLab	0.243***	0.250***	0.260***	0.277***	0.250***	0.255***
	(0.026)	(0.026)	(0.063)	(0.067)	(0.030)	(0.031)
L.lnAge	−0.068***	−0.071***	−0.084***	−0.100***	−0.067***	−0.068***
	(0.006)	(0.006)	(0.018)	(0.017)	(0.006)	(0.006)
L.lnKPS		0.006***		0.014**		0.006***
		(0.002)		(0.006)		(0.002)
Constant	6.073***	6.119***	6.757***	6.688***	6.149***	6.200***
	(0.538)	(0.542)	(1.270)	(1.286)	(0.620)	(0.624)
Obs	69,053	69,053	8,386	8,386	60,667	60,667
AR(2)	0.036	0.033	0.446	0.438	0.055	0.052
AR(3)	0.291	0.307			0.201	0.212
Hansentest	0.120	0.149	0.457	0.440	0.442	0.496

Lastly, when comparing the effects of patent flow and stock, the coefficient of the flow variable appears to be slightly larger in general. This may be due to the fact that the patent stock is calculated from the patent flows of several years using depreciation. Theoretically, the difference in these coefficients may vary depending on the depreciation rate.

5. Summary and conclusion

South Korea is vigorously focusing on technology development and innovation, competing for the first or second place globally in terms of R&D intensity. This effort is manifesting in increased patent filings and exports to major countries around the world. South Korea is already among the top five countries in the world in terms of patent filings, and these innovative activities are becoming the foundation of South Korea's economic development.

In this situation, this study constructs corporate financial data and patent data into one integrated data, and uses this to study the impact of patent applications on exports and sales of Korean manufacturing companies over a period of 21 years from 1999 to 2019. In particular, considering the characteristics of the industry and patents, the industry was classified into the entire manufacturing industry, ICT industry, and non-ICT industry, and patents were divided into overseas patents and domestic patents. We also analyzed the effects of patents considering both patent flow and patent stock. The key findings can be summarized as follows.

First, both overseas and domestic patents were found to have a positive effect on the exports and sales of Korean manufacturing companies. This means that patents are a variable that can represent the level of technology and have a positive effect on corporate performance in the Korean manufacturing industry.

Second, overseas patents have a more significant impact on exports and sales compared to domestic patents. This can be attributed to the high costs associated with overseas patent applications and maintenance, making companies prioritize high-tech patents for international filings.

Third, patents had a greater impact on exports and sales in the ICT industry than in the non-ICT industry. This greater impact seems to be because ICT is an important field that improves the productivity of other fields as a foundational technology for the entire industry.

From the analysis of this study, it is evident that patents are playing an important role in the exports and sales of companies throughout the manufacturing sector. This indicates that R&D investment and the resulting technological development are essential for the success of the South Korean economy. Consequently, there is a need for support in patent applications, especially in overseas patent filings, to secure technological leadership in competitive global markets, build an industry structure resilient to external shocks, and sustain continuous economic growth.

Appendix

Table A: Number of patent applications by industry from 1999 to 2019

	Whole			ICT			non-ICT		
	Overseas patent	Domestic patent	Total patent	Overseas patent	Domestic patent	Total patent	Overseas patent	Domestic patent	Total patent
1999	5,732	24,711	30,443	5,095	14,360	19,455	637	10,351	10,988
2000	5,921	22,360	28,281	4,827	9,977	14,804	1,094	12,383	13,477
2001	7,722	24,522	32,244	6,411	10,872	17,283	1,311	13,650	14,961
2002	10,961	25,099	36,060	9,249	11,876	21,125	1,712	13,223	14,935
2003	16,197	29,606	45,803	14,028	14,841	28,869	2,169	14,765	16,934
2004	22,605	34,034	56,639	18,890	19,652	38,542	3,715	14,382	18,097
2005	30,244	37,562	67,806	23,897	23,198	47,095	6,347	14,364	20,711
2006	34,624	39,266	73,890	27,286	22,385	49,671	7,338	16,881	24,219

Table A: Continued

	Whole			ICT			non-ICT		
2007	31,197	38,251	69,448	25,130	20,556	45,686	6,067	17,695	23,762
2008	27,798	33,873	61,671	21,936	15,886	37,822	5,862	17,987	23,849
2009	24,897	29,211	54,108	19,116	13,184	32,300	5,781	16,027	21,808
2010	31,013	31,968	62,981	23,904	13,133	37,037	7,109	18,835	25,944
2011	35,840	36,183	72,023	27,083	13,172	40,255	8,757	23,011	31,768
2012	37,378	39,192	76,570	27,514	12,752	40,266	9,864	26,440	36,304
2013	44,619	41,049	85,668	32,464	13,506	45,970	12,155	27,543	39,698
2014	45,356	40,534	85,890	31,627	13,104	44,731	13,729	27,430	41,159
2015	43,151	38,621	81,772	31,489	11,907	43,396	11,662	26,714	38,376
2016	41,707	36,783	78,490	29,790	10,536	40,326	11,917	26,247	38,164
2017	39,324	36,489	75,813	26,497	9,705	36,202	12,827	26,784	39,611
2018	43,168	36,851	80,019	27,821	10,320	38,141	15,347	26,531	41,878
2019	47,543	37,390	84,933	32,084	10,599	42,683	15,459	26,791	42,250

References

Blind, K., & Jungmittag, A. (2005). Trade and the impact of innovations and standards: The case of Germany and the UK. *Applied Economics*, *37*(12), 1385–1398.

Brunel, C., & Zylkin, T. (2022). Do cross-border patents promote trade?. *Canadian Journal of Economics/Revue canadienne d'économique*, *55*(1), 379–418.

Choi, K. Y. (2022). *Cold peace*. Inmun Gongkan.

Chung, W. J., & Hyeon-Jun, J. (2014). ICT standard competition and its implication. *ICT & Media Policy*, *26*(7).

Cockburn, I. M., & Griliches, Z. (1987). *Industry effects and appropriability measures in the stock markets valuation of R&D and patents*. Working paper N° 2465, National Bureau of Economic Research.

Crass, D., & Peters, B. (2014). *Intangible assets and firm-level productivity*. ZEW-Centre for European Economic Research Discussion Paper (14–120).

Dechezleprêtre, A., Hémous, D., Olsen, M., & Zanella, C. (2021). *Induced automation: Evidence from firm-level patent data*. University of Zurich, Department of Economics, Working Paper N° 384.

Evans, D. S. (1987). Tests of alternative theories of firm growth. *Journal of Political Economy*, *95*(4), 657–674.

Frietsch, R., Neuhäusler, P., Jung, T., & Van Looy, B. (2014). Patent indicators for macroeconomic growth—the value of patents estimated by export volume. *Technovation*, *34*(9), 546–558.

Griliches, Z., Pakes, A., & Hall, B. H. (1986). *The value of patents as indicators of inventive activity*. Working paper N° 2083, National Bureau of Economic Research.

Grossman, G. M., & Helpman, E. (1993). *Innovation and growth in the global economy*. MIT press.

Gruber, W., Mehta, D., & Vernon, R. (1967). The R & D factor in international trade and international investment of United States industries. *Journal of Political Economy*, *75*(1), 20–37.

Hall, B. H., Jaffe, A., & Trajtenberg, M. (2005). Market value and patent citations. *The RAND Journal of Economics*, *36*(1), 16–38.

Harhoff, D., Scherer, F. M., & Vopel, K. (2003). Citations, family size, opposition and the value of patent rights. *Research Policy*, *32*(8), 1343–1363.

Ji, H. K., Oh, D. K., Kim, D. Y., Hwang, D. H., Cha, J. S., Kim, J. T., & Choi, Y. H. (2019). Importance of ICT as a future technology source and the promotion of competitiveness. *Electronics and Telecommunications Trends*, *34*(2), 1–9.

Josheski, D., & Koteski, C. (2011). The causal relationship between patent growth and growth of GDP with quarterly data in the G7 countries: Cointegration, ARDL and error correction models. *MPRA Paper N° 33153* (September 4, 2011).

Kim, T., Maskus, K. E., & Oh, K. Y. (2009). Effects of patents on productivity growth in Korean manufacturing: A panel data analysis. *Pacific Economic Review*, *14*(2), 137–154.

Kim, T., Maskus, K., & Oh, K. Y. (2014). Effects of knowledge spillovers on knowledge production and productivity growth in Korean manufacturing firms. *Asian Economic Journal*, *28*(1), 63–79.

Kim, W. K., & Kim, J. W. (2017). An empirical study on the relationship between intellectual property rights and productivity. *Review of Institution and Economics*, *11*(3), 121–152.

Kim, Y. K., Lee, K., Park, W. G., & Choo, K. (2012). Appropriate intellectual property protection and economic growth in countries at different levels of development. *Research Policy*, *41*(2), 358–375.

Kretschmer, T. (2012). *Information and communication technologies and productivity growth: A survey of the literature.* OECD Digital Economy Papers, N° 195.

Lach, S. (1995). Patents and productivity growth at the industry level: A first look. *Economics Letters, 49*(1), 101–108.

Lee, J., & Habte-Giorgis, B. (2004). Empirical approach to the sequential relationships between firm strategy, export activity, and performance in US manufacturing firms. *International Business Review, 13*(1), 101–129.

Lee, K., Kang, R., & Park, D. (2022). How industrial design matters for firm growth at different stages of development: Evidence from Korea, 1970s to 2010s. *Asian Economic Journal, 36*(2), 101–126.

Lee, S. W., & Park, S. K. (2019). *A study on the effect of intellectual property on economic growth: a study on innovation and economies,* Korea Institute of Intellectual Property, Discussion paper.

Lema, R., Pietrobelli, C., Rabellotti, R., & Vezzani, A. (2021). Deepening or delinking? Innovative capacity and global value chain participation in the IT industry. *Industrial and Corporate Change, 30*(4), 1065–1083.

Lucas Jr, R. E. (1988). On the mechanics of economic development. *Journal of Monetary Economics, 22*(1), 3–42.

Madsen, J. B. (2008). Economic growth, TFP convergence and the world export of ideas: a century of evidence. *Scandinavian Journal of Economics, 110*(1), 145–167.

Mun, H. J., & Choe, S. K. (2017). A study on the relationship between international patenting and export performance. *Korea Trade Review, 42*(3), 49–74.

Oh, K. Y., & Kim, T. G. (2005). Patents and productivity growth in information and communication technology industry of Korea: A panel data study. *International Telecommunications Policy Review, 12*(4), 59–85.

Pakes, A., & Griliches, Z. (1980). Patents and R&D at the firm level: A first report. *Economics Letters, 5*(4), 377–381.

Putnam, J. D. (1996). *The value of international patent rights.* Yale University.

Reddy, K., Chundakkadan, R., & Sasidharan, S. (2021). Firm innovation and global value chain participation. *Small Business Economics, 57*(4), 1995–2015.

Romer, P. M. (1986). Increasing returns and long-run growth. *Journal of Political Economy*, *94*(5), 1002–1037.

Solow, R. M. (1956). A contribution to the theory of economic growth. *The Quarterly Journal of Economics*, *70*(1), 65–94.

Sudsawasd, S., & Chaisrisawatsuk, S. (2014). Foreign direct investment, intellectual property rights, and productivity growth. *Journal of International Commerce, Economics and Policy*, *5*(03), 1440009.

Tajoli, L., & Felice, G. (2018). Global value chains participation and knowledge spillovers in developed and developing countries: An empirical investigation. *The European Journal of Development Research*, *30*, 505–532.

Ulku, H. (2004). *R&D, innovation, and economic growth: An empirical analysis*. IMF Working Paper, No. 2004–185, Washington, DC.

von Laer, M., Blind, K., & Ramel, F. (2022). Standard essential patents and global ICT value chains with a focus on the catching-up of China. *Telecommunications Policy*, *46*(2), 102110.

Wakelin, K. (2001). Productivity growth and R&D expenditure in UK manufacturing firms. *Research Policy*, *30*(7), 1079–1090.

Wu, C., Kim, T., & Oh, K. (2019). Shift from input-based growth to productivity-based growth in Korean manufacturing industry. *Asian Economic Journal*, *33*(4), 363–379.

Xu, B., & Chiang, E. P. (2005). Trade, patents and international technology diffusion. *The Journal of International Trade & Economic Development*, *14*(1), 115–135.

Chapter 6

Innovation systems in Japan

Nhan Thanh Thi Nguyen, Giang Ngan Hoang
and Duong Thuy Thi Nguyen

Abstract: The content of this book chapter refers to innovation systems in Japan, starting from presenting the general innovative context in Japan to introducing the innovation development management systems in Japan at each level: national, local, and enterprise. The cities introduced are Tokyo, Kansai, Osaka, Kyoto, and Kobe. At the business level, KEIDANREN (Japan Business Federation), a comprehensive economic organization whose members are companies and industry associations nationwide, is considered a typical example of efforts in innovation that contribute to promoting sustainable growth of the Japanese economy. A case study of PayPay Corporation is presented as a Japanese company that develops electronic payment services and provides new technology solutions to change the payment habits of Japanese consumers.

Keywords: National Innovation System, Regional Innovation System, Innovation Ecosystem

1. An overview of Japan and innovative context

1.1. An overview of Japan

Japan is an island nation in East Asia. Located in the Pacific Ocean, it borders China, North Korea, South Korea, Russia, Taiwan, the Sea of Japan, the Sea of Okhotsk, and the East China Sea. It is an archipelago of 6,852 islands, most of which are mountainous, and many are volcanic. The government system is a parliamentary government with a constitutional monarchy; the chief of state is the emperor, and the head of government is the prime minister. Japan has a market economy in which the prices of goods and services are determined by a free price system. Japan is a member of the Asia-Pacific Economic Cooperation (APEC) and the Trans-Pacific Partnership (TPP)[1].

Japan is widely recognized as a prominent global economic powerhouse, boasting a substantial size and advanced level of development. The nation possesses a highly educated and diligent labor force, and its substantial and prosperous populace positions it as one of the largest consumer marketplaces globally. From 1968 to 2010, Japan's economy held the second largest position in the world, trailing only the United States. The country's estimated gross domestic product (GDP) in 2016 amounted to USD 4.7 trillion, while its population of 126.9 million experiences a commendable level of prosperity, demonstrated by a GDP per capita of just under USD 40,000 in 2015.

The phenomenon of manufacturing has emerged as a prominent and globally recognized aspect of Japan's economic expansion. Presently, Japan holds a prominent position on the global stage as a frontrunner in the production of electrical appliances and electronics, automobiles, ships, machine tools, optical and precision equipment, machinery, and chemicals. In recent years, Japan has experienced a decline in its economic edge in the manufacturing sector, as it has been surpassed by China, the Republic of Korea, and other economies known for their manufacturing capabilities. Japanese companies have responded to this trend to some extent by relocating their manufacturing operations to countries with lower production costs. The service industry in Japan, encompassing financial services among others, has assumed a significantly more prominent position in the country's economy, constituting approximately 75 % of its gross domestic product. The Tokyo Stock Exchange is widely recognized as a prominent global hub for financial activities[2].

1.2. Innovative context in Japan

Japan possesses a flourishing startup ecosystem characterized by a progressively expanding community of entrepreneurs, investors, and support entities. It has a rich historical background characterized by significant advancements in technology, a legacy that is evident in the diverse range of thriving companies currently operating in the country.

---

[1]   Retrieved from https://globaledge.msu.edu/countries/japan
[2]   Retrieved from https://asialinkbusiness.com.au/japan/getting-started-in-japan/japans-economy?doNothing=1

Japan's innovation system evolved under both domestic and foreign pressures over a long period to become a major technological manufacturing powerhouse. The relocation of manufacturing activities overseas to expand market presence sparked debates as it led to a decline in the domestic industry, with large enterprises struggling to keep pace with rapid market changes and a shortage of innovative startups. However, despite concerns about U.S. dominance in emerging high-tech industries, Japan's export product structure indicated value-added technological innovation (Whittaker, 2001).

Japan's technology innovation system comprises many parts: companies, universities, research institutes, the government (Macdowall, 1984). Japan enacted a law to encourage technology transfer from universities to the industrial sector. Universities were treated as national research institutes, empowered to effectively control technological resources, including those developed using government funds. Professors were granted more freedom in research and technology transfer (Whittaker, 2001).

Japan had over 10,000 startups in 2022, according to data from CBS Insights in October 2022. Japan accounts for a mere 0.5 % of 1,191 global unicorns (a private unlisted startup with a market value of USD 1 billion or more), with a total of 6 such businesses as of October 2022 (see Table 6.1). The aforementioned percentage experienced a decline from the initial six-month period of 2022, during which Japan accounted for 8 out of 943 unicorn startups worldwide (see Figure 6.1). This figure was quite diminutive, representing just 0.5 % of the whole population of unicorn startups worldwide[3].

---

[3] Retrieved from https://www.ejable.com/tech-corner/miscellaneous/startups-and-star tup-ecosystem-in-japan/

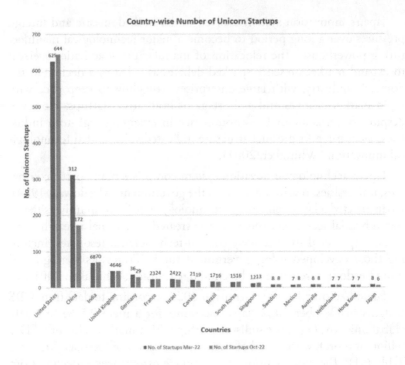

Figure 6.1: Country-wise number of unicorn startups

Source: https://www.ejable.com/tech-corner/miscellaneous/startups-and-startup-ecosys
tem-in-japan/

Name	Founded	Valuation (October 2022)	Products/Services
SmartNews	June 2012	USD 2.00 billion	App to discover and deliver top 0.01% news from around the world.
Preferred Networks	March 2014	USD 2.00 billion	Developing practical, real-world applications of deep learning, robotics, and other advanced technologies.
SmartHR	January 2013	USD 1.60 billion	HR cloud software optimized for labor management solutions
Spiber	September 2007	USD 1.22 billion	New-generation biomaterial development (Spiber's Brewed Protein™)
Opn	2013	USD 1.00 billion	Fintech solutions and products
Playco	2020	USD 1.00 billion	The instant gaming company focused on building games people can play together without additional app downloads.

Table 6.1: Japan's unicorn startups by October 2022

Source: https://www.ejable.com/tech-corner/miscellaneous/startups-and-startup-ecosystem-in-japan/

One of the key factors influencing startups in Japan is the culture. Japan is widely recognized as a nation characterized by a propensity for risk aversion. Consequently, a limited number of individuals in Japan considered pursuing entrepreneurship as a means of initiating their own enterprises. Furthermore, it is important to note that a startup, characterized by its novel ideas and approaches, inherently entails a higher degree of risk than a conventional company model. This element also contributes to the resistance among many Japanese individuals against establishing a startup enterprise. However, the context has shown a significant change recently. In the initial six months of 2021, a total funding amount of 3,234 million Japanese Yen (equivalent to 3.01 billion US dollars) was reported, with 1,014 Japanese firms being the recipients of such capital. During the initial six months of 2021, the performance pertaining to the acquired funding reached its peak[4]. The current state of Japan's startup ecosystem, therefore, exhibits promising prospects.

Japanese companies have successfully aligned themselves with the proposed innovation model. The support for the model from Japanese data is strong enough to suggest that certain general management factors will be implemented for successful innovation. The success of Japanese businesses in both domestic and international markets is closely linked to the innovation of appropriate business models. A tightly structured business production process from ideation to strategy development, resource concentration, organizational implementation, and systematic value creation is considered the key innovation approach for Japanese enterprises to assert their position (Ota *et al.*, 2013).

2. Innovation development management system in Japan

2.1. National level

2.1.1. J-startup

Startups have a pivotal role in driving societal transformation and addressing social challenges through innovative approaches. The J-Startup project aims to consolidate public and private resources in order to provide support to companies exhibiting significant potential. The ultimate objective of this effort is to cultivate globally recognised startup entities that contribute novel and valuable solutions to the international community.

The J-Startup programme aims to foster a positive perception of entrepreneurial endeavours and strengthen Japan's startup ecosystem through the emergence of prosperous Japanese firms (Ministry of Economy, Trade and Industry, 2018a).

2.1.2. Startup City Project

The objective of the "Startup City Project" is to establish a vibrant startup environment in Japan.

---

[4] Retrieved from https://www.ejable.com/tech-corner/miscellaneous/startups-and-startup-ecosystem-in-japan/

The Japanese government has designated eight cities as Startup Cities including Tokyo, Central, Kansai, Fukuoka, Sapporo, Sendai, Hiroshima, and Kitakyushu and is offering comprehensive assistance in fostering the development of their entrepreneurial ecosystems through collaboration with local governments, universities, and the corporate sector.

"In order to further promote open innovation in Japan, we have decided to praise the highly original and leading efforts expected as a role model in the future as the "Japan Open Innovation Award". In this award, the ministerial award, the minister's award, the economic organization, the president's award of academic organizations, etc. for each field of responsibility, etc. In addition to commending, the best of each award will be commended as the Prime Minister's Award" (Ministry of Economy, Trade and Industry, 2021).

2.1.3. Next Innovator

The Next Innovator is an annual event starting from 2018 organized by the Ministry of Economy, Trade and Industry (METI) with the aim of fostering individuals who possess the requisite mindset, knowledge, and skills deemed essential for innovation. These individuals should demonstrate a strong determination to challenge established frameworks in order to address significant problems that cannot be resolved by an individual alone. Furthermore, they should exhibit self-motivation to persistently undertake new challenges and engage in proactive endeavours. In particular, the Japan External Trade Organization (JETRO) also joined METI to hold the Start Next Innovator 2020 to search for innovators who were able to identify commercial opportunities that lie beyond the confines of established organisational and industrial frameworks and generate novel and transformative values against the challenges caused by the coronavirus disease (Ministry of Economy, Trade and Industry, 2020).

2.2. Local level

2.2.1. Tokyo

Tokyo, the capital of Japan, is one of the world's largest cities with a population of 13.95 million (see Figure 6.2). Its GDP is valued at 108.2 trillion yen (in fiscal year 2018), exceeding the GDP of the Netherlands.

Tokyo has approximately 3,000 large corporations, each with capital of 1 billion yen or more, representing around half of the total number of companies in Japan. An international business center, Tokyo is also home to 76 % of the foreign-affiliated companies in Japan, with over 2,400. Tokyo is the world's leading city in the number of Fortune Global 500 companies[5].

Given these strengths, Tokyo has set an ambitious objective of becoming the most conducive city for startups globally. To achieve this, the city plans to establish a new facility dedicated to supporting young firms and significantly enhance its procurement from these companies. Tokyo aims to amplify the number of unicorns and new business ventures in the capital by a factor of ten within a span of five years.

Reasons to move your startup to Tokyo

1. **Market Access:** *Japan is the third largest economy in the world, and much of this activity is concentrated in Tokyo. Tokyo's stock market boasts high-quality liquidity: there are 3,700 listed companies (second in the world); the total market value is 600 trillion yen ($4.4 trillion and ranks third in the world); and stock trading value per day is 3 trillion yen ($22.3 million and the first in Asia).*

2. **Technical Infrastructure:** *Cloud technology and 5G have been widely adopted in Japan. The government has set a target of 95 % 5G coverage nationwide by 2024. Alibaba Cloud, Tencent Holdings, Equinix, and Google all have plans to open new data centers in Japan. The Equinix project, scheduled to open in 2024, will be its 15th international business exchange data center in Tokyo.*

3. **Dedicated Support:** *The e-Business Concierge chatbot provides English information 24 hours a day, 365 days a year. TOKYO Business Development Center offers support to foreign companies considering expansion in Tokyo. The Fundraising Support for Foreign Entrepreneurs Project provides financial support to foreign entrepreneurs. The Tokyo Metropolitan Government's Special Zone system makes it easier for foreigners to start a business here (Office for Startup and Global Financial City Strategy, 2022).*

---

[5]   Retrieved from https://j-startup-city.go.jp/city/tokyo/

Figure 6.2: Tokyo
Source: https://www.goodhousekeeping.com/uk/lifestyle/travel/g41225336/pictures-of-tokyo/

2.2.2. Kansai area

The Kansai region in Japan is recognised as a significant economic hub, consisting of 10 prefectures (Fukui, Mie, Shiga, Kyoto, Osaka, Hyogo, Nara, Wakayama, Tottori, and Tokushima Prefectures). It is also characterized by a thriving startup ecosystem, connected by the organization named The Kansai Startup Ecosystem. Kansai Startup Mashups (see Figure 6.3) is a special event with the aim of supporting the birth of unicorn companies from the Kansai region by creating a startup ecosystem for the Expo 2025 and beyond, through maximizing the synergy of the unique cultures of Osaka, Kyoto and Kobe[6].

---

[6] Retrieved from https://www.starecokansai.com/keihanshin/kansaistartupmashups-en/

Figure 6.3: Kansai startup mashups
Source: https://www.innovation-osaka.jp/

2.2.3. Osaka

The historical significance of entrepreneurship in Osaka (see Figure 6.4) has consistently played a pivotal role, with its amicable and inclusive culture fostering a conducive environment for the establishment and growth of companies.

Osaka, recognised as the designated city for hosting the 2025 World Expo, boasts a diverse array of prominent corporations and esteemed academic institutions, with a special emphasis on the domain of life sciences. Additionally, it possesses a substantial market size.

The city of Osaka and its surrounding ecosystem offer global businesses the potential to achieve success within the Japanese market[7].

---

[7]   Retrieved from https://j-startup-city.go.jp/city/kansai/

Figure 6.4: Osaka
Source: https://www.touristinjapan.com/dotonbori-osaka/

2.2.4. Kyoto

Kyoto is home to a total of 194 startup companies (see Figure 6.5). This figure corresponds to around 9 % of the total number of startups in Japan. According to the rankings, Kyoto is positioned as the third most prominent startup environment in Japan.

Kyoto boasts a varied industrial landscape that encompasses a wide range of areas, including biotechnology, precision machining, robotics, artificial intelligence, gaming, and cuisine. The city has garnered acknowledgment for its notable achievements in the industrial sector, securing the 49th position on a global scale in the Hardware and Internet of Things (IoT) industries. Although Kyoto's startup ecosystem is not as developed as that of other players in Northeast Asia, it is now undergoing a consistent growth trajectory.

The collaborative initiative known as the Startup Capital Kyoto, which involves JETRO Kyoto, Kyoto Prefecture, and Kyoto Municipal City, was established with the aim of supporting foreign entrepreneurs in the process of establishing their firms in the city. This project offers co-working spaces, assistance in establishing companies, consultations, and connections to Kyoto's startup environment[8].

Figure 6.5: Kyoto
Source: https://rove.me/to/kyoto

2.2.5. Kobe

The city of Hyogo Kobe (see Figure 6.6) has been actively engaged in a range of pioneering endeavours aimed at transforming itself into an innovative urban center that surpasses the limitations often associated with local governance. As an illustration, various endeavours have been undertaken, such as accelerating the expansion of entrepreneurial ventures in Japan and abroad, fostering collaborations between governmental entities and startups to address administrative challenges, and providing financial assistance through investment funds.

Furthermore, the UNOPS worldwide Innovation Centre was established with the objective of addressing the challenges posed by the Sustainable Development Goals (SDGs) through the use of innovative technologies. This initiative is anticipated to serve as a platform for accessing the worldwide market pertaining to SDG-related concerns[9].

---

[8]   Retrieved from https://www.startupblink.com/startup-ecosystem/kyoto-jp
[9]   Retrieved from https://j-startup-city.go.jp/city/kansai/

Figure 6.6: Kobe
Source: https://www.hotels.com/go/japan/best-kobe-things-to-do

2.2.6. Other prefectures

Furthermore, apart from offering appealing compensation packages to entrepreneurs in major urban areas, there has been an implementation of visa-related regulations with the aim of fostering international companies in Japan.

Mie Prefecture, Hokkaido Government, and Ibaraki Prefecture have been newly certified for Startup Visa, one of the International Startup Activity Promotion Projects issued and enforced on December 28, 2018 (see Figure 6.7).

With this new certification, foreign entrepreneurs are able to stay in Japan for up to one year in Mie Prefecture, Hokkaido Government, and Ibaraki Prefecture (Ministry of Economy, Trade and Industry, 2018b).

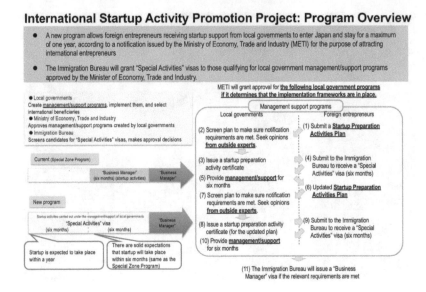

Figure 6.7: International startup activity promotion project
Source: J-Startup

2.3. Enterprise level

With regard to enterprise level, KEIDANREN (Japan Business Federation) – a comprehensive economic organization with a membership comprised of 1,512 representative companies of Japan, 107 nationwide industrial associations and the regional economic organizations for all 47 prefectures, can be considered the portrayal of businesses in Japan (see Figure 6.8). The primary objective of this organisation is to leverage the resources and energies of firms, individuals, and local communities to facilitate corporate initiatives that promote sustainable growth of the Japanese economy and enhance the overall quality of life of the Japanese population. In order to achieve its objectives, KEIDANREN endeavours to foster agreement throughout the business community about a range of significant domestic and international matters, with the aim of facilitating their efficient and timely settlement. Simultaneously, it engages in communication with a diverse array of stakeholders, encompassing political leaders, administrators, labour unions, and citizens[10].

---

[10]   https://www.keidanren.or.jp/en/profile/pro001.html

Organization Chart

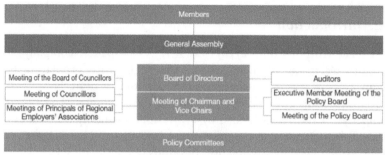

Figure 6.8: KEIDANREN Organizational chart
Source: https://www.keidanren.or.jp/en/profile/pro001.html

"*As a securities company with a mission to enrich society through our expertise in the capital markets, I believe the strengthening of the startup ecosystem is crucial to revitalize the Japanese economy. Addressing this issue jointly between the public and private sectors should be a priority.*" – said Koji NAGAI, Vice Chair of the Board of Councillors, Keidanren Chairman of the Board of Directors, Nomura Holdings, Inc.

In March 2022, Keidanren unveiled its "*Vision for Startup Breakthrough*" emphasizing the imperative of fortifying the startup eco-system as a means to invigorate the Japanese economy and restore its global competitiveness. There is a considerable level of anticipation over the potential for these public-private ventures to advance even further in the future (Holdings & Inc, 2022). In order to promote investment in startup enterprises, it is crucial to recruit foreign investors with the requisite expertise and capacity to impartially assess privately-held firms, therefore expanding the investor pool within the Japanese financial system. To cultivate a recurring pattern of economic expansion, it is crucial to invigorate the financial markets, which function as a facilitator for the economy, and encourage proactive investment in entrepreneurial endeavours.

3. Case study of innovation in Japan – PayPay

3.1. Introduction

PayPay Corporation (PayPay株式会社) is a Japanese company that develops electronic payment services owned by LY Corporation (see Figure 6.9). It was established in 2018 as a joint venture between the SoftBank Group and Yahoo Japan through Z Holdings, their holding company[11]. PayPay was funded by 8 investors, including SoftBank and Tokai Tokyo Financial as the most recent investors and has raised a total of 53.5 billion yen in funding over 6 rounds[12].

Figure 6.9: Logo of PayPay
Source: https://paypay.ne.jp/

PayPay is a convenient and intelligent payment solution that eliminates the need to carry a wallet. By simply displaying a barcode or QR code on a smartphone, users may effortlessly complete transactions. Also, with regard to payment methods, there are several options available such as via bank accounts, credit cards, or charging cash from ATM (see Figure 6.10). As noted on PayPay's website, there are 5 reasons that you should use PayPay in Japan:

1. ***Can be used at stores nationwide****: It can be used at various shops such as convenience stores, drug stores, and restaurants. In addition, it also supports payment of internet services and utility charges.*
2. ***Save money on shopping****: Earn PayPay points when you shop. We also offer great deals and coupons!*
3. ***Safe and secure to use****: In order to ensure your peace of mind, we have implemented measures to protect information and prevent unauthorized use, as well as a compensation system.*

---

[11] Retrieved from https://en.wikipedia.org/wiki/PayPay
[12] Retrieved from https://www.crunchbase.com/organization/paypay/company_financials

4. You can send your balance to friends and family: *You can easily send your balance to someone far away. No need for troublesome bills or coins.*

5. Besides shopping: *You can use various functions from the PayPay app, from paying utility bills to ordering delivery to investing!*

Figure 6.10: Smart features of PayPay
Source: https://about.paypay.ne.jp/pr/20200428/02/

3.2. SWOT analysis

3.2.1. Strengths

First, PayPay owned a strong customer base of SoftBank and Yahoo! Wallet which comprised approximately 40 million accounts[13]. Furthermore, it benefitted from the strong reputation of its co-founder, Softbank, which is one of the largest banks in Japan.

Second, in terms of affiliated stores, the initial expenditures associated with setting up the system are relatively modest, as the retailer is simply required to prominently display the code within their establishment. Furthermore, the provision of this service was offered at no cost

---

[13] Retrieved from https://www.softbank.jp/en/corp/news/press/sbkk/2018/2018 0727_01/

to affiliated stores throughout the initial three-year period following its commencement.

Third, for customers, they have gained the ability to access services offered by a diverse array of establishments, encompassing both nationwide retail chains and local merchants operating within specific regions with three different payments methods (credit cards, electronic money, or cash directly charged from ATM).

Fourth, concerning technological background, Paytm's consumer-centric technology can be utilised to develop a mobile payment system and facilitate the expansion of mobile payment services in Japan.

3.2.2. Weaknesses

Despite exhibiting several characteristics, PayPay was deemed to lack significant differentiation from its competitors. The initial step involves engaging in negotiations with various retail establishments to establish affiliations, thereby enabling customers to use PayPay as a viable payment option. Customers simply download PayPay application onto their smartphones and establish a connection between their bank accounts or credit cards and their PayPay accounts. Subsequently, they may conveniently make payments by utilising the QR code displayed inside the application, so obviating the necessity of physically handling cash or cards. The business model of using QR code payment technology on smartphones is not fundamentally distinct from that of other electronic payment service providers.

3.2.3. Opportunities

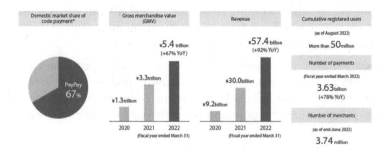

Figure 6.11: Ratio of PayPay gross merchandise value (2021) as a percentage of total merchandise transaction value in the code-based payment market
Source: https://www.softbank.jp/

PayPay has experienced significant growth (see Figure 6.11) and has emerged as one of Japan's leading cashless payment systems, boasting a user base that comprises over 50 % of the country's smartphone users and this figure is predicted to increase. With a three-layered revenue model (see Figure 6.12), PayPay's revenue is expected not only from payment fees, merchant services like other e-payment service providers but also from financial services such as insurance, personal and business loans[14].

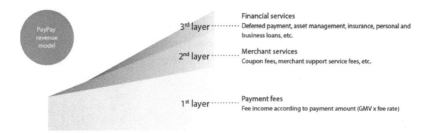

Figure 6.12: PayPay's three-layered revenue model
Source: https://www.softbank.jp/

3.2.4. Threats

Since its inception, PayPay has faced significant competition from many domestic competitors such as Line Pay, Rakuten Pay, and Amazon Pay, as well as overseas competitors like WeChat Pay and AliPay. These competitors additionally possess a substantial consumer base and exhibit superior technological features, hence enabling them to potentially establish market dominance at any given moment.

Despite the challenges and vulnerabilities that PayPay encounters, it is indisputable that the platform has achieved a significant advancement in the digital market within Japan, a nation that has traditionally relied on cash transactions. Until October 2023, the number of registered users has already reached a significant milestone of 60 million (PayPay)[15]. Sharing about PayPay's goal in the near future, Hirofumi Fujii, Division Head of the Marketing Division, PayPay stated in an interview in April

---

[14] Retrieved from https://www.softbank.jp/en/corp/ir/documents/integrated_reports/fy2022/nakayama/

[15] Retrieved from https://paypay.ne.jp/

2023: *"Cash still accounts for 40 to 50 % of Japan's personal consumption, with over 100 trillion yen spent annually. If we take the lead in this shift to cashlessness and get half the market share, we can increase our GMV by 50 trillion yen. We would definitely like to work strategically in this domain"*[16].

Thus, through SWTO analysis, it is possible to draw lessons learned from PayPay in innovation, from the advantage of owning a large customer and the reputation of co-owned partners, and affiliated stores to create a consumer-centric technology ecosystem platform. However, PayPay has a lack of big differences compared to the competition. Face with opportunities to increase the number of electronic payment users and its position as a pioneering business, PayPay needs outstanding innovations to contribute to changing the culture of using cash that still dominates the Japanese market.

References

Holdings, N., & Inc. (2022). Keidanren: *Strengthening the startup ecosystem.* Retrieved from: https://www.keidanren.or.jp/en/journal/2022/05_kantou gen.html

MacDowall, J. (1984). The technology innovation system in Japan. *Journal of Product Innovation Management, 1*(3), 165–172.

Ministry of Economy, Trade and Industry. (2018a). *J-Startup.* Retrieved from: https://www.j-startup.go.jp/en/about/

Ministry of Economy, Trade and Industry. (2018b). *Three new startup visas have been certified. J-Startup.* Retrieved from: https://www.j-startup.go.jp/en/news/news_200302.html

Ministry of Economy, Trade and Industry. (2020). *"Start Next Innovator 2020" Program Starts.* Retrieved from: https://go.gale.com/ps/i.do?id= GALE|A627962133&sid=sitemap&v=2.1&it=r&p=AONE&sw=w&userGroupName=anon%7E3ac6e84b&aty=open-web-entry

Ministry of Economy, Trade and Industry. (2021). *J-Startup City Project Japan.* Retrieved from: https://j-startup-city.csti-startup-policy.go.jp/

Office for Startup and Global Financial City Strategy. (2022). *Startup Genome Tokyo.* Retrieved from: https://startupgenome.com/ecosystems/tokyo

---

[16] Retrieved from https://insideout.paypay.ne.jp/en/2023/04/11/leader-interview_vo l09-en/

Ota, M., Hazama, Y., & Samson, D. (2013). Japanese innovation processes. *International Journal of Operations & Production Management, 33*(3), 275–295.

Whittaker, D. H. (2001). *Crisis and innovation in Japan: A new future through techno-entrepreneurship?*. MIT Japan Program, Working Paper Series 01.02

Chapter 7

The role of Bio-Circular-Green economy in fostering business innovations towards post Covid-19 economic recovery and sustainable development: The case of Thailand

Supawan Saelim

Abstract: Thai government has placed Bio-Circular-Green (BCG) economy as the national agenda and the core of the Thailand's post Covid-19 economic recovery in 2021. BCG is aimed at turning Thailand's comparative advantage in biological and cultural diversity into new sustainable and inclusive growth engines with technology and innovation. In addition, BCG is also in line with Thailand's growth path towards achieving climate goals of carbon neutrality by 2050 and net-zero emissions by 2065. BCG focuses on four strategic sectors, namely (i) agriculture and food; (ii) wellness and medicine; (iii) energy, materials and biochemicals; and (iv) tourism and creative economy. Accordingly, the BCG Action Plan 2021–2027 was implemented in Thailand with key strategies to promote sustainability of biological resources, strengthen communities and grassroots, enhance the competitiveness of Thai BGC industries and build resilience to global changes by employing science, technology, and innovation. BCG policy measures include support BCG startups, create digital repository, and employ big data analysis, create demand for innovative goods and services through the government procurement program, tax and investment incentives. This chapter will introduce Thailand's BCG policies and action plan as well as investment ecosystems supporting business innovations related to BCG, including the lessons learned and policy recommendations for fostering business innovations related to BCG.

Keywords: Bio-Circular-Green (BCG) Economy, Sustainable Development, Business Innovation.

1. Introducing Thailand's Bio-Circular-Green economic model

In 2021, the Thai government has placed Bio-Circular-Green economic model (BCG) as the national agenda and the core of the Thailand's post Covid-19 economic recovery. The BCG has been applied for the development of bioeconomy, circular economy, and green economy in Thailand, aligning to the United Nation's Sustainable Development Goals (SDGs) and a key principle for Thailand's social and economic development so-called the Sufficiency Economy Philosophy (SEP). The adoption of BCG economic model aims to turn Thailand's comparative advantage in biological and cultural diversity into new sustainable and inclusive growth engines with technology and innovation. In addition, BCG is also in line with Thailand's growth path towards achieving climate goals of carbon neutrality by 2050 and net-zero emissions by 2065.

The term 'Bio' refers to bioeconomy such as the use and conversion of biological resources for production of value-added products. 'Circular' refers to circular economy such as the reuse and recycling of materials to maximize the resources. 'Green' refers to green economy such as the deployment of renewable energy and sustainable development principle. Thailand aims to integrate these three key concepts for the development of high-value products and services that conserve natural and biological resources, use less resources as input and are environmentally friendly while retaining Thailand's unique attributes on cultural and social identity (Dharmapiya *et al.*, 2022).

BCG focuses on four strategic sectors, namely (i) agriculture and food; (ii) wellness and medicine; (iii) bioenergy, biomaterials and biochemistry; and (iv) tourism and the creative economy. These four sectors have a total economic value of about Baht 3.4 trillion or 21 % of Thailand's GDP, and are expected to rise to Baht 4.4 trillion or 24 % of GDP by 2027. These four sectors drive the BCG strategy together with other drivers such as talent and entrepreneurial development, area-based development and frontier research, as summarized in the Figure 7.1.

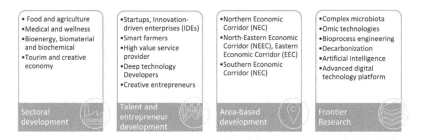

Figure 7.1: Drivers for BCG Strategy
Source: Author's illustration from NXPO (2023)

BCG Action Plan 2021–2027, endorsed by the Cabinet in 2022, has already been implemented in Thailand (NSTDA, 2022). The plan outlines key strategies to promote sustainability of biological resources, strengthen communities and grassroots, enhance the competitiveness of Thailand's BCG industries and build resilience to global changes by employing science, technology, and innovation. BCG policy measures include the support to BCG startups, creation of digital repositories, employment of big data analysis, promotion of demand for innovative goods and services through the government procurement program, tax and investment incentives.

The BCG Action plan aims to add Baht 1 trillion contribution to Thailand's GDP. The economic targets of five strategic sectors in the BCG Action Plan are summarized (NSTDA, 2022) as follows:

Sector 1 – Agriculture and food: Diversification of agricultural products, a real-time production monitoring and traceability system, Good Agricultural Practice (GAP), adopting green manufacturing practices, novel healthy food products.

■ *Economic targets by 2027*: Raise GDP from Baht 1.3 trillion to Baht 1.6 trillion for the agriculture sector and from Baht 0.6 trillion to 0.9 trillion for food products.

Sector 2 – Health and wellness: Manpower and technological capacity building to promote R&D in drugs, vaccines, biopharmaceuticals and medical devices, and the use of genetic data.

■ *Economic targets by 2027*: Raise GDP from drugs and medical supplies from Baht 40 billion to Baht 90 billion.

Sector 3 – Energy, Material and Biochemicals: Renewable energy, community-based power plants with smart microgrid, blockchain technology and energy storage research, conversion of biomass and agriculture by-products to high-value materials and chemicals such as bioplastics, fiber, pharmaceuticals and oleochemicals.

■ *Economic targets by 2027*: Potentially raise GDP to Baht 260 billion from Baht 110 billion.

Section 4 – Tourism and Creative Economy: Promotion of secondary cities, employment of technology and innovation in tourism and ecosystem management, adoption of sustainable tourism, creative economy to create high-value goods and services.

■ *Economic targets by 2027*: Potentially raise GDP to Baht 1.2 trillion from Baht 1 trillion.

Section 5 – Circular economy: Business opportunities for a new economy and create green jobs.

■ *Economic targets by 2027*: At least 1 % contribution to the GDP in 2027.

In addition to the contribution to GDP, BCG Action plan also aims to achieve the following goals by 2027 (Sirilertworakul, 2021):

■ **Sustainability of resources:** Reduce natural resource consumption by a quarter, cut down GHG emissions by at least 20 % and add at least 0.5 million hectares of forest area.

■ **Socioeconomic prosperity:** Improve income inequality of 10 million people, reduce the undernourished population share to 5 %, improve health inequality of at least 300,000 people and increase the number of energy self-sufficient community by 20 %.

■ **Sustainable economic growth:** Increase the share of high-value products and services to at least 20 % and generate at least 50 % more income for the grassroots.

■ **Self-reliance:** Improve skill of at least 1 million workers, increase additional 1,000 startups and innovation-driven enterprises (IDEs), reduce imports of medical and health supplies by at least 20 %.

Proposed BCG actions could be consolidated into 13 measures (NSTDA, 2022) as follows:

Measure 1: Create digital repository of bioresources, cultural capital and local wisdom and employ big data analytics to serve the purposes of conservation, restoration and utilization of these assets to strengthen a local economy and tourism industry.

Measure 2: Replenish national resources by introducing forestry carbon projects to attract private sector participation and accelerating research and development in plant and animal breeding and resource management.

Measure 3: Develop the BCG corridor by building a regional economic corridor and employing BCG approach to develop and improve goods and services.

Measure 4: Transform the agricultural system to produce premium and safe products, diversify farm products, increase farmers' access to knowledge and technology and promote sustainable agriculture.

Measure 5: Improve quality and safety of street food and local food products through food machinery and Good Hygiene Practices (GHP) compliance.

Measure 6: Build a bio-based economy by employing advanced technology to develop and manufacture high-value products such as functional ingredients, functional food, biochemicals such as oleochemicals, biomaterials such as carbon-based materials, drugs and vaccines.

Measure 7: Create demand for innovative goods and services through the government procurement program, tax and investment incentive, and instruments such as carbon pricing and the polluter pays principle.

Measure 8: Promote sustainable and green tourism and establish a one-time payment system to support big data analysis.

Measure 9: Promote the development and manufacturing of sustainable goods and services by employing green technologies, green finance and circular design.

Measure 10: Raise the standards of products and services to comply with international requirements by investing in infrastructure and healthy innovation ecosystem.

Measure 11: Support BCG startups with skill development program for entrepreneurs and increase access to technology, infrastructure, experts and finance.

Measure 12: Develop manpower to support the BCG model at all levels, from grassroots to startups and deep technology.

Measure 13: Promote international collaboration in all facets, including knowledge creation and talent mobility.

These measures indicate new business opportunities aligning to the BCG, ranging from potential investment in specific sectors to capacity building and campaigning activities.

2. Current investment ecosystems supporting business innovations related to BCG

Thailand's Board of Investment (BOI) plays a prominent role in supporting new BCG business opportunities as a "promoter" proving tax and non-tax benefits, an "integrator" of investment support tools, a "facilitator" providing services and a "connector" linking industries to create business opportunities (BOI, 2022a). In October 2022, BOI approved a new 5-year investment promotion strategy (2023–2027) with the focus on innovative, competitive, and inclusive approach to the new economy. This strategy will encourage technological advances, the transition to green and smart industries, talent development as well as creativity and innovation with the aim of transforming Thailand into a regional hub for business, trade and logistics (BOI, 2022a). BOI identified seven pillars of investment promotion strategy for the New Economy (BOI, 2022b) as follows:

Pillar 1 Restructure industries and strengthen supply chain

Pillar 2 Accelerate industrial transition to smart and sustainable industries

Pillar 3 Promote Thailand as an International business center and the regional gateway for trade and investment

Pillar 4 Enhance the competitiveness of SMEs and startups and connects to global market

Pillar 5 Promote investment based on the potential of each area to generate inclusive growth

Pillar 6 Promote investments in community development programs

Pillar 7 Promote Thai overseas investment to expand business opportunities

These 7 pillars also aim to strengthen the country's status as regional hubs for business, namely TECH hub, BCG hub, Talent hub, Logistic and Business hub and Creative hub. BOI introduced measures to support local economic development and strengthen community enterprises, agriculture and food processing business and community-based tourism, technological upgrade to comply with international standards.

In October 2023, BOI published the new 5 key strategies and agendas for transition to new industries. The 5 key strategic industries (BOI, 2023) are as follows:

(1) **BCG:** Advancing ASEAN's "BCG Capital" – Promote investments in Biocomplex, the Economic Corridors in the four regions and expand measures to cover the community forest management and PM 2.5 reduction.

(2) **Automotive:** Developing a Premier Global Automotive Manufacturing center – Promote a complete EV production systems and management of used EV batteries.

(3) **Electronics:** Evolving into ASEAN's Smart Electronics, Manufacturing Hub and Pioneering the development of the Upstream Electronics Industry in Thailand.

(4) **Digital and Creative:** Transforming into ASEAN's Digital and Creative Center – Attract investments in hyperscale data center and cloud services and promote a fully integrated digital industry.

(5) **Regional Headquarters & International Business Center:** Positioning Thailand as an International Business Hub.

Along with 5 strategic industries, BOI also announced 5 key agendas for promoting the transition to new industries as follows (BOI, 2023).

(1) **Green Transformation:** Endorsing policy targets of carbon neutrality by 2050 and net zero emissions by 2065.

(2) **Technology Development:** Supporting 1,000 Innovation Driven Enterprises (IDEs) with an annual revenue of Baht 1 billion.

(3) **Talent Development and Attraction:** Becoming Regional Talent Hub.

(4) **Cluster-based investment:** Decentralizing investments and distributing growth based on local potential across the country.

(5) **Ease of Investment:** Positioning as the ASEAN's Trade & Investment Gateway.

BCG investment activities aligned with various investment promotion strategies and policies during 2023–2027. BOI classified 55 eligible activities under the concept of BCG economy in the five following sectors: agriculture and agricultural products, bio-based industry, medical industry, paper industry, energy and public utilities. These eligible activities, examples shown in Figure 7.2, will be entitled to obtain the tax benefits such as corporate income tax exemption ranging from 3 to 8 years (BOI, 2022c). Environmentally friendly activities could also be classified as BCG.

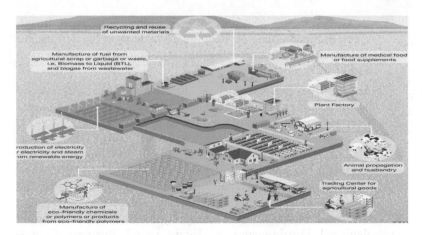

Figure 7.2: Examples of BOI- promoted projects under the concept of BCG
Source: BOI (2022c)

The value of investment application in BCG during 2015–2021 totaled about Baht 7 trillion, showing a positive growth trend, particularly in 2021 (Thatpitakkul, 2024). During the first 9 months of 2023, there were 254 investment proposals categorized as BCG projects with a total value of Baht 73.3 billion. Approved investment projects will be entitled to obtain various incentives (such as corporate income tax (CIT) exemption and exemption of import duties on machinery and raw materials) under different incentive schemes summarized in Table 7.1.

Table 7.1: Types of BOI investment incentive schemes

Activity-based incentives	Technology-based incentives	Merit-based incentives	Area-based incentives
■ Bio and medical industries	■ Biotechnology	■ R&D	■ EEC 3 provinces
■ Advanced manufacturing industries	■ Nanotechnology	■ IP licensing	■ SEZ 10 provinces
■ Basic and supporting industries.	■ Advanced material technology	■ Advanced technology training	■ Southern border provinces
■ Digital, creative industries, and high-value services	■ Digital technology	■ Development of local suppliers	■ 20 provinces with the lowest income
		■ Product and packaging design	■ Industrial Estates/ Zones
		■ Donations to technology and human resource development funds	■ Science and Technology zones

Table 7.1: Continued

Activity-based incentives	Technology-based incentives	Merit-based incentives	Area-based incentives
Incentive: Not more than 8 years CIT exemption, exception import duties on machinery and raw materials	Incentive: 10 years CIT exemption	Incentive: Additional CIT exemption period based on investment capital expenditure	

Source: Thatpitakkul (2024)

Business opportunities for BCG Economy that will be eligible for investment incentives from BOI are listed in Table 7.2.

Table 7.2: List of BCG activities

Bioeconomy	Circular Economy	Green Economy
Bioenergy and biofuels: ■ Electricity from biomass or stream ■ Fuel from agriculture products **Biotechnology R&D Agriculture** ■ Active ingredients from natural raw materials ■ Medical food ■ High-tech natural extract ■ Biological fertilizer, organic fertilizer, biopesticide **Plant & Animal** ■ R&D activity and/or manufacturing using biotechnology	**Circular energy and fuels** ■ Electricity or electricity and stream from garbage or refuse derived fuel ■ Fuel from agricultural scrap or garbage or waste ■ Biomass briquettes and pellets **Waste and recycling management** **Products from circular process** ■ Recycled plastic pellets with properties equivalent to virgin plastic pellets ■ Recycled pulp with R&D process in the project ■ Agricultural by-products or waste products **Waste & recycling** ■ Waste treatment or disposal ■ Recycling and reuse of unwanted materials	**Green energy** ■ Electricity or electricity and stream from renewable energy **Green management** ■ Energy Service Company (ESCO) ■ CCUS ■ Agro-Industrial Zone ■ Cold Storage facilities and Cold Storage transport **Product from saving energy** ■ Fuel cell ■ Energy-saving parts for automobiles ■ High density energy storage ■ Solar cells and/or raw materials for solar cells ■ Energy-saving home appliances **Eco-friendly chemicals/polymers** ■ Bio plastics ■ Eco-friendly pulp ■ Products from eco-friendly polymers, pulp and paper

Source: Author illustration from Thatpitakkul (2024)

Support startups are identified as key action plan under the BCG Action Plan and also key strategies in BOI investment promotion policies. Figure 7.3 summarized the success factors and government support for the startup ecosystem in Thailand.

Figure 7.3: Success factors and government support for Thai startup ecosystem
Source: Fingerle *et al.* (2023)

As lack of funding and access to capital is the key challenge for BCG startups, the Thai government provides investment and funding support through various government agencies. As featured in the work of Figerle *et al.* (2023), the BOI offers co-financing up to a maximum of USD 132,000 for startups' human capital expenses, and the national Digital Economy Promotion Agency (DEPA) provides convertible grants to startups that can be returned as soft loans with low rates or as equity. In addition, the National Innovation Agency (NIA) offers a maximum funding of Baht 1.5 million to startups and SMEs with projects focused on transformative, productivity and value-added innovation and provides grants for social innovation projects. In addition to corporate income tax exemption incentives provided by BOI, incentives for startups are also in the form of tax incentives such as tax exemptions to SMEs that use DEPA-certified startups' services for digitalization, tax reduction for SMEs that provide digital skills training, capital gain tax exemption for startups whose core business is technology and innovation.

The government has also budgeted for investments related to BCG and sustainable development. In 2020, the government's budget was allocated to BCG-related investments such as development and efficiency enhancement initiatives in renewable energy (Baht 357 million), green industry program (Baht 24.8 million), eco-industrial towns (Baht

21.2 million), smart farmers (Baht 48 million), promotion of bioeconomy as a new source of regional income (Baht 10 million), etc. (PAGE, 2023).

In October 2022, the BCG Policy Board approved several budgets on new initiatives to drive three BCG strategic areas (NSTDA, 2024) as follows:

- **Drug and Vaccines:** A government budget of Baht 661.79 million was approved to set up Thailand's first active pharmaceutical ingredients (API) manufacturing facility to strengthen the national health security. This Baht 1-billion investment project will be jointly contributed by PTT Public Co. Ltd, Innobic (Asia) Co. Ltd, the Government Pharmaceutical Organization (GPO) and National Science and Technology Agency (NSTDA). This project expects to benefit 4 million Thai people.

- **Agriculture:** A budget of Baht 50 million was approved to upgrade vaccine production infrastructure to support the production of autogenous vaccines to manage infectious diseases in farm animals.

- **Innovation, Infrastructure and Facilities:** The government was requested to remove tax barriers to promote the joint investment for the construction of a Baht 20 billion bio-polyethylene (Bio-PE) production plant with annual production capacity of 200,000 tons.

In addition, financial institutions, including the Bank for Agriculture Cooperatives and the Export-Import Bank of Thailand, are expected to offer loans to BCG businesses totaling Baht 100 billion by 2027 (NSTDA, 2024).

3. Case studies of BCG business innovations in Thailand

The BCG and SEP strategies have promoted various government initiatives and new business innovations in practice, thanks to policy and financial support. This section will provide examples of illustrative case studies in various economic sectors and areas in Thailand, summarized from the report on Thailand's BCG transformation: 40 Case Studies on the Bio-Circular-Green Strategy and the Sufficiency Economy Philosophy in Action (Dharmapiya et al., 2022). Figure 7.4 summarizes BCG and SEP strategies implemented in seven key economic sectors and areas.

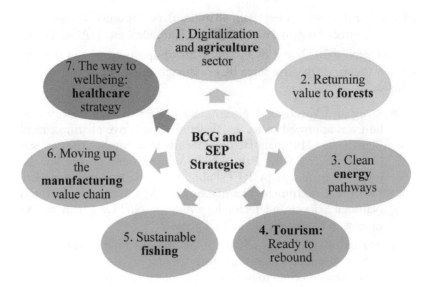

Figure 7.4: BCG and SEP Strategies in seven key economic sectors or areas

3.1. Agriculture – Digitalization and agriculture sector

Digitalization plays a prominent role in transforming the agricultural sector, driving innovations based on sensor technology and the Internet of Things that improve cultivation yields and farm management systems. Aligning with BCG's goals of reducing natural resource consumption and improve income inequality, technologies such as drones, Apps and machine learning will enable faster and more accurate cultivation, cost reductions in labor and materials through using less fertilizers and pesticides, and less water. In addition, artificial intelligence (AI) and other technologies help farmers to grow higher-value products and increase diversity of farming, leading to less impacts from global price volatility as well as potential epidemics and disasters from forecast data.

Digitalization helps improve productivity and reduce the costs of farming, thereby raising farmers' income. However, key challenges exist in the digitalization of the agricultural sector such as lack of access to new technologies, lack of finance, lack of technological skills and the risks of uncertain incomes due to commodity market volatility. Figure 7.5 illustrates some innovative business ideas with potential technological solutions that help address key challenges in the agricultural sector.

•Declining labor force due to urbainzation and aging rural population
•Pollution and pesticide poisoning
•Climate change impacts
•Biodiversity loss
•Low productivity and low profits

•Automatic systems that reduce labor burdens
•Precision farming that reduces the use of chemicals
•AI that helps forecaset weather and disasters and precision farming that uses less water and reduces carbon footprint
•Apps that enables farmers to increase productivity
•Increase high-value products and reducing costs

Figure 7.5: Innovative business ideas with technological solutions in the agriculture sector
Source: Author's illustration from Dharmapiya *et al.* (2022)

3.1.1. Case study: Aromatic Farm in Ratchaburi

A small startup, Aromatic farm, has become a BCG Business Award winning company in 2021 at the Thailand Top SME Awards. Aromatic farm switched from traditional chemical-based coconut farm to an aromatic coconut farm that is free of chemical. Aligning with BCG strategy, Aromatic farm employs natural farming methods with the help of technology to increase productivity and profits, along with good manufacturing practice, building a network of like-minded farms and waste management. Within three years after turning into an organic farm, Aromatic farm increased more than 80 % of coconut yields from 5,000 coconuts to 9,000 coconuts and the organic coconut prices are higher. The success of an aromatic farm has built a network of 34 plantations totaling 1,020 rai of coconut farms, including nine learning stations for knowledge exchange. A summary of the BCG implementation in this case includes as following:

- **Technology:** Aromatic farm uses QR codes to record data specific to each tree, enabling farmers with improved production schedules and greater accuracy of seasonal yield checks as well as real-time solutions such as when fertilizer should be added.

- **Organic:** Moving from the old chemical-based farming to an organic farming practice, yields increase, and profits are higher, increasing organic farming incomes.

- **Value-added products:** Aromatic farm offers five types of products made from organic coconut such as ready-to-eat coconut pieces,

coconut flesh for bakeries, coconut jelly for restaurants and households, and coconut ice-cream.

• **Waste management:** Aromatic farm recycles 90 % of the waste that
the farm produces. Biofertilizers could be made from food waste.

3.2. Forests – Returning value to forests

Thailand's forest ecosystem has been significantly depleted over the
past decades due to commercial exploitation, urbanization, unsustainable
agriculture practices and the growth of unsustainable tourism. Forests
are the main sources of biodiversity and biological repositories. These
biobanks could be a source of innovative and high-value products for
Thailand. The main challenges facing Thailand's forests include (i) unsustainable agricultural practices and deforestation, including monocrop-
ping and the use of pesticides as well as slash-and-burn farming (ii) illegal
logging that continues to grow partly due to high demand for luxurious
wooden furniture (iii) vested interests leading to untransparent assessments of Environmental Impact Assessments (EIAs). The protection and
conservation of biodiversity are therefore highlighted as a key BCG strategy. In addition, BCG strategy also includes the improvement of community forest, of which there are more than 10,000 community forest
sites in Thailand. The BCG strategy also encourages capacity building
for those working in the forests, leading to better forest management and
the creation of courses in specialized skills such as systems biology and
bioinformatics.

3.2.1. Case Study: Doi Tung Development Project (DTDP)

As one of the oldest and best-known social enterprises in Thailand,
the Doi Tung Development Project (DTDP) successfully encouraged
ethic people living in the mountainous Golden Triangle region to turn
to economic crops that created a sustainable income source and do not
harm the forests. The DTDP also led to an increase in the reforested
areas. Products purchased from ethnic populations are sold under the
well-known Doi Tung brand and Doi Tung products are also certified
by the United Nations Office on Drugs and Crime (UNODC) in recognition of their success in solving ethnic problems through peaceful and
sustainable development methods. The DTDP has aligned itself with the
BCG action strategy as follows:

- **Value-added products:** Foster the cultivation of high-value economic crops such as macadamias and arabica coffees.
- **Experiential tourism:** Promote authentic and immersive tourism with the transformation of ethnic villages.
- **Local economy:** Promote business units run in harmony with local people, economy, society and environment, including business units on handicrafts, processed food, agriculture and tourism.
- **Capacity building:** Support young people to learn about farming and hosting tourists.

3.3. Tourism – Ready to rebound

Before the Covid-19 pandemic, Thailand's tourism sector was concentrated in only 5 provinces with the greatest tourist records in 2019 but were also under pressures on natural resources. The government plans to address the imbalance, mass-market tourism and environmental problems in Thailand with BCG strategies, including ramping up technological innovations, promoting new forms of digital storytelling, boosting tourists in niche markets in Thailand such as wellness and culinary tourism. The implementation of BCG strategy in the tourism sector will have significant impacts on the environment and biodiversity, high-technology innovation growth, the creative economy and soft power development. Four pillars of BCG strategy are identified in the tourism sector (Dharmapiya *et al.*, 2022) as follows:

- **Pillar 1**: Promote secondary destinations with the cultural and historical distinctiveness, including the promotion of unique productions and activities in each region.
- **Pillar 2**: Develop new sustainable tourism products and activities such as knowledge-based tourism and senior tourism.
- **Pillar 3**: Create new inter-province transport systems and use technology to better manage tourists and sites.
- **Pillar 4**: Promote new forms of tourism such as 'world-class events' tied to the creative economy or agritourism.

To align with BCG action plan, the following four actions should be focused to promote the BCG in Thailand's tourism sector (Dharmapiya *et al.*, 2022).

Action 1 – Legal remedies to reduce environmental impacts: Examples of actions include:

    a. A new law penalizing bringing single-use plastics into national parks;

    b. Closing a famous island for months and popular national parks during the monsoon season for site recovery.

Action 2 – Three new niche markets to attract high-yield tourists, reduce strain on natural resources and support sustainability: Three new niche markets are as follows:

    a. *Culinary tourism*: promote Thai food with a cultural and historical experience to develop tourism;

    a. *Medical tourism*: develop technologies and new services to attract medical tourists such as elderly tourists from high-income countries;

    b. *Wellness tourism:* provide wellness activities such as yoga, spa, detox programs, meditation retreats as well as new value-added products and therapies that align with BCG's strategies.

Action 3 – New stories for a new digital era to promote tourism: Examples of actions include:

    a. The "Unseen Thailand" campaign to promote secondary destinations by using online media such as YouTubers, podcasters and TikTokers;

    b. Availability of online trip information and booking;

    c. New contact-free payment systems developed by the hospitality.

Action 4 – Community-based tourism

    a. Shifting visitors away from popular hotspots to community-based tourism for local experiences such as local food, traditional skills like rice plating and fishing and grassroots experience in homestays.

3.3.1. Case study: Sampran model of organic tourism

A family-owned business "Suan Sampran" or "Rose Garden" has transformed its hotel business into an ecotourism destination or organic tourism, which offers not only accommodation with nature but also an experience of Thai culture through local food with organic ingredients and local activities. The Sampran model is an example of a new inclusive business model for hotels and restaurants to connect with local organic farmers, enhance customers' experience and participating in the organic ecosystem (Suan Sampran, 2024). There are about 193 farming families from 16 different geographic and farming practice groups joining in this organic community. During the Covid-19 crisis, this community worked together to sell their products directly to individual customers. Currently, "the Sookjai market" generates income of over Baht 30 million for organic vendors annually and serves organic food to about 1,400 customers every weekend on average. In addition, about 19 hotels and three exhibition centers purchase 300 tons of organic products annually through this network. A summary of BCG implementation in this case includes:

- **Revolutionizing the food system:** Sampran Model transforms the entire good system, encouraging organic farming with a fair price and trade and collaborating with organic farmers and main stakeholders to foster an organic society. Suan Sampran grew its own rice, vegetables, fruits and herbs through its own Patom Organic Farm and also bought organic ingredients directly from farmers.
- **Growing organic community and network:** Suan Sampran established Sookjai Farmers' Market that creates approximately Baht 3 million per month for organic farmers and communities, building a network of organic producers with HORECA (Business-hotels, restaurants and catering), farmers, public and private sectors, the media and academia. Sampran Model Academy was also established as a learning exchange platform on topics such as inclusive business, circular economy and learning organization.
- **Digital platform:** The Thai Organic Consumer Association (TOCA) platform was launched in 2020 to bring organic farmers, businesses and consumers together via a mobile application that links the whole organic value chain. TOCA can be used to track various activities such as planting, harvesting and watering, building users' trust in the entire food chain from start to finish and help customers see their contribution.
- **Experiential tourism:** Sampran model offers tourists experience with nature as well as traditional culture, architecture and food.
- **Waste management:** Sampran model recycles all food waste into organic fertilizers, animal and wormery feeds. It also recycles used

vegetable oils into biodiesel. The use of foam packaging, plastic straws and plastic bottles is not allowed in Suan Sampran.

3.4. Manufacturing – Moving up the manufacturing value chain

Manufacturing contributed to about a quarter of Thailand's GDP. Major manufacturing companies are operating in the Industrial/ Economic Zones which provide investment incentives. As area-based development is one of the key drivers for BCG strategy in Thailand, the development of economic corridors plays significant roles in driving innovation and technologies of industries in these areas.

3.4.1. Case Study: The Eastern Economic Corridor of Innovation (EECi)

The Thai government launched the Eastern Economic Corridor of Innovation (EECi) in 2017 to drive innovation and technology in three eastern provinces, Chachoengsao, Chonburi and Rayong, promoting industries towards a sustainable economy with the support on research, infrastructure, localization and commercialization of technology and innovation. The EECi support BCG through 3 key strategies:

- **Adding value to the agriculture sector**: Promoting biorefineries and establishing a biotechnology platform with an investment of around Baht 3 billion from the government. BCG activities include modern agriculture and advanced biotechnology.

- **Supporting industrial transformation:** Promoting automation and computer-based manufacturing and establishing support- ing facilities such as Sustainable Manufacturing Center (SMC), Alternative Battery Pilot Plant, 3-GeV Synchrotron facility sup- porting research that enhance functions in various industries such as pharmaceuticals and high-protein foods. BCG activities include batteries and modern transport and automation, robotics and smart electronics.

- **Supporting future industries:** Focusing on technology for forward-looking industries such as aviation, unmanned aerial vehicles (drones), health and wellness and providing businesses with access to advanced infrastructure and labs. BCG activities include aviation and aerospace as well as medical device and supplies.

3.5. Healthcare – The way to wellbeing: Healthcare strategy

The BCG strategy for the healthcare economy in Thailand aims to create greater autonomy in the manufacturing of medicines, develop new treatment modalities and become a center for services and research. As the largest importer and exporter of medical devices in ASEAN by value (Dharmapiya *et al.*, 2022), Thailand aims to increase domestic production of pharmaceuticals and medical equipment, enabling Thai with better access to medical care at more affordable prices. In addition, Thailand has the opportunity to better capitalize various medical principles and practice with regards to Thai traditional medicine. The BCG strategy outlines (i) OMICs technology that expands biological knowledge such as genes, proteins and metabolites and (ii) genome editing and synthetic biology, which promote the production of biopharmaceutical products as areas of healthcare research that benefit the Thai economy.

In Thailand, there is also a large gap between urban and rural areas in the healthcare sector. The rural areas face different challenges due to the lack of infrastructure and the inability to retain healthcare professionals in rural locations. Therefore, the main BCG strategy for urban and rural areas is different. Strategies for urban area focus on developing more downstream medical products (such as drugs, vaccines, CT scan machines, bone replacement materials, etc.), strengthening research and development capacity with digital platforms, and targeting high-income and aging tourists. Meanwhile, strategies for rural areas focus on fostering collaboration between different sectors such as Quality of Life Development Committee, healthcare professionals, police, teachers and monks.

3.5.1. Case study: Chao Phraya Abhaibhubejhr Hospital Foundation (CAF) for traditional Thai herbs

CAF, commonly known as "Abhaibhubejhr", a pioneer in herbal medicine in Thailand, has planted herbs to produce medicines, providing affordable medicines to the Thai people and disseminating local wisdom. Examples of herbs used by Abhaibhubejhr enterprise include Indian gooseberries to make cough syrups and mangosteen peels for treating wounds. During the Covid-19 pandemic, this enterprise was the first local organization to raise awareness about the potential use of green chiretta to strengthen the immune system. The secret of this enterprise's success lies on the transformation of the organic herbs and plants they harvest into modern medicinal forms such as pills, balms, sprays, creams and soaps. In 2021, Abhaibhubejhr achieved an impressive sale of Baht 400 million. In the future, there will be a list of herbal remedies recommended by this enterprise and further research will be conducted on the medical uses of plants from an 83 Rai herbal garden in Khao Yai province. A summary of the BCG implementation in this case includes:

- **Autonomous manufacturing:** This enterprise produces herbal medicines to treat basic illnesses, initiating the whole processes starting from R&D and planting herbs. The foundation also runs 'Mo Ya Noi' camp to educate children to conserve forests and trees, which are sources of useful herbs and plants.
- **Alternative treatments:** The enterprise uses Thailand's biodiversity to highlight the wisdom of ancient knowledge and healing practices.
- **Local economy:** The enterprise buys organic products from villagers and support them as retailers.
- **Biobank:** The enterprise established a garden full of plants with medicinal properties for future research. The foundation received a donation of 83 Rai in Khao Yai for turning it into a herbal garden.

4. Policy recommendations for fostering business innovations related to BCG

During post Covid-19 economic recovery, Thailand has set clear policy targets and action plans on supporting BCG as the national agenda that aligns with sustainable development goals or SDGs as well as historical SEP principles. Accordingly, various government entities offer comprehensive policy and investment incentives that promote BCG- related business innovations.

To complete the ecosystem supporting business innovations, Figure 7.6 illustrates BCG enabling ecosystem factors in addition to policy support investment measures. Amendments of regulatory framework supporting BCG activities are required to build an innovative ecosystem, providing mandatory requirements to shift away from resource-intensive activities towards bioeconomy, circular practice, or green economy. Examples of regulatory reforms include a regulation offering 90 % carbon credit to enterprises participating in forestry carbon projects, deregulation of denatured alcohol to increase ethanal value creation, regulation for green industry adoption (Meerod, 2024). In addition, infrastructure readiness and facility development have enabled advanced technology discovery and deployment in businesses. The national biobank of Thailand is a case in point: it supports infrastructure for the conversion and research of Thailand's biological resources using cutting-edge technologies, and serves as a platform for the current and future development of the national bioeconomy. Meanwhile, capacity building is essential to prepare the workforce, including entrepreneurs, to support new businesses and technology adoption in businesses. At the same time, collaboration with global and international partners will help leap benefits of the development of new technology and know-how in the country.

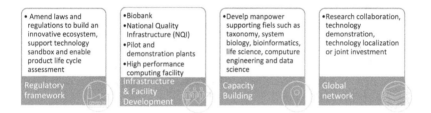

Figure 7.6: BCG enabling ecosystem factors
Source: Author's illustration from NXPO (2023)

References

BOI. (2022a, October 17). *Thailand BOI approves new 5-year investment promotion strategy focused on innovative, competitive and inclusive approach to new economy*. Retrieved from Press release: https://www.boi.go.th/index. php?page=boi_event_detail&module=news&topic_id=133090&langu age=en#:~:text=The%20new%20investment%20promotion%20strat egy,into%20account%20environmental%20and%20social

BOI. (2022b, November). *7 Pillars of investment promotion strategy for the new economy*. Retrieved from Thailand Board of Investment: https://www. boi.go.th/upload/content/7_Pillars_of_New_BOI_Strategy.pdf

BOI. (2022c, August 8). *BOI Go green under the concept of BCG*. Retrieved from: https://www.boi.go.th/upload/content/BOIBCGEN2021_608272 20decab.pdf

BOI. (2023, October). *5 Strategic industries, key agendas for transition to the new industries.* Retrieved from Thailand Board of Investment: https://www.boi.go.th/upload/content/5%20Strategic%20Industries.pdf

Dharmapiya, P., Bilyala, K., Crosbie-Jones, M., Gray, G., Siripark, P., Thaitrakulpanich, S., Wichayapinyo, N., & Wongrujirawanich, S. (2022). *Thailand's BCG transformation: 40 case studies on the Bio-Circular-Green Strategy and the sufficiency economy philosophy in action.* Retrieved from: https://sudsesc.nida.ac.th/main/images/books/Thailand%E2%80%99s%20BCG%20Transformation.pdf

Fingerle, B., Stegmann, H., Vasiksiri, W., & von Rohr, J. (2023, December). *Getting ready for business: Firming up Thailand's startup ecosystem.* Retrieved from: https://web-assets.bcg.com/5a/86/254846794c1eaeaf033d88a1992b/getting-ready-for-business-firming-up-thailand-startup-ecosystem.pdf

Meerod, W. (2024, March 8). *Supporting policies for BCG economy in Thailand.* Retrieved from National Center of Genetic Engineering and Biotechnology (BIOTEC): https://www.boi.go.th/upload/content/Supporting%20policies%20for%20BCG%20Economy%20in%20Thailand%20(BIOTEC).pdf

NSTDA. (2022). *Bio-Circular-Green economy action plan 2021–2027 summary.* Retrieved from: https://www.nstda.or.th/en/images/pdf/bcg_action_plan.pdf

NSTDA. (2024, March). *BCG policy board greenlights new measures to drive BCG agenda.* Retrieved from NSTDA: https://www.bcg.in.th/eng/bcg-policy-board-greenlights-new-measures-to-drive-bcg-agenda/

NXPO. (2023, December). *BCG in action.* Retrieved from Office of National Higher Education Science Research and Innovation Policy Council: https://www.nxpo.or.th/th/en/bcg-in-action/

PAGE. (2023). *Green Economy Policy Scoping Report of Thailand: Opportunities and options for macroeconomic and sectoral policy reform to advance an inclusive green economy.* Retrieved from Partnership for Action on Green Economy (PAGE): https://www.un-page.org/static/f7fa322e4cd34477028dba022dc0a55f/green-economy-policy-scoping-report-of-thailand-06102023-compressed.pdf

Sirilertworakul, N. (2021). *BCG model: Fostering sustainable development in Thai economy.* Retrieved from Trade and Development Regional Forum

2021: https://www.itd.or.th/en/itd-data-center/bcg-model-fostering-sust
ainable-development-in-thai-economy/

Suan Sampran. (2024, March). *Sustainability – Sampran model and organic tourism.* Retrieved from: https://suansampran.com/sustainability/

Thatpitakkul, S. (2024, March 17). *Opportunities and investment support measures for the BCG economy.* Retrieved from Thailand Board of Investment: https://www.boi.go.th/upload/content/Opportunities%20 and%20Investment%20Support%20Measures%20for%20the%20 BCG%20Economy%20BOI.pdf

Chapter 8

Innovation models in rural area of Vietnam

HUNG MANH HOANG, SON THI KIM LE,
TRANG NHU NGUYEN AND VAN THI HONG BUI

Abstract: This chapter firstly analyzes the national innovation system of Vietnam with an emphasis on startup innovation ecosystem and innovation strategy in the agriculture sector as well as in rural areas. Several innovation programs and projects at national and regional level have been highlighted in which focus on Green Innovation, Circular Economy and Social Innovation. Innovation activities emphasize sustainable development and focus on: exploiting digital technology in production (Big Data, IoT, AI, new generation biotechnology…); innovation in market access (e-commerce platforms and online sales channels are widely deployed at the national level); international cooperation in scientific research and technology transfer (CGIAR, GIZ…). To clarify for the effectiveness of these programs, two case studies on Innovation in the agriculture sector and a startup handicraft in rural areas have been explored.

Keywords: National Innovation System, Regional Innovation System, Agriculture, Sustainable Innovation.

1. National innovation system

1.1. Overview of Vietnam's national innovation system

Vietnam, a Southeast Asian country with a population of approximately 100 million people, has experienced rapid economic growth in various key sectors. In recent years, the country has shifted its focus towards fostering innovation to drive growth and development. As a result, by 2023, Vietnam has become one of the most promising destinations for innovation and tech investment in Southeast Asia (NIC, 2023). One of the significant developments in Vietnam's innovation and tech investment landscape in 2023 is the rising innovation ecosystem (InnoLab.Asia, 2023).

Recognizing innovation as a national priority, the Vietnamese government has actively promoted innovation and entrepreneurship through various initiatives and policies. Specifically, the government has implemented numerous investment programs to enhance innovation indexes and build a high-quality workforce to support innovation. Additionally, digital transformation support programs have spurred scientific research, innovative startups and the transformation of technology, production processes, and business operations management on digital platforms, with the aim of enhancing production capabilities and competitiveness of enterprises. The government has implemented several initiatives to encourage and support the growth of the country's technology sector, which has attracted a considerable amount of investment in recent years. In 2023, Vietnamese startups secured $634 million in funding, and Vietnam ranked 3rd in Southeast Asia in deal count (NIC, 2023).

As a result, Vietnam has made significant strides in improving innovation indexes, positioning itself as a country that is quickly catching up with the rest of the world in this area. According to the Global Innovation Index 2023 (GII 2023) report by the World Intellectual Property Organization (WIPO), Vietnam consistently held the 42nd position in 2019 and 2020, followed by 44th in 2021 and 48th in 2022 in terms of innovation. Vietnam, alongside other countries like Kenya and India, has been recognized for achieving innovative milestones for ten consecutive years from 2011 to 2020, particularly in the innovation indexes related to markets and businesses. In 2023, Vietnam climbed two positions compared to 2022, securing the 46th rank out of 132 countries and economies. According to this ranking, Vietnam stands as the second among 37 economies classified as low to middle-income countries, trailing behind India. Within the ASEAN region, Vietnam is positioned after Singapore (5th), Malaysia (36th), and Thailand (43rd). Vietnam holds the 10th position among 16 economies in Southeast Asia, East Asia, and the Pacific.

Currently, Vietnam is one of the seven middle-income countries that have made the most progress in innovation in the past decade. It is also one of the three countries that hold a remarkable record of outstanding achievements in development for 13 consecutive years (Economic & Forecast Review, 2024a). Notably, Vietnam's key strengths in innovation include high-tech exports (ranked 3rd), labour productivity growth (ranked 4th), and high-tech imports (ranked 4th) (WIPO, 2023).

Vietnam is currently considered an attractive innovation ecosystem due to the rapid development of the digital economy and the strong growth in the technology sector. The country's focus on digital transformation and emerging technologies presents significant opportunities for investors. As a result, a record amount of over 1.4 billion USD flowed into Vietnam's innovative startup sector in 2021.

Thanks to the "Startup Nation" initiated since 2016 to support the development of 5,000 startups by 2025, Vietnam has been continuing to attract the attention of international investors as one of the three pillars of the Southeast Asian Startup Triangle (Vietnam – Singapore – Indonesia). This program offers various incentives such as tax breaks, funding, and mentoring to help startups succeed. Vietnam has built and developed a startup ecosystem with over 3,000 startups in various fields such as fintech, e-commerce, health tech, and logistics. Vietnam has a growing number of accelerators, incubators, and co-working spaces that support startups. Some of the most popular accelerators in Vietnam include 500 Startups, VIISA, and Topica Founder Institute (InnoLab.Asia, 2023). As of Dec 2023, the startup ecosystem comprises over 3,000 startups, 70 technology and business incubators, 40 startup accelerators, 140 universities with creative spaces for student startups, 291 industrial parks, and 4 national high-tech parks, etc. (NSSC, 2023).

Alongside the innovative startup ecosystem and a young, tech-savvy population, Vietnam is well-positioned to further develop in the technology sector. Vietnam, therefore, has strongly focused on digital transformation in recent years. The government has implemented various measures to encourage digitization across different sectors, including education, healthcare, and finance. This has created opportunities for tech companies in Vietnam, particularly in the areas of cloud computing, artificial intelligence, and big data analytics. Notably, there are several industries in Vietnam that offer significant opportunities for tech investment, including fintech, e-commerce, and logistics.

Vietnam's national innovation system consists of four main components: (1) Policy-making agencies (Party and State at various levels, such as ministries, sectors, and local authorities), (2) Research and development organizations and universities, (3) Large, small, and medium-sized enterprises, science and technology enterprises, high-tech enterprises, and innovative startups, (4) Intermediary support organizations such as financial institutions; intellectual property, standards, quality measurement and inspection agencies; high-tech parks, incubators, innovation promotion organizations, innovation and startup support centers, consulting intermediaries, brokers, technology exchange platforms… (CIEM, 2019).

1.2. Innovation system in agriculture and rural areas

Agriculture continues to be regarded as a crucial sector of Vietnam's economy. Presently, Vietnam is promoting agricultural development in rural areas through innovative approaches in production, aiming to facilitate economic restructuring in these regions. Vietnam has placed significant emphasis on promoting innovation in agriculture, encompassing aspects from production to business, investment, and services.

Innovation in production. Vietnam is currently at the initial stage of integrating advanced technologies into agricultural production, such as the application of ecological and organic solutions, the utilization of high-tech methods in agricultural production, the implementation of programs for the development of the biotechnology industry and the application of cutting-edge technology, as well as the Digital Transformation and the adoption of high-tech agricultural practices.

Innovation in consumption. Vietnam has established special task forces to proactively coordinate and support localities in the introduction, promotion, and consumption of One Commune One Product (OCOP) and organic agricultural products. These task forces organize conferences, forums, and information exchanges to discuss solutions in production, processing, and consumption, concurrently building brands, trademarks, and geographical indications. To expand the market and enhance consumer access, promotional activities are intensified through reputable e-commerce platforms such as Postmart, Vosco, Shopee, Tiki, Lazada, or Live Stream trade promotion programs at farmers' fields. This approach effectively promotes agricultural products widely and facilitates the online shopping process.

International collaboration in scientific research and technology transfer. Vietnam has actively collaborated with international organizations and partners, such as the Vietnam National Innovation Center (NIC), CGIAR, and the German Corporation for International Cooperation – The Deutsche Gesellschaft für Internationale Zusammenarbeit (GIZ), to promote scientific research and implement sustainable development projects in agriculture.

1.3. Several programs focus on innovation

The green innovation in agriculture and food project (GIC). The GIC Vietnam Project is focused on promoting and enhancing the application of innovative solutions in agriculture, with the specific goal of assisting farmers in improving product quality and increasing income. GIC Vietnam places emphasis on innovative approaches that align with market demands, such as promoting high-demand rice varieties, improving agricultural standards, adhering to food safety and quality certifications, and providing services for small-scale farmers with a business-oriented approach. The project also implements initiatives to minimize environmental impacts in agriculture. To optimize resource utilization, the project strongly advocates for the application of Internet of Things (IoT) technology. Initiatives involving alert systems and mobile applications are employed to assist farmers in managing and tracing the origin of their products, accessing market information, conducting online sales, and participating in electronic trading platforms. Additionally, the project supports the connection between producers and customers both domestically and internationally, integrating with innovative solutions to create nationwide models that promote the effectiveness of innovation in agriculture (Vietnam Agriculture News, 2021).

The promotion of innovation and investment in agricultural technology program – GRAFT challenge. This program connects leading Agricultural Technology businesses with resources and supportive partners to address crucial challenges in Vietnam's agricultural sector. GRAFT is implemented under the Aus4Innovation Program, a collaboration between the Australian and Vietnamese governments, aimed at facilitating the testing of new models in public-private partnerships, enhancing Vietnam's capabilities in data forecasting, scenario building, commercialization, and innovation policy. Through the Aus4Innovation Program, GRAFT supports businesses in addressing urgent challenges in Vietnam's agriculture, including improving the quality and cost of input materials, minimizing post-harvest losses, and building consumer trust. Simultaneously, it tackles specific challenges within each sector: crop cultivation, aquaculture, and livestock farming. The program contributes to fostering collaboration between the public and private sectors, thereby enhancing innovation in Vietnam's agricultural industry (CESTI, 2022).

Although facing initial challenges in implementing innovation in rural areas, Vietnam has achieved positive results. In 2023, Vietnam completed the execution of 362 science and technology tasks at the ministry level and 140 agricultural promotion projects, successfully completed 55 science and technology tasks (including 44 topics, 05 pilot production projects, and 06 environmental tasks). The outcomes encompass 69 new plant varieties, 42 technological advancements, 19 technological processes, 12 technical guidebooks, and 23 reference books, along with over 1,100 articles published in domestic and international journals. Currently, Vietnam has 12 high-tech agricultural application regions recognized by localities, and 51 high-tech agricultural application regions recognized by the Ministry of Agriculture and Rural Development. Scientific and technological advancements have contributed over 30 % of the value-added in agricultural production and 38 % in the production of plant varieties and livestock (Economy & Forecast Review, 2024b). Due to the adoption of advanced technology, the loss of agricultural products, particularly rice, has experienced a significant decrease, falling below 10 % (Vietnam Agriculture Newspaper, 2022a).

1.4. Innovation for sustainable development in Vietnam and government programs supporting innovation systems.

In addition to the rapid development of the innovation system in specific areas such as fintech, e-commerce, health tech, and logistics, etc., current innovation programs and activities are increasingly emphasizing sustainable development. Stemming from this direction, combined with the global trend of sustainable development in all sectors, innovation models such as Green Innovation, Circular Economy, and Social Innovation are gradually becoming popular in Vietnam.

For example, innovation is one of the most important keywords in Vietnam, as reflected in national development strategies, government action plans, international cooperation activities, investment attraction, and research in science and technology. Green innovation encompasses various forms of innovation that contribute to the production of products, services, or critical processes aimed at minimizing the environmental impact and degradation, while optimizing the use of natural resources. Specifically, this includes technological innovations for energy conservation, pollution reduction, waste recycling, designing green products, and developing environmental management activities for businesses to enhance sustainability.

In terms of the Vietnamese government, numerous policies for developing green innovation markets have been implemented, including:

- Policies for environmental standards, product standards, including 13 Vietnamese standards, and 59 Vietnamese environmental standards;
- Climate policies, such as the Green Growth National Action Plan, documents, regulations supporting energy efficiency;
- Support policies for green production and consumption, such as the National Action Plan on Sustainable Production and Consumption (2021–2030);
- The Law on Environmental Protection 2020 regulating green procurement, circular economy, extended producer responsibility;
- The Vietnam Green Label Program encouraging businesses to design and produce environmentally friendly products;
- Current Law on Corporate Income Tax with various incentive policies, encouraging innovative approaches towards green growth.

Furthermore, Vietnam currently has several prominent programs to promote green innovation, such as the Green Innovation Fellowship (aimed at identifying, promoting, and applying green innovation solutions to foster sustainable development for Vietnamese businesses and the region); the Green Growth Show 2023 exhibition (introducing over 100 technologies from organizations and businesses, providing energy-saving solutions, recycling materials, and environmental protection services); the Net Zero Challenge (focused on finding climate change mitigation technology solutions and sustainable development goals); the Vietnam Circular Economy Network (designed as a public-private partnership, aiming to facilitate the transition to a circular economy in Vietnam, promoting green innovation for small and medium-sized enterprises (SMEs)), etc.

Regarding the development of a circular economy, by the end of 2023, the Vietnamese government has issued policies and laws related to circular economy development, including Law on Protection of the Environment 2005 and 2015, Law on Minerals 2010, Law on Water Resources 2012, and Land Law 2013. Circular economy-related contents are also explicitly mentioned in various strategic documents such as the Vietnam Sustainable Development Strategy for 2011–2020, the National strategy on environmental protection to 2020 with visions to 2030, the Green Growth Strategy, the National Strategy for Integrated Solid Waste Management to 2025 with visions to 2050.

As a result, various circular economy models are gradually forming and developing, even though they are still in a rudimentary stage. Examples include the development of solar and wind energy models replacing fossil fuels, utilizing by-products in production for industrial and construction purposes, ecological industrial zone models, recycling waste into consumer products or handicrafts, and green consumer models focusing on the use of renewable and energy-efficient products (trends such as replacing plastic straws with bamboo or paper, transitioning from plastic bags to organic products, designing eco-friendly homes, utilizing natural wind and light, etc.).

Aligned with the concept of sustainable development, an increasing number of Vietnamese businesses, especially startups, prioritize social impact entrepreneurship, addressing societal issues such as environmental pollution, climate change, and providing employment for vulnerable groups. Social enterprises are considered innovative solutions for sustainable social problem-solving, as they offer essential, low-cost products and services for low-income individuals, provide public services, particularly in the healthcare sector and social assistance, enhance community welfare by reconnecting socially marginalized individuals, and offer training and employment opportunities for the disadvantaged. In Vietnam, despite various supportive policies for businesses leveraging social resources for business purposes, the number of enterprises taking this approach remains limited due to factors such as limited awareness of social enterprises, limited accessibility to capital, lack of resources, management skills, and support services for communication, networking, and product distribution.

In spite of numerous challenges, some social enterprises in Vietnam are making efforts to address social issues through advanced solutions and innovative business models. Examples include:

- KOTO (Know One Teach One) Social Enterprise: Originating from a sandwich shop, creating employment opportunities for at-risk youth, KOTO has evolved into a non-profit social enterprise, receiving numerous awards. It provides continuous vocational training programs lasting 24 months in the fields of restaurants, hotels as well as basic life skills and English for disadvantaged youth, particularly those aged 16 to 22.

- Kym Viet Joint Stock Company (established in late 2013) specializes in producing stuffed animal toys crafted by the hands and minds of individuals with disabilities. It simultaneously provides training services for people with disabilities in fabric handicrafts, supporting community integration for disabled individuals, and additional services such as educational tours.
- Mekong Plus Social Enterprise, under the brand Mekong Quilts, focuses on handmade products created in various projects, including blankets, bamboo products, and traditional crafts. These endeavours provide stable jobs and income for impoverished women in rural areas within the community development projects of the NGO Mekong Plus.
- Solar Serve, a solar energy services company, has succeeded with solar-powered stoves designed to serve poor communities and people in regions facing severe deforestation. This initiative aims to reduce the reliance on forest wood for fuel, mitigate indoor air pollution, and bring tangible economic benefits to impoverished communities, especially in coastal and off-grid mountainous areas.

Social enterprises are thus seen as unique business models focusing on positive values within the social community.

2. Regional innovation systems

2.1. Disadvantages of rural areas

In the past decade, Vietnamese agriculture has made significant advancements, but it continues to face numerous limitations and challenges, highlighting the imperative for innovation and creativity.

2.1.1. Resources for rural development are both scarce and weak

The urbanization and industrialization processes have attracted several resources and led to fierce competition for the resources of rural agriculture such as land, water, trained young labour force, and capital. The result is a gradual decline in the resources available for the development of rural agriculture.

The workforce is weak in terms of education and skills. The trend of labour migration from rural to urban areas has resulted in the fact that the remaining labour force is mainly made of people too young or too old to work, those lacking the necessary health conditions, or students who are still attending school. As a result, it leads to low labour productivity. Nearly 70 % of the workforce has not undergone any specialized training, with only 4 % having received training. Those with a university degree constitute about 9 % of the labour force. The labour market experiences a surplus of unskilled labour with low educational attainment while facing a severe shortage of high-quality labour. Additionally, a prevalent trend in rural areas is the return of labour (due to expired contracts, age, occupational accidents, etc.) from foreign-invested enterprises which primarily attract untrained labour, thereby creating challenges in addressing employment and social welfare issues in rural areas (Bui, 2022).

2.1.2. Low income

The average income of farmers is low and not yet equal to 1/3 of the average income of workers in the industrial and service sectors. The poverty rate is still primarily concentrated among rural residents, with over 90 % of the country's poor households living in rural areas, especially in ethnic minority areas and mountainous regions. Compared to other segments of society, farmers remain a vulnerable group facing many risks in both production and daily life (Le, 2022).

2.1.3. Environmental pollution in rural areas

Environmental pollution in rural areas has become a serious issue due to various agricultural activities. The excessive use of pesticides and fertilizers has led to the contamination of water sources such as rivers, lakes, canals, and ditches, significantly impacting water quality and public health. The unplanned development of industries and craft villages without proper waste management systems contributes to environmental pollution. Moreover, environmental management faces a lack of personnel. Vietnam currently has only about 30 environmental management officials per one million people, which is lower than some other ASEAN countries with 70 officials per one million people. Efforts are needed to address these issues and implement effective environmental conservation measures (Le, 2022).

2.2. Solutions

2.2.1. Innovation in building and developing rural areas – the New Rural Program.

Recognizing the crucial role of agriculture and rural areas in the country's economic development, Vietnam has outlined the strategy to build new rural areas (NRAs). This marks a significant step for innovative transformation in the field of agriculture and rural development in Vietnam. The specific goal for the period 2021–2025 is to shape smart new rural areas towards urbanization and digital transformation, aiming for smart NRAs beyond 2025 (GSO, 2021).

The process of digital transformation in rural Vietnam is still in its early stages, undergoing preparation and implementation steps. The Vietnamese government has formulated policies to support digital transformation in rural areas. Several noteworthy policies include:

- *Financial support policy*: Providing financial assistance to empower farmers for investments in technological solutions;

- *Training policy*: Focused on elevating technological skills within the rural farming community;

- *High technology industry support program*: Creating favorable conditions and providing support for high-tech enterprises and research and development projects in the agricultural sector;

- *Entrepreneurship and innovation promotion policy in agriculture*: Facilitating startup enterprises and innovative projects related to digital agriculture.

The results from the 2010–2020 period showed diversity in research and implementation of technology in rural areas. Research projects have significantly contributed to improving economic efficiency and addressing environmental conservation issues. Digital technology and competitive economic models play a crucial role in the innovation of rural areas. Specific results include the completion of theoretical foundations for 15 NRAs models, improvement policies in 26 research projects, 45 research projects on science and technology solutions for NRAs, and the application of research results in 66 NRAs projects. In addition, there have been 159 production models transferred and recommended by research projects, along with 200 processes and technological solutions. Moreover, a total of 1,735 technical structures, machinery, and equipment have been successfully transferred (Nguyen, 2021).

During the 2020–2023 period, Vietnam continued to witness innovation and development in the field of agriculture and rural areas. Vietnam has produced 148 recognized plant varieties and 36 technological advancements approved to enhance productivity and ensure the quality of products for both domestic consumption and export (Ministry of Agriculture and Rural Development, 2022). The NRAs results until 2023 report positive outcomes, approximately 78 % of communes meeting NRAs standards, including 1,612 communes reaching advanced NRAs standards and 256 communes meeting exemplary NRAs standards. Additionally, 270 district-level units were recognized for meeting NRAs standards (Ministry of Agriculture and Rural Development, 2023).

In general, the innovative transformation within Vietnamese New Rural Areas has made significant contributions, encompassing the enhancement of agricultural efficiency, environmental conservation, and the promotion of agricultural product exports. The overarching goal is to establish a smart and sustainable new rural area.

2.2.2. Innovation in agricultural production development

√ *Developing ecological, organic, and smart agriculture*

The efforts to develop agriculture in Vietnam during the period 2021–2025 have outlined significant objectives. In this period, innovation in ecological, organic, and smart agriculture have played a pivotal role.

One of the key directions is the adoption of ecological and organic solutions, coupled with high technology, which has brought forth new opportunities for the agricultural sector. The integration of Big Data, IoT, and AI has given rise to intelligent and efficient agricultural models, covering aspects from farm management to crop and livestock care. Furthermore, initiatives such as the development of the Biotechnology Industry and the application of new-generation technologies contribute to the industry's overall innovation. Bio-based fertilizers, biopesticides, and next-generation vaccines play a crucial role in optimizing agricultural production while minimizing adverse environmental impacts.

Numerous high-tech agricultural models, invested by enterprises such as TH (milk), Dabaco (livestock farming), Nafoods (fruit cultivation and processing), Masan (slaughter and processing), Central South (shrimp), Vingroup (vegetables), Ba Huan (livestock), among others. Up to now, Vietnam has five high-tech agriculture application zones (HTAAZ) designated by the Prime Minister's decision (Hau Giang, Phu Yen, Bac Lieu, Thai Nguyen, Quang Ninh) and one Forestry Urban Development Center in North Central Vietnam. There are 690 agricultural production regions, with 499 regions applying HTAAZ; 290 enterprises in agriculture applying HTAAZ engaged in production (including 70 HTAAZ enterprises); and 1,930 agricultural cooperatives in HTAAZ (Ministry of Agriculture and Rural Development, 2023)

✓ *Developing value chain linkages*

The establishment of value chain linkages is considered an innovative approach in the development of Vietnam's agriculture by creating relationships from production to consumption, aiming to maximize value. Vietnam has successfully implemented several exemplary models of value chain linkage (Ministry of Agriculture and Rural Development, 2023):

- *Safe agricultural supply chain and the "Clean Agriculture for Vietnamese, for the World" Program*: Vietnam has established and developed a model of a safe and clean Agricultural, Forestry, and Aquatic Product Supply Chain with 2,510 safe supply chains, attracting the participation of over 300 companies and 150 cooperatives. This contributes to creating a system for the production and consumption of clean and safe food.

- *Development of production-consumption cooperation and linkages*: The promotion of cooperative development and production-consumption linkages has involved 2,204 cooperatives, 517 cooperative groups, 1,091 businesses, and 186,829 farmers. This has created a system that connects producers with consumers. As of now, 2,146 projects have been approved, including 1,504 projects related to cultivation, 489 projects related to livestock farming, 61 projects related to forestry, and 92 projects related to aquaculture.

- *Agricultural enterprise development*: In 2023, Vietnam had an additional 1,400 agricultural enterprises, bringing the total to over 16,100 enterprises, marking a 7.3 % increase compared to 2022. This growth is coupled with the emergence of 96 Agricultural Cooperative Alliances and more than 20,500 agricultural cooperatives, including 2,500 cooperatives applying high technology and digital transformation. These developments hold the promise of bringing innovative changes, enhancing value-added, and expanding market opportunities for the agricultural sector in the near future.

√ *Developing craft villages, "One Commune, One Product" program (OCOP)*
– *Developing craft villages*

Conserving and developing craft villages play a crucial role in promoting economic restructuring, job creation, and improving the livelihoods of people in rural areas. Additionally, it contributes to preserving and safeguarding the landscape and spatial characteristics of craft villages, thereby contributing to the development of new rural areas. The conservation of cultural values in craft villages has created a strong motivation to maintain and promote the traditional cultural identity.

Vietnam has implemented several policies to innovate and develop craft villages, which include supporting technology transfer, adopting advanced machinery, and connecting these craft villages with domestic and international markets through e-commerce platforms. Until 2021, Vietnam had recognized 211 traditional crafts, with 2,031 traditional craft villages being acknowledged. The current production organization in these craft villages is predominantly based on household production, with small and very small scales. However, there is a significant trend towards transitioning to collaborative production models (Ministry of Industry and Trade, 2021).

– *"One Commune, One Product" program (OCOP)*

The 'One Commune, One Product' (OCOP) program focuses on developing local products with unique characteristics and high economic value. Initiated in 2008 and approved for the 2021–2025 period, OCOP has become a vital tool for reshaping the economic landscape in rural areas, yielding positive results.

The program has implemented several innovative activities to achieve its goals, including the development of region-specific product groups and the application of science and technology in the production process. It also aims to enhance logistic capabilities and undergo digital transformation, incorporating features such as source traceability, promotion, and commercial activities through e-commerce and virtual exhibitions.

The implemented approach has yielded noteworthy results such as:

– *Product rating and classification*: OCOP products have been evaluated and classified by all 63 provinces and cities by July 2023. Out of 9,852 OCOP products, 63 provinces and cities have rated them, with 9,852 products achieving a rating of 3 stars or higher.

- *Diverse participation*: The program has attracted diverse participants, including 5,069 OCOP entities. Of these, 38.5 % are Cooperative Groups (HTX), 24.4 % are businesses, and 34.1 % are production facilities/business households, with the remaining being cooperative groups.

- *Positive impact on rural economic development*: The OCOP program has positively impacted rural economic development by tapping into the potential of land, resources, and competitive advantages. The integration of "multi-value" in OCOP products has linked agricultural development with services and tourism, promoting the livelihoods of rural residents.

- *Development of rural tourism*: Additionally, the OCOP program has spurred the development of rural tourism. Through OCOP, many regions have actively developed community tourism service groups and tourist destinations. Currently, 65 OCOP products in the community tourism and tourist destination group have been evaluated and recognized by localities. These products leverage natural conditions, agricultural production, culture, and traditional craft villages to create distinctive rural tourist destinations, such as the Northern Mountainous Region and the Mekong Delta (Ministry of Agriculture and Rural Development, 2023).

3. Case study of innovation models in rural area of Vietnam

3.1. Case study 1: TH Truemilk

3.1.1. Introduction and background

TH Joint Stock Company, known as TH True MILK, is a key entity within the TH Group (True Happiness) in Vietnam. Established on February 24, 2009, it holds the distinction of being the pioneering company within the TH Group to initiate an investment project in industrial dairy farming, adopt modern milk processing technology, and establish a comprehensive and systematic distribution network.

TH True MILK's main office is located in Nghia Dan, Nghe An, with high-tech dairy farms and milk processing facilities spread across various provinces in Vietnam, including Ha Giang, Cao Bang, Tuyen Quang, Thanh Hoa, Nghe An, Kontum, Phu Yen, Lam Dong, and An Giang. Driven by the ambition to become a global company, TH True MILK extends its operations beyond domestic production and markets. Starting from 2016, TH has signed cooperative agreements and initiated the construction of a dairy farm system in the provinces of Russia. The dairy farm system is being developed in regions such as Kaluga, Moscow, Primorsky, and the Republic of Bashkortostan.

Over the past decade (2009–2023), TH True MILK has earned the trust of customers with its clean milk brand, currently holding a significant market share of 45 % in the domestic fresh milk segment (Vietnam Agriculture News, 2022b). It is recognized as a strong brand for fresh and clean milk alongside many longstanding dairy producers in Vietnam. Presently, the TH True milk brand offers a diverse range of products, including various milk products (fresh pasteurized milk, UHT milk, Topkid fresh milk, yogurt, ice cream, milk with grains), cheese and butter products (natural butter, Mozzarella cheese sticks), ice cream products (cinnamon snail ice cream, assorted stick ice cream, box ice cream), beverages (TH True Juice, TH True Juice milk, TH True Rice), and TH True purified water.

During the rapid 10-year development period, with a widespread production system and a large market share, TH True MILK has achieved numerous significant awards, affirming its success and position in the market. Some notable awards received: Certification for the Largest High-tech Concentrated Dairy Farming Cluster in Asia by the Asian Record Organization, "Product of the Year" awards consecutively from 2015 to 2019 at the World Food Exhibition in Moscow, Best ASEAN Food Award from the ASEAN Food Science and Technology Association in 2015, Asia-Pacific's International Quality Award (Global Performance Excellence Award – GPEA) in 2021 in the highest category – WORLD CLASS AWARD – for large-scale production, presented by the Asia-Pacific Quality Organization (APQO), National Brand Honors for six consecutive years (2014–2018) in Vietnam awarded by the Prime Minister, Commendation from the Prime Minister in 2019 and the Second-class Labour Medal presented by the state in 2019, etc. These awards received over the years serve as evidence of the continuous proactive and innovative capabilities of the TH Group as a whole and TH True MILK in particular.

3.1.2. Innovation model/project

✓ Innovative Imprint

The success of TH True MILK is built upon the strategic development mindset of the TH Group. The project "Dairy farming and high-tech milk processing on an industrial scale" in Nghe An province has harnessed global technological advancements, incorporating manufacturing technology, scientific management, and artificial intelligence. This approach has transformed TH True MILK into a model of green economy, circular economy, and has created many innovative imprints: *(i) Clean fresh milk*; *(ii) Sugar-free*. Replacing sweeteners derived from sugar with natural sweetness from Stevia or natural sweetness from rice; *(iii) Nutrition for the Vietnamese*. Standardizing research on milk products for the school milk program; *(iv) Organic*. TH True MILK is the first and only enterprise in Vietnam with a herd of dairy cows converted to organic farming according to European standards EC 834–2007, EC 889–2008, and U.S. standards JSDA-NOP in Vietnam.

✓ Innovation model through the implementation of a closed-loop production process with modern management and manufacturing technology.

The revolutionary imprint of TH True MILK is ensured by applying modern production and management technology. The entire closed-loop production process covers everything from raw materials, through processing, manufacturing, quality control, to the final product.

(i) **Cattle breed.** Cattle with clearly traced origins are imported from countries such as New Zealand, the US, Australia, Canada, …

(ii) **Raw materials.** TH is self-sufficient in raw materials. All TH's fields are integrated into the GPS and Google Map systems to determine optimal cultivation directions for large-scale machinery. In the care process, TH uses modern sensor technology from Israel (Mottes) or the US (Hobolink), or Australia (FieldNET) to measure soil moisture, allowing checking soil conditions through mobile devices and receiving alerts when soil moisture decreases. The automatic irrigation system based on demand and soil moisture is synchronized, using PIVOT, REEL HOSE integrated irrigation and fertilization systems. The harvesting phase involves the use of a continuous harvesting machine (cutting, grinding, spraying onto trucks) at a speed of 2 tons/minute, utilized in raw material harvesting at TH True MILK.

(iii) **Nutrition.** The feed formula for each cattle group and the mixing process are controlled by the Skiold software system from Denmark. Control of the intake of fine feed ingredients, grinding, and blending of fine feed formulas based on the Nutritional Dynamic System software from Italy. The 1-ONE software from Israel manages the blending and spreading of feed.

(iv) **Water source.** The water source is treated using Amiad water filtration technology to ensure clean, pure, and safe water for the cattle.

(v) **Farm sheds**. TH adheres to advanced global standards and specifications for livestock barns farming sheds. Cattle are free to move in barns with roofs, equipped with cooling fans, and are provided with music and daily cooling baths. The TH Group has invested, installed, and operated the "Solar Roof Farm Energy" project, which produces electricity while reducing heat absorption for cattle sheds, increasing animal welfare, and reducing heat stress during the summer.

(vi) **Herd management.** The Afifarm herd management technology from Afimilk (Israel) is applied. Cattle are tagged with electronic chips (Afitag) on their legs to monitor health, nutritional regimes, and milk production. TH True MILK utilizes AI cameras to detect and count the number of cattle feeding in specific areas. The fan/misting system is controlled to turn on/off and adjust power according to needs, helping save electricity and water costs and treat wastewater. AI cameras monitor the amount of food in each area and provide timely warnings to ensure sufficient food for the cattle.

(vii) **Health care.** The international standard veterinary center and laboratory allow for rapid diagnosis, disease research, and treatment for cattle.

(viii) **Milk extraction.** A fully automated milking system is employed to increase productivity and ensure the quality of milk.

(ix) **Transportation.** Fresh milk is transported through a refrigerated pipeline and refrigerated tanks (20°C–40°C) to the factory.

(x) **Dairy factory.** Modern production technology and equipment imported from G7 countries and Europe. The entire operating system complies with ISO 9001 standards. Products are produced and managed according to ISO 22000 standards to meet strict food safety standards.

✓ *Innovation with a green and circular economic development model*

TH True MILK is actively promoting the development of a circular economy in Vietnam, aiming for sustainable development, environmental protection, and contributing to green growth. In the circular production chain at TH True MILK (see Figure 8.1), by-products and waste from this process become the input materials for another process. As a result, the lifecycle of materials is extended as much as possible before being discharged into the environment, thereby minimizing emissions.

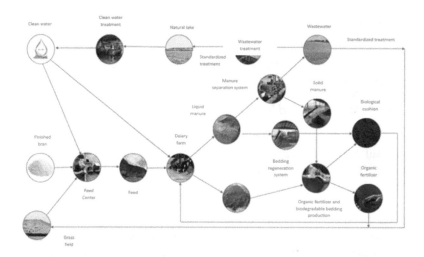

Figure 8.1: Circular production processes in the milk production chain
Source: TH True MILK's seminar report (2021)

The TH farm implements a closed-loop circular model, converting all organic materials and livestock waste into bio-bedding for the farm and organic fertilizer. Livestock wastewater is reused to improve arable land and then treated to meet environmental standards before being returned to nature. Cow manure is collected, composted, and processed without using chemicals to create bio-bedding and organic fertilizer for barns and fields. The treated wastewater becomes a liquid fertilizer source rich in nutrients beneficial to crops. This helps reduce reliance on chemical fertilizers, minimizing negative impacts on soil and the environment. TH's organic fertilizer is produced through a biological decomposition process, free of pathogens and weed seeds. This product not only improves the soil but also enhances crop productivity, ensuring the sustainability of the agricultural system.

This circular economic model of TH True Milk plays a crucial role in establishing a sustainable production system and improving the environment, demonstrating the company's strong commitment to social responsibility. By integrating the principles of the circular economy, the company simultaneously minimizes waste and actively utilizes resources and materials, transforming former waste sources into value. TH True MILK's production model is evidence that innovative thinking is essential not only for business development but also as a significant driver in building a green and sustainable economy.

3.2. Case study 2: Maypaperflower – Traditional handmade paper flowers brand

3.2.1. Introduction and background

Maypaperflower is a Vietnamese brand that specializes in creating beautiful handmade paper flowers. The brand is under control of the Innodir Trading and Services Limited Company, founded in 2020. Maypaperflower's products are known for its intricate designs, vibrant colors, and the unique process with Vietnamese traditional techniques passed down through generations. Maypaperflower has gained recognition not only in Vietnam but also globally and has appeared on various nationwide TV shows and events. The brand's products have been exported to over 14 countries around the world such as Europe, the United States, Malaysia, and beyond.

Mission: Preserving Vietnam's traditional craft villages; creating income for vulnerable groups; and promoting a harmonious, nature-respecting, and environment – friendly lifestyle.

Vision: Maypaperflower aspires to become a prestigious destination for visitors to experience the process of making artificial flowers, where the beauty of traditional art seamlessly intertwines with exquisite innovation, bringing a harmonious blend of heritage and contemporary charm, evoking a sense of timeless elegance and artistic wonder.

Some notable awards Maypaperflower achieved are: Top 29 businesses in Vietnam creating strong social impact recognized by the United Nations, UNDP, and the Canadian government; and the Impactful

Social Business Idea and Innovative Social Business Concept prize at the Social Business Creation 2023, etc.

✓ *Idea*

Maypaperflower originates from a project pioneering the preservation and innovation of handmade paper flower art in Thanh Tien Village, Hue. Thanks to ongoing innovation and the specific support for potential entrepreneurs from government and society, Maypaperflower turned an idea into a beneficial business specializing in traditional paper flowers production.

What sparked the inspiration for Maypaperflower?

Firstly, Maypaperflower inherited an over 300-year-old bougainvillea village in Thua Thien Hue. Despite its survival through tough periods, Thanh Tien village has fallen in catching up with updated trends in modern society. Furthermore, the lack of exposure and marketing opportunities limits their image and recognition nationwide. This makes it difficult for traditional craftsmen to remain their business, not talking about the enlargement. Not only that, the application of technology in production is still adventurous while the process of making paper flowers is complicated and laborious. This makes fewer and fewer people pursue the craft of making paper flowers, and it becomes harder to regenerate skilled craftsmen. As a result, the craft village is in danger of being wiped off the map.

Secondly, the inspiration for the project also stems from rural issues, specifically gender inequality and the disabled employee's disadvantages. When it comes to gender inequality, the issue revolves around households failing to remunerate female employees, and their much lower average income than male in similar positions. As for the employment opportunities for individuals with physical disadvantages, Vietnam currently harbours a population exceeding 7 million with disabilities. Nevertheless, only 31.7 % of those with moderate disabilities and merely 7.8 % of those grappling with severe disabilities (individuals experiencing partial or diminished functionality yet still capable of work) are employed (Communist Party of Vietnam, 2023).

Finally, Maypaperflower is motivated by the environmental pollution issues caused by traditional craft villages in Vietnam, where 95 % of production activities contribute to environmental pollution, with over 50 % causing serious pollution (Central Council of Theoretical Studies, 2021).

✓ *Overview of Thanh Tien village and its traditional art*

Thanh Tien Village is a traditional craft village in Hue, Vietnam, which is famous for its art of making paper flowers. The village has a history of more than 300 years of paper flower-making traditions, and the art has been passed down through generations. The paper flowers made in Thanh Tien are used for various purposes, such as decoration, ancestor worship, and religious ceremonies. Paper flowers are an important part of the local culture and are highly valued for their beauty and craftsmanship. Today, Thanh Tien village is a popular tourist attraction and a must-visit destination for those interested in learning about traditional Vietnamese handicrafts.

✓ *Maypaperflower: A social business*

In 2020, Innodir Trading and Services Limited Company was established with the goal of turning a traditional craft into a modern and sustainable business. How can a once-deemed unfeasible social idea scale up to become a renowned paper flower production business that receives hundreds of orders each month as it does today? The answer is Innovation. One of the supporting factors for Maypaperflower's innovation process is the National Innovation System (NIS). Specifically, Maypaperflower has received support (in finance, technology, marketing, etc.) from key entities such as the Ministry of Planning and Investment, the People's Committee of Thua Thien Hue Province, and the Hue Department of Science and Technology, etc.; intermediary organizations like the Startup Vietnam Foundation (SVF), etc. and several domestic universities.

✓ *Products*

Maypaperflower currently offers a diverse range of products (see Figure 8.2). Maypaperflower's main product lines are paper flower shadow boxes, flower stems, and painting products combined with paper flowers, corsage from paper, etc.

Figure 8.2: Products image

Source: Author's synthesis based on the report from Maypaperflower team (2023)

3.2.2. Innovation model/project

✓ *Innovation in the business production model*

The Maypaperflower's innovation model focuses on the transformation of its business production paradigm. Precisely, Maypaperflower has innovated the conventional handmade paper flower business model with consideration of Environment, Society, and Governance (ESG) factors. This shift replaces the household model with a modern and sustainable business orientation.

Figure 8.3: Business model
Source: CEO/Founder of Maypaperflower

Figure 8.3 shows the structure of the main blocks within the company currently, with:

Business & communication department: is responsible for market development, customer demand, and legal constraints such as intellectual property ownership, contract compliance, and market requirements for product quality.

Design & quality management department: is in charge of product design, quality check, etc.

Craft village department: manages the input of raw materials to craft villages; observes and urges the process; appreciates working conditions, and social welfare.

Processing supervision department at the production facility: is responsible for manual production processes at the main facility, including assembly and recycling steps.

Finished product inspection department: inspects product quality based on samples before packaging.

√ *Production specialization*

The brand splits the production process into stages and trains workers specific skills according to those stages. Instead of having staff gather at the factory, Maypaperflower developed a model that allows them to do their jobs personally at home. Each worker is responsible for only one component of the final product, which requires a couple of days to be totally instructed. This approach, known as specialization, helps with the product quality enhancement while maximizing productivity and lower costs.

✓ *Innovation in R&D*

Maypaperflower has collaborated with universities for market research, product design, and innovation suggestions in traditional handmade product production and business. The primary objective is to integrate modern practical design into traditional-themed paper flower products. The meticulously handcrafted designs further set Maypaperflower apart, capturing the intricacy and beauty of real flowers in a unique and artistic way.

Moreover, Maypaperflower differentiates itself from competitors through its eco-friendly and sustainable approach. Maypaperflower uses FSC certified paper, organic paper (from banana stalks, silk mulberry stems) as input materials for manufacturing.

✓ *Innovation in product consumption phase*

(1) Opening showrooms and participating in international and domestic exhibitions and trade fairs to explore markets; (2) Collaborating with rural tourism programs for selling products to tourists, and utilizing e-commerce platforms for domestic and international sales.

✓ *Applying technology in keeping traditional paper flower-making techniques*

The brand has digitized the paper flower-making processes: transforming long-standing traditional paper flower crafting experiences and techniques, along with contemporary designs, into three-dimensional simulated designs on paper according to common standards and specific technical specifications; subsequently, digitizing these designs into an application with a dedicated cloud storage system.

✓ *Implementing MIS (Management Information System) into traditional paper flower management and production*

This is a system which is used to manage production processes and inventory. It supports the logistics of goods receipt and delivery through QR code scanning technology, with several features such as *Remote Production Management*: assigns tasks to individual personnel through the app; *Warehouse Management Model*: remotely manages capacity to deliver goods and real-time inventory reporting; *Tools to report progress on specific orders and forecast potential capacity*: reduces shortages in critical processes, enabling adjustments to synchronize production.

3.2.3. Innovation effectiveness

- ✓ **Economic effectiveness:** Average Annual Growth Rate is 54,6 % per year; Net Sales for 2022 reached about 1.3 billion VND and for the first 6-month of 2023 was about 1.2 billion VND. Maypaperflower has successfully built its brand and registered the "Maypaperflower" trademark with the National Office of Intellectual Property of Vietnam. Moreover, it also received the "Handicrafts Identification Seal of Hue" from the Ministry of Industry and Trade in October 2023.

- ✓ **Social effectiveness:** Maypaperflower has preserved over 200 traditional paper flower making techniques; created employment opportunities for 23 local workers, including women and people with disabilities. The brand also engages in other social responsibilities such as promoting education and providing vocational training in the traditional art of making paper flowers for students and individuals with disabilities.

- ✓ **Environment effectiveness:** Maypaperflower uses FSC-certified paper and paper made from agricultural by-products, helping to minimize environmental impact.

Maypaperflower is a representative brand in applying innovation models in craft, making a significant contribution to the preservation, promotion, and globalization of traditional Vietnamese paper flower craftsmanship. The strength of Maypaperflower's innovation model lies not only in maintaining traditional and avant-garde artistic values but also in its integration into society and the environment in terms of sustainability, the next generation, long-term value.

References

Bui, X. D. (2022). Quality of rural human resources in Vietnam: Current situation and solutions. *Journal of Social Sciences* (in Vietnamese), *6*, 25–32.

Central Council of Theoretical Studies. (2021). Some environmental issues in Vietnam today – current situation and solutions. Retrieved from https://hdll.vn/vi/nghien-cuu---trao-doi/mot-so-van-de-ve-moi-truong-o-viet-nam-hien-nay--thuc-trang-va-giai-phap.html on 25 March, 2021.

CESTI. (2022). *Empowering agrotech businesses in Vietnam.* Retrieved from https://cesti.gov.vn/bai-viet/CTDS1/chap-canh-cho-doanh-nghiep-cong-nghe-nong-nghiep-tai-viet-nam-01011424-0000-0000-0000-000000000 000 on 25 December 2023.

CIEM – Central Institute for Economic Management. (2019). *Current status and national innovation systems: Issues raised.* Retrieved from https://ciem.org.vn/tin-tuc/8929/thuc-trang-va-nhung-he-thong-doi-moi-sang-tao-quoc-giavan-de-dt-ra?newsgroup=Th%C3%B4ng%20tin%20-%20T%C6%B0%20li%E1%BB%87u on 20 December 2023.

Communist Party of Vietnam. (2023). *The forum: "ESG – Employment Opportunities and Challenges for People with Disabilities".* Retrieved from https://dangcongsan.vn/xa-hoi/dien-dan-esg-co-hoi-va-thach-thuc-viec-lam-cho-nguoi-khuyet-tat-653993.html on 1 December, 2023.

Economy & Forecast Review. (2024a). *The overview of open innovation ecosystem in 2023: Many challenges for businesses.* Retrieved from https://kinhtevadubao.vn/buc-tranh-he-sinh-thai-doi-moi-sang-tao-mo-nam-2023-nhieu-thach-thuc-cho-doanh-nghiep-28012.html on 20 December 2023.

Economy & Forecast Review. (2024b). *High-tech agriculture in Vietnam: Difficulties and prospects.* Retrieved from https://kinhtevadu bao.vn/nong-nghiep-ung-dung-cong-nghe-cao-o-viet-nam-kho-khan-va-trien-vong-28355.html on 15 March 2024.

GSO. (2021). *Building new countryside achieving 'significant, comprehensive, and historic' results.* Retrieved from https://www.gso.gov.vn/du-lieu-va-so-lieu-thong-ke/2021/09/xay-dung-nong-thon-moi-dat-ket-qua-to-lon-toan-dien-va-mang-tinh-lich-su/ on December 25, 2023.

InnoLab.Asia. (2023). *Vietnam's innovation and tech investment landscape in 2023.* Retrieved from https://innolab.asia/2023/05/19/vietnams-innovat ion-and-tech-investment-landscape-in-2023/ on 20 December 2023.

Le, V. L. (2022). Issues in agricultural development, farmers, and rural areas in Vietnam today. *Journal of Political Science*, 3 (online).

Maypaperflower Team. (2023). Maypaperflower's business description report. *Social Business Creation 2023*, August 2023.

Ministry of Agriculture and Rural Development. (2022). Approval of the digital transformation program for new rural construction, towards smart new countryside phase 2021–2025. Retrieved from https://mard.gov.vn/Pages/phe-duyet-chuong-trinh-chuyen-doi-so-trong-xay-dung-nong-thon-moi-huong-toi-nong-thon-moi-thong-minh--.aspx?item=6 on January 20, 2024.

Ministry of Agriculture and Rural Development. (2023). *Report summarizing the implementation of the agricultural and rural development plan for 2023 and outlining the plan for 2024*, 38p.

Ministry of Industry and Trade. (2021). *Developing the micro-industry sector and craft villages: A direction to transform the rural landscape and accelerate economic restructuring.* Retrieved from http://arit.gov.vn/tin-tuc/phat-trien-nganh-nghe-ttcn-va-cac-lang-nghe-dang-la-huong-di-giup-thay-doi-bo-mat-nong-thon-day-manh-qua-trinh-chuyen-dich-co-cau-kinh-te-e52277bf_4309/ on January 23, 2024.

Nguyen, H. S. (2021). *Assessing the impact of the science and technology program serving new countryside construction on agricultural growth, results of new countryside construction in the 2010–2020 period, and proposing the framework of the science and technology program serving new countryside construction for the 2021–2025 period*, Ministry-level Project, Ministry of Agriculture and Rural Development.

NIC. (2023). *Vietnam innovation & tech investment report 2023*. Retrieved from https://nic.gov.vn/wp-content/uploads/2023/03/VIE_Vietnam-Innovation-Tech-Investment-Report-2023-1.pdf on 20 December 2023.

NSSC. (2023). *Techfest – Whise program 2023*. Retrieved from https://nssc.gov.vn/techfest/chuong-trinh-dau-an-techfest-whise-2023/ on 23 December 2023.

TH True Milk. (2021). Report on sustainable development models, including green economy, knowledge economy, circular economy, etc., within the TH Group. *Smart Agriculture Workshop: Potential and Reality*, November 2021, Hanoi, Vietnam.

Vietnam Agriculture News. (2021). *Agricultural and rural development 2021–2025: Shifting towards a robust agricultural economy*. Retrieved from https://nongnghiep.vn/phat-trien-nong-nghiep-nong-thon-2021-2025-chuyen-manh-sang-kinh-te-nong-nghiep-d309037.html on December 23, 2023.

Vietnam Agriculture News. (2022a). *Harnessing the role of science and technology in building the new countryside*. Retrieved from: https://nongnghiep.vn/phat-huy-vai-tro-cua-khoa-hoc-cong-nghe-trong-xay-dung-nong-thon-moi-d332711.html on January 20, 2024.

Vietnam Agriculture News. (2022b). *Over a decade of TH true MILK: Pure milk from a world-record farm.* Retrieved from https://nongnghiep.vn/hon-1-thap-ky-th-true-milk-dong-sua-sach-tu-trang-trai-dat-ky-luc-the-gioi-d321310.html on January 20, 2024.

WIPO. (2023). *Global innovation index 2023: Innovation in the face of uncertainty.* Retrieved from: https://www.wipo.int/edocs/pubdocs/en/wipo-pub-2000-2023-en-main-report-global-innovation-index-2023-16th-edition.pdf on 20 December 2023.

List of Authors

Anedda Raffaele is a PhD student in Economics at ENSTA Paris. His work focuses on the impact of the 4th Industrial Revolution (artificial intelligence, additive manufacturing, Internet of Things, etc.) on technological innovation in firms and industries.
E-mail: raffa.anedda@gmail.com

Bai Yun received her Ph.D. from Chungnam National University, Daejeon City, South Korea with a focus on the economic effects of patents and is currently a lecturer in the Department of International Trade. Her primary research topic is the relationship between trade and patents.
E-mail: baiyun0202@gmail.com

Bui Van Thi Hong is a third-year student majoring in Agricultural Economics at the Faculty of Real Estate and Resource Economics, National Economics University, Vietnam. Her research focuses on Agribusiness Administration, Innovation and Sustainable Development.
E-mail: buithihongvan03@gmail.com

Chen Jin is Professor of Innovation Management at the School of Economics and Management and Research Center for Technological Innovation, Tsinghua University, Beijing, China. His research and teaching mainly focuses on management of technological innovation. He is currently the Editor-in-Chief of the International Journal of Innovation and Technology Management and International Journal of Innovation Studies.
E-mail: chenjin@sem.tsinghua.edu.cn

Hoang Hung Manh is currently a lecturer in National Economics University, Vietnam. He received his PhD in Agricultural Economics from National Economics University. Her research interests are Applied Agricultural Economics, Agribusiness Administration and Natural Resource Economic.
E-mail: hunghm@neu.edu.vn

Hoang Ngan Giang is a Master of Engineering from Tokyo University of Agriculture and Technology. She is currently an Independent researcher at Kodaira-shi, Tokyo, Japan. Her research focuses on Natural resources management, Science-technology-innovation policies.
Email: ms.giang@gmail.com

Jiang Pingping is a Graduate student in School of Management, Jiangsu University, China. She is a member of the Chinese Society of Science and Technology Policy Research. Her research interests cover ESG and Green innovation. She won the second prize for excellent paper at the 2023 East Asian Economic and Management Cooperation International Forum.
Email: jpp1635821038@163.com.

Le N. Dieu Anh is PhD in Economics and currently a lecturer at the Department of Economics, Thuong Mai University, Ha Noi, Vietnam. Her research fields are Trade and Economic development.
E-mail: dieuanh.ln@tmu.edu.vn

Le Son Thi Kim is currently associate professor at Research centre on Innovation and Industrial Strategies ISI /Lab.RII and International business school ISCID-CO, University of Littoral Côte d'Opale, France. Her research focuses on Innovation Management in limited-resource contexts and circular economy. She is an administrative member of Research Network on Innovation (RNI).
E-mail: sontk.le@univ-littoral.fr

Lebert Didier is Professor of Economics at ENSTA Paris. His research focuses on the economics of innovation. He uses mathematical graph theory to identify relational structures within innovation ecosystems at the firm and regional levels.
E-mail: didier.lebert@ensta-paris.fr

Liu Yurui is a Master candidate in School of Economics and Management, University of Science and Technology Beijing, China. His research interests cover innovation behaviour. He has published paper in Environment, Development and Sustainability. He won the third prize for excellent paper at the 2023 East Asian Economic and Management Cooperation International Forum.
E-mail: lyr15907068126@163.com

Long Xingle is an Associate professor and PhD supervisor in School of Management, Jiangsu University, China. His research fields cover innovation and sustainable development. He has published papers in Environmental and Resource Economics, Business Strategy and the Environment, awarded as Highly Cited Chinese Scholars in 2022 and 2023 (Elsevier).
E-mail: longxingle@163.com

Nguyen Duong Thi Thuy is a Master of Business Administration from Kwansei Gakuin University, Japan. She is currently a lecturer at STEP International School, Osaka, Japan. Her research interests are Consumer Behaviour and Innovation Management.
E-mail: duongngt03@gmail.com

Nguyen Nhan Thi Thanh is PhD in Economics and currently a lecturer at Institute of Business Administration, Thuongmai University (TMU), Hanoi, Vietnam. Her main research interests are Management, Leadership, Consumer Behaviour.
E-mail: nhan.ntt@tmu.edu.vn

Nguyen Trang Nhu is currently a lecturer in Hanoi Architectural University, Vietnam. She received her PhD in Agricultural Economics from National Economics University. Her research interests are Applied Agricultural Economics and Development Economic.
E-mail: nhutrangktnn@gmail.com

Nguyen P. Lien is currently a lecturer at the Department of Marketing, Thuong Mai University, Ha Noi, Vietnam. Her research fields are Marketing, Economics, and Business management.
E-mail: Lien.np@tmu.edu.vn

Oh Keunyeob is currently a Professor in the Department of International Trade at Chungnam National University, Daejeon City, South Korea. He was previously the Director of the Entrepreneurship Center at CNU. His main research areas the relationships among international trade, intellectual property rights, and environmental issues.
E-mail: kyoh@cnu.ac.kr

Saelim Supawan is currently a lecturer and researcher at Policy Research Center on Economy (PRO-Green) at the Faculty of Economics at

Thammasat University, Thailand. Her research focuses on Renewable
Energy and Climate Mitigation Policies, Disruptive Technologies and
Decarbonization of the Energy Sector.
E-mail: supawans@econ.tu.ac.th

Sun Jiayi is a Master candidate in School of Management, Shanghai
University, Shanghai, China. Her research interests cover innovation economics, quasi-natural experiment econometric. She has published paper
in Technological Forecasting & Social Change. She won distinguished
paper award in the 5th international conference on IR 4.0 and GVC
(ICIG2023).
E-mail: sunjiayisuda@163.com

Vu Yen is PhD in Economics and currently a lecturer at the Department
of Economics, Thuong Mai University, Ha Noi, Vietnam. Her research
fields are Trade, Investment, Economic growth and development.
E-mail: yen.vt@tmu.edu.vn

Yang Shuo is Post Doctor at the School of Economics and Management
and Research Center for Technological Innovation, Tsinghua University,
Beijing, China. Her research focuses on Managing Technological
Innovation.
E-mail: yangshuo@sem.tsinghua.edu.cn

Titres parus

Vol. 8 – Réseau de Recherche sur l'Innovation, Sophie Boutillier, Joëlle Forest, Delphine Gallaud, Blandine Laperche, Corinne Tanguy, Leïla Temri (dir.), *Principes d'économie de l'innovation*, 2014.

Vol. 7 – Michel Santi, *Capitalism without Conscience*, 2013.

Vol. 6 – Arnaud Diemer, Jean-Pierre Potier, Léon Walras, *Un siècle après (1910–2010)*, 2013.

Vol. 5 – Sophie Boutillier, Faridah Djellal, Dimitri Uzunidis (Réseau de Recherche sur l'Innovation) (dir.), *L'innovation. Analyser, anticiper, agir*, 2013.

Vol. 4 – Aurélie Trouvé, Marielle Berriet-Solliec, Denis Lépicier (dir.), *Le développement rural en Europe. Quel avenir pour le deuxième pilier de la Politique agricole commune ?*, 2013.

Vol. 3 – Sophie Boutillier, Faridah Djellal, Faïz Gallouj, Blandine Laperche, Dimitri Uzunidis (dir.), *L'innovation verte. De la théorie aux bonnes pratiques*, 2012.

Vol. 2 – Faridah Djellal, Faïz Gallouj, *La productivité à l'épreuve des services*, 2012.

Vol. 1 – Abdelillah Hamdouch, Sophie Reboud, Corinne Tanguy (dir.), *PME, dynamiques entrepreneuriales et innovation*, 2011.